Bison Hunting at Cooper Site

May 1993, excavation at the Cooper site. This crew, and the one that followed in 1994, consisted of a mixture of professional and avocational archaeologists. (Photo by Terrell Nowka)

Bison Hunting at Cooper Site

Where Lightning Bolts Drew Thundering Herds

Leland C. Bement

with a contribution by Brian J. Carter

Foreword by Solveig A. Turpin

University of Oklahoma Press : Norman

Library of Congress Cataloging-in-Publication Data

Bement, Leland C.

Bison hunting at Cooper site : where lightning bolts drew thundering herds / Leland C. Bement ; with a contribution by Brian J. Carter ; foreword by Solveig A. Turpin.

p. cm.

Includes bibliographical references and index.

ISBN 0-8061-3102-0 (cloth)

ISBN 0-8061-3053-9 (paper)

1. Cooper Site (Okla.) 2. Folsom culture—Oklahoma—North Canadian River Watershed. 3. American bison hunting—Oklahoma—North Canadian River Watershed. 4. Animal remains (Archaeology)—Oklahoma—North Canadian River Watershed. 5. North Canadian River Watershed (Okla.)—Antiquities I. Carter, Brian J. II. Title.

E99.F65 B45 1999

976.6'1—ddc21

98-43323

CIP

The paper in this book meets the guidelines for permanence and durability of the Committee on Production Guidelines for Book Longevity of the Council on Library Resources, Inc. ∞

1 2 3 4 5 6 7 8 9 10

To Terry, Stephanie, Jason, Roy, and Terrell

Contents

Figures

Unless indicated otherwise, all illustrations are from the author's collection.

Tables

Foreword

SOLVEIG A. TURPIN
UNIVERSITY OF TEXAS

The Cooper site ranks as one of the most important archaeological sites in the New World, bringing information to bear upon such diverse topics as Folsom hunting strategies, seasonality and scheduling, butchering techniques, bison growth and development, territoriality, group size, lithic technology and procurement, and, most important, people's sense of the supernatural world of magic and religion. The three superimposed kills evidence use of the same locale for the same purpose, probably by the same people, permitting intrasite comparisons to be made independent of time and space. This functional redundancy reflects the intimate knowledge of the landscape expected of hunters and gatherers, identifies one fixed point in their seasonal calendar of activities, and demonstrates their control over the mass killing techniques they had developed.

Analyses of the skeletal remains and the resultant profile of herd age-sex composition provide the means for determining the cyclical seasonality of the hunts that ended with mass slaughter at the Cooper site. Similarly, the gourmet butchering techniques indicated by the patterned distribution of cut marks and degree of articulation led Bement to postulate seasonal aggregations with their concomitant increase in the number of people participating in and benefiting from communal hunts.

Based solely on the number of projectile points, the Cooper site is in the top tier of Paleoindian sites. All three bonebeds yielded Folsom points in varying stages of their useful life as well as expedient tools more readily discarded. Thus, Bement was able to elaborate and modify operational models of tool kit production, renovation, replacement, and discard with their concomitant implications about mobility patterns. Bement rightfully assumes that the driving force behind the movements of venatic people is the movement of their targeted prey and subsumes the acquisition of raw material for stone tool manufacture as a secondary or embedded task.

Much of the data generated by the Cooper site excavation and presented in this volume is of particular interest to archaeologists who specialize regionally in the Great Plains, temporally in the Paleoindian period, or topically in the human ecology of hunting people. The intricacies of skeletal and projectile point measurements, the calculations of MNIs, MAUs, and FUIs, and discussions that require the specialized vocabulary of the Plains and Paleoindian cognoscenti to conceptualize fully the technical or technological models may elude the general public and other archaeologists as well, but one product of the excavations immediately elevates the Cooper site above the mundane. The discovery of a single painted skull, erected atop the massed skeletal remains of its slaughtered herd, conferred upon these long vanished people a humanity that is not often found in the archaeological record. The lightning bolt blazened on the bleached and dried bone of an earlier kill is a talisman that has ethnographic analogs among the more recent Plains dwellers who use magic to lure bison to their death. Red ochre, the paint of choice, has magic connotations; bones are essential elements in resurrection themes in hunting and gathering belief systems of the present and the past; and geometric signs are often a symbolic representation of trance, another basic principle in animistic religions. This simple design gains meaning from its context, which in turn legitimizes the concept of hunting magic and its role in economic and social success.

Although it remains a subliminal thread and would likely be denied by the very specialists who promote it, there is a tendency to view the first explorers and colonizers of the New World as *tabulae rasae*, primitive innocents who wandered across the Bering Strait trailing big game and found themselves eventually in Tierra del Fuego. All along the way, they produced exquisite stone tools and decimated the local megafauna, showing surprising abilities for strangers in a strange land. Logic, on the other hand, suggests that such astonishing reproductive success was encouraged by a highly flexible yet well-established system of familial and societal relationships, augmented by science, art, and religion as well as by efficient economy and technology. The people of the New World were indeed culture bearers, whose intimate understanding of the natural world was probably coupled with a structured familiarity with the supernatural universe, remnants of which ethos remain in place today. It is not surprising that the Folsom hunters at the Cooper site perpetuated their ancestral belief system, encapsulating many of its precepts in the lightning bolt that drew thundering herds. What is remarkable is that this, the oldest formally painted object in North America, survived the millennia to remind us that there is more to archaeology than stones and bones.

Preface

Bones protruding from the bank of a stream terrace or the gravel of a riverbed are commonplace occurrences in Oklahoma. The age of such specimens ranges from recent to ancient—from modern farm animals to dinosaurs millions of years old. The majority of these bones draw little attention from the rancher or hiker who stumbles across them, but a deeper interest is sparked in some people and they gather up the bones and take them home. The same applies to the many prehistoric Indian artifacts found across the state each year. Sometimes interested people contact knowledgeable members of their communities, such as schoolteachers, to learn more about their finds. Often in the past, little information was available to answer the collector's questions, let alone to identify the specimens collected.

In response to this situation, in 1970, the Oklahoma State Legislature created the Oklahoma Archeological Survey. The Survey was charged with a dual mission: to research the prehistory of Oklahoma and to educate the citizenry about this heritage. The Survey also took on the task of aiding Oklahoma's communities with regulatory dictums concerning federally funded projects under the review process stemming from the Historic Preservation Act of 1966.

Hand in hand with these developments came close ties with the long-standing Oklahoma Anthropological Society. This group of citizens interested in Oklahoma's past became the logical and necessary counterpart to the Survey's staff. In many ways, the Society extends the reach of Survey into the various communities scattered across the state. At the same time, Society members became informed resources for the citizenry of each community.

The close workings of the Survey and Society often can be seen in the excavation of archaeological sites. These excavations provide an unequaled opportunity for professionals and avocationals to work side by side. The Survey also has a close relationship with the University of Oklahoma, particularly the Anthropology Department. Survey staff members teach in the department and offer field schools that provide students opportunities to experience both the monotony and the thrill of excavation.

The Cooper site excavation provided a unique opportunity for the people of Oklahoma to collaborate in the investigation of one of the earliest cultures of their prehistoric heritage. Members of the Oklahoma Anthropological Society participated as part of a three-week-long field project. Archaeology students at the University of Oklahoma participated as part of a field school. Civic groups, teachers, Native American groups, and many others toured the excavation and contributed where possible. The Cooper site is a success story of public archaeology, and the people of Oklahoma are commended for their support of this endeavor.

This book is testimony to the strength of public archaeology. Because of the close ties between the professional and nonprofessional communities, it has been written with both groups in mind. Members of the scientific community may find some portions too familiar and oversimplified. Others may complain that some sections are too complicated and technical. A glossary is provided to help in these instances. Everyone will find some parts just flat-out boring. In those cases, look at the pictures and move on. By the end, I hope all will share the sense of discovery of the Cooper site.

Acknowledgments

First, thanks are extended to Game Warden Dick James, of the Oklahoma Department of Wildlife Conservation, for bringing this important site to the attention of the archaeological community. We have learned so much from this unselfish act. The excavations and analysis of the Cooper site and its contents were made possible by the joint efforts of numerous people representing many organizations. Excavations were partially funded by Grant 5211-94 from the National Geographic Society, a University of Oklahoma Research Council grant, and the Oklahoma Archeological Survey. The Touch 'n Foam spray foam used to encase the bison bones was donated by Convenience Products of Fenton, Missouri. Special thanks are extended to Susan Levko for coordinating the foam donation. Thanks go to Steve Conrady and Eddie Wilson of the Department of Wildlife Conservation for facilitating excavations on the Hal and Fern Cooper State Wildlife Management Area. All staff members of the Oklahoma Archeological Survey have been involved in the project through fieldwork, laboratory work, discussions, and reading drafts of this book. These staff members are Don Wyckoff, Bob Brooks, Richard Drass, Larry Neal, Kent Buehler, Lois Albert, and Marjy Duncan. Debbie Farris helped keep financial matters in line, and Lisa Whitman provided unequaled efficiency in coordinating visitors and the press, and in dealing with important decisions left to her discretion while I was in the field.

Many members of the Oklahoma Anthropological Society participated in the excavations. Specific individuals to be recognized in this endeavor include Ken Bloom, Dave Morgan, Mick and Marta Sullivan, Charlie Gifford, and Sherl Holesko. I appreciate the help and enthusiasm of the Texas crew—Karl Kleinbach, Gemma Mahalchick, and Bruce Nightengale—who braved the harsh and muddy conditions of the first season. Likewise, the efforts of the long-haul crew of the second season, particularly Scott Brosowske, Jesse Ballenger, and Charlie Gifford, are appreciated. Thanks to Solveig Turpin and Kelly Scott for dropping everything and coming to look at the painted skull.

All those who provided donations—too many people to name individually—are graciously acknowledged; among them, contributors deserving special mention are Terrell Nowka, Harold Courson, Arnold Coldiron, and Pete Thurmond. Special thanks are extended to everyone who purchased point sets, donated by Paul Maxwell, and posters; a portion of the proceeds from these sales was used to offset costs of preparing the manuscript. Phil Ward III aided in the collection of soil samples and in conducting particle size analyses. Photographic plates were prepared by Color Chrome Labs of Norman, Oklahoma. Susan Basmajian donated many hours to the analysis of the bones and shared the headaches of making sense out of the data. Jennifer Coleman likewise donated her efforts in the cleaning of the bones. Chris Cook established and enhanced the computer database containing all bone measurements.

In addition to their other roles, Scott Brosowske, Pete Thurmond, Larry Neal, Kent Buehler, Terry Bement, Terrell Nowka, and Solveig Turpin read various drafts of this book, as did Robert Brooks and Arthur and Charlotte Bement. They provided valuable comments and suggestions (some of which cannot be printed). Scott also helped in the drafting of figures and compiling of tables.

George Frison and Mike Collins reviewed the manuscript and provided valuable suggestions to improve its clarity.

This book is dedicated to my wife, Terry, and our two children, Stephanie and Jason, and to my first Oklahoma friends and field crew, Roy Patterson and Terrell Nowka.

Bison Hunting at Cooper Site

CHAPTER 1

Introduction

Nearly seven decades have elapsed since the first Folsom projectile point was found in association with ancient bison remains in North America. With that discovery came proof that people had been in the New World as early as the end of the last ice age (12,000 years before present). Today, research continues into developing an understanding of the lifeways of these early inhabitants. Folsom projectile points, with their distinctive channel flakes and exquisite craftsmanship, remain the best identifier of one of these ancient cultures. Folsom points have been found up and down the Great Plains of North America from Mexico to Canada. Folsom sites in the southern plains include bison kills, processing areas, camps, and lithic quarries (Bement 1994a; Boldurian 1990; Figgins 1927; Harrison and Killen 1978; Harrison and Smith 1975; Hester 1962, 1972; Hofman, Amick, and Rose 1990; Jodry and Stanford 1992; Johnson 1987; Judge 1973; Schultz 1943; Tunnell 1977). However, finding intact deposits containing Folsom points in association with items representing other aspects of Folsom lifeways is still a rare event. For this reason, wherever the remains of large bison are found, extreme care and close scrutiny of the deposits are warranted to see if humans were involved.

In November 1992, I was taken to just this sort of place, where skeletons of large bison were observed sticking out of a bluff face along the Beaver (North Canadian) River floodplain in northwestern Oklahoma. At the time of this visit, there was no evidence that people had been responsible for the death of these animals. However, monitoring of this exposure over the next six months yielded the evidence that placed Folsom people at this kill. On April 15, 1993, the broken tip of a Folsom point was found among the debris on the sloping surface beneath the exposed bones. That single find set in motion the research that led to excavation, processing, and analysis, and to the compilation of information presented in this book. The Cooper site, named for the longtime owners of the ranch on which the find was made, was only the second Folsom-age site in Oklahoma that had intact cultural deposits; the first was the Waugh site 30 miles northwest of Cooper. Together the two permit comparative research into Folsom cultures in this area of the Great Plains.

Since its discovery, Cooper has become recognized as one of the premier Folsom sites in North America. Its three stratified Folsom-age large scale bison kills provide the unique opportunity to study change and continuity in hunting strategies, lithic technology, processing activity, and bison herd dynamics. The highly preserved bonebeds contain numerous fully articulated skeletons, allowing identification of previously unrecognized butchering patterns; assessment of new postdepositional destructive agents; and insights into *Bison antiquus* growth and development. Much of the information gleaned from Cooper bolsters existing reconstructions of Folsom lifeways while at the same time providing new avenues for investigation. The discovery of a painted skull, the oldest painted object in North America, opens doors to aspects of Folsom culture rarely seen in Paleoindian contexts.

The following chapters provide an archaeological and environmental background; introduce the site, its setting, and its history; describe the excavation techniques and results; detail the analysis of cultural, faunal, and paleoenvironmental materials; and conclude with a synthesis of regional Folsom lifeways and technology.

CHAPTER 2

Archaeological and Environmental Background

The Folsom cultural complex is one of several complexes grouped under the general category of Paleoindians. Paleoindians are the earliest documented human inhabitants of the New World. And, while there is still considerable controversy over when the first Americans arrived, it is well established that people were in North and South America by 12,000 years ago—a time roughly equivalent to the end of the last ice age (Dillehay 1989; Dillehay and Meltzer 1991; Frison 1991, 1996; Haynes 1993; Meltzer 1993).

The first groups to spread throughout the New World and for which we have a sizable amount of knowledge were members of the Clovis cultural complex. Clovis people lived alongside the soon to be extinct mammoth, mastodon, horse, camel, giant ground sloth, and large bison. Finds of Clovis points among the bones of mammoths, mastodons, and large bison at such sites as Domebo in Oklahoma (Leonhardy 1966), Murray Springs in Arizona (Haynes 1993), and Aubrey in Texas (Ferring 1989, 1990, 1994) indicate that these early people were accomplished hunters. Other aspects of their lives evolved around hunting smaller game, collecting aquatic resources, and gathering plant foods (Ferring 1990, 1994; Haynes 1993).

Following the retreat of the glacial ice sheets came a period of decreased moisture on the southern plains, with minimal seasonal variation in temperature and precipitation. Annual extremes in temperature and precipitation were less pronounced, leading to an overlap in the ranges of animals that today are found in separate, noninclusive habitats (Graham and Lundelius 1984; Lundelius 1989). Evidence from fossil plant remains and landscape reconstructions suggests that Clovis people lived in an increasingly arid environment. Reduction in the quality of grasslands and changes in habitat contributed to the demise of many animal species during this time. By the end of the Clovis period, the dominant large animal was the bison (*Bison antiquus*).

The amelioration of climatic conditions by 11,000 BP is indicated by more continuous spring discharge and by water levels in lakes (Haynes 1993; Holliday 1995; Johnson 1987). On the southern plains, the Folsom cultural complex succeeded the Clovis. Evidence is now emerging for a Goshen culture between or overlapping Clovis and Folsom on the northern plains (Frison 1996). Both of these post-Clovis groups hunted the herds of bison.

Our understanding of the Folsom complex stems from excavations at sites at or near bison kills. Technology and adaptations besides those for hunting bison are less well known, but other aspects of Folsom life assuredly included the gathering of plants and lesser animals (Ferring 1989, 1990; Johnson 1987). Unfortunately, plant remains are rarely preserved in the archaeological record. However, stone tool design and usewear indicate that plant resources were routinely gathered and utilized (Akoshima and Frison 1996; Wilmsen 1968).

In addition to increased water availability in the Folsom period, environmental reconstructions suggest that temperature and rainfall fluctuated seasonally (Holliday 1995). Different food resources became available during specific seasons of the year. Seasonal food availability may have led to more structured movement of bison and human groups.

The complexity of the Folsom bison hunting adaptation can be seen in the organization of lithic technology and landform use. Folsom hunters, like other bison-hunting groups, understood their prey and used this knowledge to enhance success rates of hunts. They knew how to manipulate bison herds of differing sizes. At Lubbock Lake and Blackwater Draw, small bison groups (< 6 animals) were ambushed near lake edges (Agogino 1968; Hester 1972; Johnson 1987; Stanford et al. 1986). At Bonfire Shelter, larger groups (20–50 animals) were possibly stampeded over a cliff (Dibble and Lorrain 1968) or maneuvered and trapped in the large rockshelter (Bement 1986); groups of similar size were run into dead-end arroyos and into sand dune traps (Frison 1991; Frison and Stanford 1982; Hofman et al. 1991).

Cultural developments following Folsom times (ca. 10,000 BP) continued to target bison as a key game animal. Large kills containing more than one hundred animals are seen in the late Paleoindian cultures known as Plainview, Agate Basin, Hell Gap, Alberta, and Cody (Agenbroad 1978; Frison 1991, 1996; Frison and Stanford 1982; Sellards, Evans, and Meade 1947; Wheat 1967, 1972). Even with these cultures, more is known about their hunting technology than their plant and other resource utilization. The environmental conditions during these times (10,000–7,000 BP) remained seasonally varied, with a gradual drying trend. Hunting techniques continued to include arroyo and sand dune traps (Frison 1974, 1991; Frison and Stanford 1982; Wheat 1972, 1978). The Olsen-Chubbuck site in eastern Colorado provided evidence for the use of an arroyo jump—a variation of the cliff jump utilizing a steep gully wall (Wheat 1972). Several sites, including Jones-Miller in Colorado, provided no evidence of the type of enclosure utilized but it is postulated that the animals were driven into a corral in a fashion similar to that used by historic groups on the northern plains (Frison 1991; Stanford 1978, 1984).

A hiatus in large-scale bison kills is seen from 7,000 to 2,500 BP. After 2,500 BP, southern plains large kills are known from Bonfire Shelter, Twilla, and several other sites in Texas, and from the Certain site in Oklahoma (Bement and Buehler 1994; Buehler 1997; Dibble and Lorrain 1968; Hughes 1977). Kills are more common on the northern plains than on the southern plains (Davis and Wilson 1978; Frison 1991). A variation on the jump technique is seen at the Vore site, where bison were stampeded into a deep, steep-walled, sinkhole (Frison 1991; Reher and Frison 1980).

Large-scale bison kills remained a component of northern plains economy throughout the early historic period when European traders and explorers recorded eyewitness accounts of these events. Kill techniques included all types developed by earlier groups as well as chases in which equestrian hunters pursued the herds, killing as many bison as possible. Of course, this technique was made possible by acquisition of the horse from Europeans.

Site Setting

The Cooper site, 34HP45, is located along the floodplain margin of the Beaver River in northwestern Oklahoma (fig. 1). The site is in the

Figure 1. The Cooper site in northwestern Oklahoma is located in the northeast portion of the southern plains.

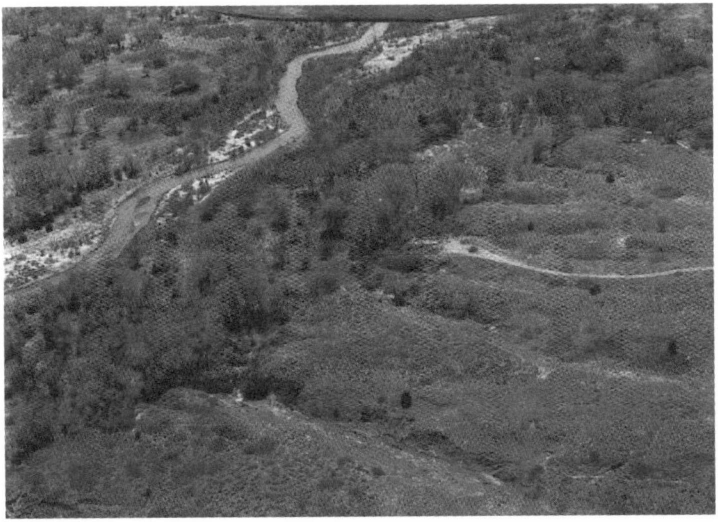

Figure 2. An aerial photophraph of the Cooper site area shows the distinct floodplain boundary formed by the bluff line. The site is at the end of the dirt road.

Western Sand Dune Belts province, which is bordered on the west by the High Plains and Western Sandstone Hills and on the east by the Cimarron Gypsum Hills and Central Redbed Plains (Curtis and Ham 1979). Eolian sands blown from dried riverbeds and adjacent Quaternary alluvial deposits form the hummocky sand dunes of the Western Sand Dune Belts province. The region is underlain by sandstones, limestones, and shales of Pennsylvanian and Permian age.

The site deposits are in a bluff bordering the Beaver River floodplain (fig. 2). The bluff is one of many forming a boundary created by the widening of the floodplain through the lateral cutting of the river channel. Short drainages, usually less than half a mile long, channel runoff onto the floodplain from hills above and to the north of the bluff line.

Soil development on the bluff consists of a shallow organic zone accumulating on top of moderately deep to deep eolian sands. With low rainfall (< 20 inches a year) and temperature extremes (below 0°F minimum during the winter, and over 100°F during the summer), the sandy soils support a sparse vegetation cover dominated by xeric species including sagebrush, yucca, short grasses, and various stunted shrubs of oak. The riparian zone supports lush vegetation, including an overstory of oaks, hickory, and cottonwood, a midstory of juniper and vines, and tall grasses in occasionally flooded areas.

CHAPTER 3

History of Site Investigation and Discoveries

Activities leading up to the discovery of the Cooper site began with the purchase of over 16,000 acres of the Cooper ranch by the Oklahoma Department of Wildlife Conservation to establish a wildlife area with public hunting access. Agency personnel toured the ranch and were shown many of its interesting characteristics, including sand-capped hills, the expansive floodplain, permanent water, and quality wildlife habitats. One point of interest was a bluff along the northern margin of the Beaver River riparian zone. Bones of large animals—horse, cattle, or bison bones—were eroding from high in the bluff and cascading to the floodplain floor below. The resultant steep sediment slump beneath the exposure was littered with bone fragments.

In November of 1992 while en route from the dedication ceremony of the Lunceford Playa conservation project, where I learned of the bone deposit, I stopped in Woodward, Oklahoma, to contact Dick James, the game warden familiar with the exposure. He agreed to show me the bone deposit, and off we went. Following the unimproved pasture roads that crisscross the ranch, we forded the Beaver River and headed to the distinctive red cliffs of a bluff line along a bend in the river. Stopping about a half-mile from the exposure, we descended on foot onto the densely vegetated floodplain and proceeded along the base of the sheer bluff face. The bluff, 6 to 7 meters high, is composed of a base of Permian red sandstone, overlain in some areas by massive colluvial deposits filling ancient gullies, and capped by white sandy eolian deposits. The modern river channel meanders from the base of the bluff near where the truck was parked to over 100 m away from the bluff at the point of the bone exposure.

Just as it had been described, the bone exposure consisted of vertebrae and leg bones sticking out of the bluff face some 6 m above the level surface of the floodplain (fig. 3). A steep, sandy slump talus had accumulated at the base of the cliff face and extended to the bone exposure. The surface of this displaced colluvial material was littered with bone fragments. More complete bones recently released from the bluff face had rolled down the slope, coming to rest at the base of a tree on the floodplain. It was quickly apparent that the bones were from bison. The profile afforded by the bluff face indicated that the bones were contained in an ancient arroyo, but it was not immediately discernible whether they were the result of human activity or a natural catastrophe. At this stage, all that was known was that there was an extensive deposit of bison bone contained in the fill of an old gully. We collected bone from the surface of the eroded slope to be used in determining the species of bison and for radiocarbon dating.

At the Oklahoma Archeological Survey in Norman, a bone sample was submitted for radiocarbon dating. The remaining elements were measured and compared to bone measurements of modern bison (*Bison bison*) and two species of extinct bison (*B. antiquus* and *B. occidentalis*) provided in Jerry McDonald's *North American Bison* (1981). Bone measurements compared favorably with the upper size range of *B. antiquus*, implying that the bones represent a species of bison that became extinct on the southern plains between 5,000 and 7,000 years ago. The radiocarbon date from our sample seemed to corroborate this: the age came back at 7020 ± 120 radiocarbon years BP (Beta-60260).

We still did not have any evidence that the bison had fallen victim to human hunters. However, the age of the bone and the species of bison indicated that if human groups were involved, they would probably be members of the Cody Complex—a late Paleoindian culture of accomplished bison hunters (Wheat 1972).

With these developments in mind, Survey Director Don Wyckoff, Oklahoma State Archaeologist Robert Brooks, and I returned to the site for further consultation. We agreed that the deposit should be visited at regular intervals to see if any cultural materials eroded out and to monitor any disturbance to the deposits after the area was opened to the public. At this point, the deposits were viewed as acultural—not the result of human activity. After all, a similar bone deposit along the Cimarron River had failed to yield evidence of

Figure 3. Dick James inspects the bones eroding from high on the bluff face. Closer in, the bones appear to be in good condition.

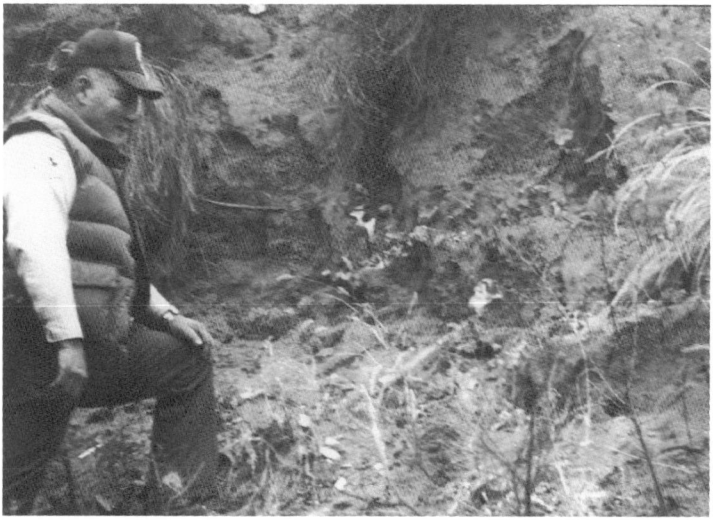

prehistoric people after several investigative endeavors. Wyckoff jokingly attributed the Cooper bonebed to animals killed by a lightning strike—a portent of what was to come.

The next visit to the bone exposure came on tax day, April 15, 1993. The wildlife area—now named the Hal and Fern Cooper Wildlife Management Area—had been opened for the spring turkey hunt.

Kent Buehler of the Archeological Survey, Eddie Wilson, manager of the wildlife area, and I followed the footprints of many turkey hunters along the bluff face to the bone exposure. Most of the tracks kept going. However, the keen eye of one hunter was not lost on the bone deposits. One small area of exposed bone had been pulled from the bank; the bones still lay beneath their extraction point. Less than a meter downslope from the recent bone pile was the tip of a Folsom projectile point. Whether the point fell with the bones that had recently been removed or was already on the surface will never be known. What was certain, however, was that the bones were the result of Folsom age bison kill. The Folsom culture is known to be between 10,200 and 10,900 years old (Haynes et al. 1992). As already indicated, the Cooper site, as it was now called, was only the second Folsom bison kill site known in Oklahoma. The first, the Waugh site, was discovered in 1991 and remains to be fully investigated (Hofman, Carter, and Hill 1992; Hill and Hofman 1997).

The discovery of the Folsom point fragment catapulted the bone exposure from an anomalous bison deposit needing monitoring to a singularly important site in need of protection. Immediate action was required to inhibit further erosion and to avert what was now called site vandalism (before this it had merely been a case of someone pulling some bone from the wall). The effects of erosion were readily apparent. The problem of vandalism emerged as a greater concern. By the time the Folsom point was discovered, a new entrance to the management area had been constructed on the north side of the river, allowing easy access to the far reaches of the hunting area. Management headquarters was on the larger acreage south of the Beaver River. Manpower to protect the site consisted of Wilson, who was in charge of the entire area of more than 16,000 acres, and a handful of game wardens, including Dick James, who patrolled the whole district. Protection of the site was not assured, especially if word got out that a Folsom point had been found.

The 1993 Excavation

Immediate steps were taken to assess the extent of the site deposits and to formulate an erosion abatement plan. From April 26 through May 26, 1993, volunteers from the Oklahoma Anthropological Society and archaeologists from the Archeological Survey conducted preliminary excavation of the Cooper site. For several reasons, the first task was to screen the slump material. Most important, profiling the site deposits would turn the bluff face into a vertical cliff that isolated the bone exposure out of reach of people on the floodplain. Screening of the slump also removed all bone and artifacts that might attract the attention of passersby. This activity was immediately rewarded by the recovery of a complete, although heavily reworked, Folsom point on the first day.

Concurrently, we set a permanent horizontal and vertical datum on the first ridge top west of the site (fig. 4). A grid with 2 m increments was placed over the site area and initial coring of deposits away from the bluff face was undertaken to determine the horizontal expanse of the bone deposit. Coring indicated that the bones were limited to an area less than 6 m north-south by 8 m east-west. Because of the small size of the bone deposits, it was decided that the eastern half would be exposed to provide a glimpse of the nature of the bonebed and to provide intersecting profiles of overlying deposits.

As the 1.5 m overburden was being removed by hand, the slump excavators cleaned the bluff face and exposed a second layer of bison bone (Bement 1994a) that had been hidden from view by the slump deposits. The presence of two bone deposits prompted numerous questions concerning which layer had produced the Folsom points. Were both bonebeds of Folsom age, or did the upper one merely consist of bones from a single kill that had been redeposited from an upslope position?

As cleaning of the bluff face progressed, it became clear that the bone deposits were in the fill of an ancient arroyo. Each bonebed defined the bottom of the arroyo at the time of the kill. The sheer face provided a profile that transected the old gully from east to west. The western wall of the arroyo inclined sharply, while the eastern edge had been removed by a modern gully. The bluff face was produced by the lateral movement of the Beaver River, which, through its meandering,

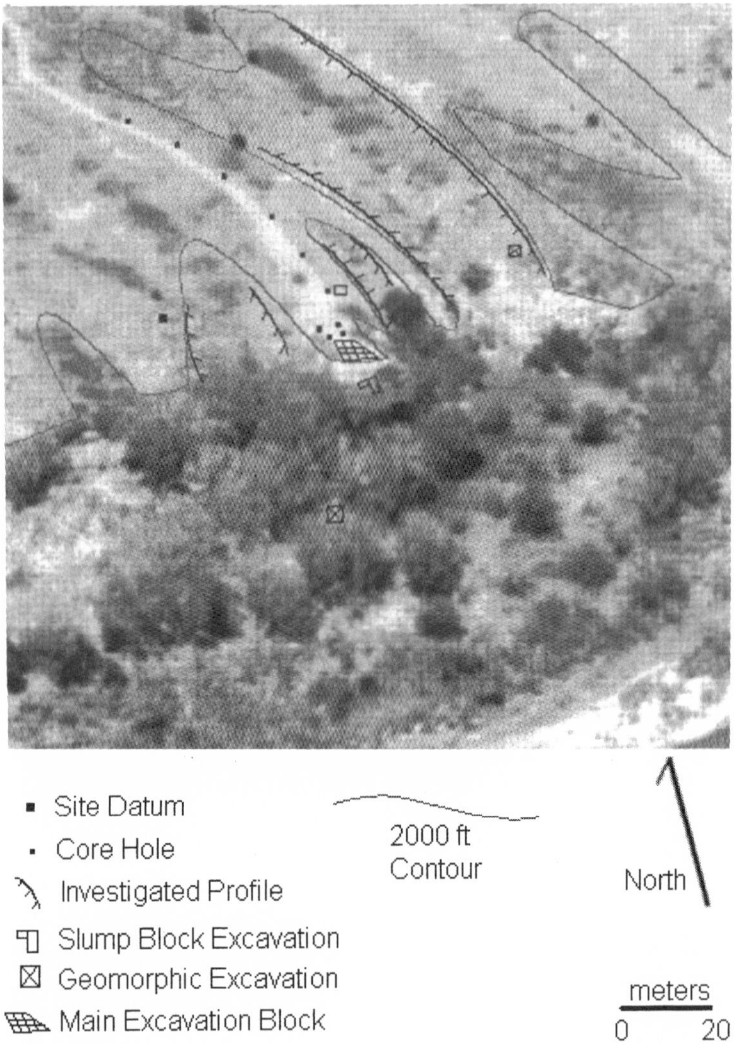

Figure 4. This plan view map of the site area identifies key areas that were investigated.

had truncated the ancient gully until the bedrock bench underlying the upper end of the arroyo was encountered.

The second bonebed could be traced until it joined the upper bonebed along the western wall of the arroyo. There, the two bonebeds intermingled and would be difficult to separate.

Excavation of the eastern half of the upper bonebed progressed by uncovering the bone and fine-mesh screening of all sediments. None of the bone was to be removed, but detailed plan maps and photo-documentation was performed. The intersecting profiles were drawn. The sandy deposits noted at the top of the bluff had an abrupt boundary with the underlying gully fill, which indicated that the arroyo fill had been truncated by erosion at some time in the past. This abrupt boundary was over 1 m above the upper bonebed. Numerous gopher runs crossed the boundary between the two deposits and continued downward to the bonebed below (fig. 5).

The first Folsom point discovered while excavating the upper bonebed (point C, fig. 33) came from a gopher burrow above a bison skull. Although this find suggested that the upper bone deposit was of Folsom age, its location within a gopher burrow meant it could have been transported upward from the second bonebed. It would be two more days before a Folsom point was found in situ in the upper bonebed.

A balk 1 m wide was left in place as the overburden was removed from the western portion of the site, the area that provided a window to the intermingling of the two bonebeds. It was here that the first in situ Folsom point was discovered (point D, fig. 27), providing definite proof that the upper bonebed was the work of Folsom hunters. The cultural association of the second bonebed remained unknown.

Our initial views of the upper bonebed were dominated by skulls and articulated skeletons. Many of the animals were lying on their stomachs with their hind legs folded underneath (fig. 6a). Others were on one side with legs outstretched (fig. 6b). The large number of articulations dictated that all bones be left in situ until the entire bonebed was cleaned to avoid problems in identifying individual animals later during analysis. This situation had a profound effect on the method employed to preserve the site. Initially, we had thought we could uncover the surface of the bonebed, map it in place, and remove a meter-wide strip along its eastern and southern margins where

Figure 5. A profile view from early in the excavation shows the windblown sand overlying the red gully deposits. Note the filled gopher runs. Excavations are just starting to expose bones of the upper kill.

modern erosion had exposed the bone. The remainder of the bonebed would be reburied and preserved until funds were available for more extensive excavations. However, with the discovery of the articulated skeletons, we realized that removal of the meter-wide strip would mean dismantling otherwise complete skeletons, thus increasing the risk of information loss regardless of the exactness or thoroughness of documentation.

At this juncture, the word went out that we needed emergency funds to allow the excavation to continue for a month. Response among the citizens of Oklahoma and members of the archaeological community was surprisingly swift and was sufficient to allow excavations to continue until the last week of May. Professional archaeologists from Texas joined our team of volunteers and Oklahoma archaeologists to complete the excavation season. The goal was to remove articulated skeletons from the exposed areas and along the bluff edge of the upper bonebed.

A

B

Figure 6. Here are examples of hind legs folded under the animal (a) and outstretched legs within the Upper Kill (b).

Nature provided us with a little down time to coordinate fund-raising and personnel recruitment. One of the first tornadoes of the year bore down on the communities of Fort Supply and May. The Cooper site lies just north of one and east of the other. The tornado passed right over the site and our camp. Baseball-sized hail, high tornadic winds, rain, and commotion was followed by one hour of continuous pelting of the area with marble-sized hail. As we watched the storm build, we made many snide comments about the little fluff clouds as they raced overhead. A word to the wise: never make fun of fluff clouds. The aftermath of the storm saw shredded tents, trees stripped of leaves and small to medium branches, and a hail-dented university truck with a shattered windshield. On our way to the site we stepped over numerous dead and injured birds, including a hawk that sought refuge under a large juniper tree.

Damage from the storm was evident when we reached the site. The plastic cover placed over one completely articulated skeleton was intact. The remainder of the site, however, had felt the full brunt of the storm. Skulls and pelvi were rendered into piles of bone scrap (fig. 7). Ribs were fragmented and displaced across the bonebed. Only the thick-walled long bones of the legs seemed undamaged. Some of the hail left spherical impacts on the bone similar to those produced by hammerstones or expediency tools. Fortunately, the excavation area was not washed by fast-moving runoff. Although some washing of small bone fragments was noted, most of the displacement was attributed to impact hurling. Many of the bones were reburied during the storm and needed to be reexcavated. The soft mud in the bonebed and around the site was marked with hundreds—if not thousands—of holes produced by marble- and larger-sized hail. Small bone fragments were driven up to 3 centimeters into the matrix by the force of the hail. A single resharpening flake was washed out by the storm.

Tornadic storm damage is not one of the taphonomic agents usually covered in the archaeological literature, but that day proved how these storms can devastate an exposed bone deposit. The damage sustained at Cooper may be analogous to destruction seen at other bonebed sites, suggesting a possible cause.

After the storm, all calmed down to the work at hand. More resharpening flakes, flake tools, and projectile point fragments surfaced as the bones from the Upper Kill were removed. A thin layer of

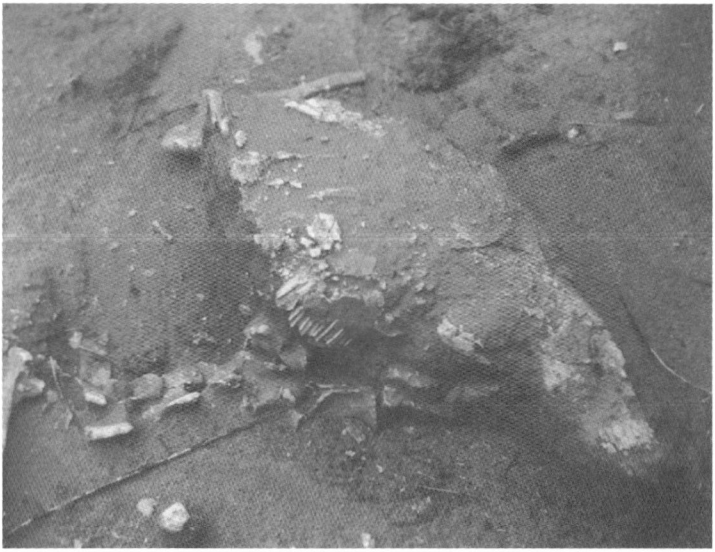

Figure 7. The mass of bone in the center of this photograph is a skull that was essentially destroyed by hail accompanying the tornado during the 1993 fieldwork.

gray sediment was visible under the skulls and most of the larger bones. This gray lense is similar to that found at the Waugh site and is attributed to the microbial decomposition of whatever meat, skin, hair, and other organic material was left on the carcasses when the bone was buried.

After the section of bonebed along the eastern margin of the site had been removed, a 50 × 50 cm area was excavated to the level of the second bone deposit. Approximately 20 cm of sterile red sandy colluvium separated the two bonebeds along the eastern edge. The gray lense under the Upper Kill was continuous in the profile. A similar gray gleyed zone appeared around the bones of the lower bonebed. The base of a translucent brown Folsom point was found on top of the bones, confirming that the second bonebed was also the result of Folsom hunters' activity.

By now, work on the bluff face had succeeded in perching the bonebeds out of reach of anyone standing on the floodplain. The

Figure 8. This cleaned bluff profile provides evidence that the bones were in an ancient gully.

cleaned profile clearly showed the outline of the ancient arroyo and the bone deposits it contained (fig. 8). The lower bone deposit was nearly twice as thick as the upper one. Interestingly, the gray deposit that was confined to a thin line under the bones of the Upper Kill began halfway through the bonebed of the lower deposit. In fact, many of the lowest bones were completely contained in the gray deposit. The reason for this would become clear when excavations resumed in 1994.

Soil scientist Brian Carter of Oklahoma State University described the first of many profiles at the site and took samples for sediment analysis. At this point, the 1993 field season drew to a close and the site was covered to protect the bonebeds from vandalism and erosion until additional funds were raised to finish the excavation. Permeable landscaping cloth was draped over the bonebed and 6 cm of dirt buried the cloth. Two layers of hog fence were placed on top of the dirt and then a meter of fill and tree brances on top of that (fig. 9).

By the end of the first field session, we had assigned two hundred bone numbers (many to articulated skeletons), uncovered at least thirteen skulls, and discovered portions of nine Folsom projectile points.

Figure 9. Dirt, hog wire fence, and tree branches were layered above the bonebed to protect the site during the year between the first and second excavations.

Word of the site had spread throughout the area as well as throughout the archaeological community. Visitation to the site was hampered only by the inclement weather. A return to the site for continued investigation was deemed the most prudent course of action considering the potential for losing information since site protection could not be guaranteed. The task of raising money to fund a second field season began.

Return to the Cooper site was slated for May 1994. That gave us one year to raise money and plan the excavation. Moral support was easier to raise than monetary support. Dennis Stanford of the Smithsonian Institution was instrumental in twisting arms for the cause. Heightened visibility of Paleoindian studies—as a result of recent excavations at Stewart's Cattle Guard site by Pegi Jodry and Dennis Stanford; the Lake Ilo project on the northern plains (Root and Emerson 1994; Root et al. 1995); the Hudson-Meng site by Larry Todd and others; and the nearby Waugh site by Jack Hofman—was a double-edged sword for fundraising. On the one hand, funding sources were swamped with proposals for Paleoindian projects. On the other hand, the private sector was eager to become involved in such studies of early peoples, which historically have been high profile and highly romanticized endeavors. Ultimately, support came from a mixture of these sources. The people of Oklahoma, the National Geographic Society, the University of Oklahoma, the Oklahoma Archeological Survey, and private donations from professional, avocational, and armchair archaeologists supplied the monies to fund the second season of excavations.

Donations other than money also greatly aided the effort. The excavation of bone is, in itself, an arduous task and requires the use of special consolidation and preservation materials. The application of spray foam insulation to archaeological situations provides a fast, easy, and light casing suitable for use on osteological materials (Bement 1985; Bement and Buehler 1994). Convenience Products, the maker of Touch 'n Foam, having supplied us with foam for use on the Late Archaic age Certain site (Bement and Buehler 1994; Buehler 1997), were equally generous in supplying several thousand dollars' worth of the product for Cooper.

The 1994 Excavation

Investigation of the Cooper site resumed on May 23, 1994. The protective measures set in place in 1993 were successful. The only erosional damage was noted along the eastern edge where the modern gully cut into site deposits. A small section of the edge of this arroyo had collapsed, taking with it several bones. Vandalism to the site was limited to probing into the floodplain deposits beneath the bluff. In all, no major damage had been inflicted to the site.

Excavation commenced with the removal of the sandy fill that had been used to cover the bonebeds. Removing the overburden was easily accomplished down to the first major barrier, the impenetrable hog fencing. Nary a single bison escaped. Subsequent removal of the dirt and landscaping cloth revealed that the bonebed was in the same condition as when we had left it. Although numerous bison remains had been collected from the upper bonebed in 1993, many more awaited removal—in particular, the bones from the western margin of the old arroyo, where the upper and second bone deposits intermingled.

Excavation and removal of the Upper Kill progressed from east to west. Working along the bluff edge proved uncomfortable since this area overlooked the 6 m vertical drop onto the floodplain. To circumvent the possibility of collapse, reinforcing bars were driven into the profile 50 cm below the lower bonebed and a 2 × 12 × 36-inch plank was laid across the bars to form a platform. An excavator on this platform could clean the bones along the bluff edge with ease.

Gopher runs could be followed across the bonebed. Apparently the bones were not a barrier to the movement of these animals. Holes had been gnawed through bones of all sizes and thickness (fig. 10). Other interesting discoveries included the skeletons of snakes, lizards, and occasionally gophers within the filled rodent tunnels. Not all of the tunnels were old or filled. Live gophers visited the excavations from time to time and lizards and snakes still emerged from open holes.

Since many of the bison skeletons were completely articulated, special attention was given to isolated and out-of-place elements. Of particular interest was a skull in the chest cavity of an articulated skeleton. This skull, minus nasals, mandibles, and hyoids, was that of a two-year-old. The base of the skull rested on the lower side ribs and its nose on the upper side ribs (figs. 11a, b). It appeared that the skull propped the chest cavity open to allow the body to cool; such a situation is consistent with what a modern hunter might do. The importance of this discovery is that it shows intentional manipulation of the carcass, including removal of the internal organs at least to the extent of allowing the insertion of the skull. The condition of the inserted skull indicates that it must have been scavenged from the exposed bone deposits of the earlier kill. Otherwise, the skull would have complete nasals and probably the mandibles would still be attached. The precise origin of the skull remains problematic.

Another intriguing discovery was the presence of an isolated pelvis (BN624) under the animals of the Upper Kill along the east edge of the bonebed. Although the legs and vertebrae were missing, the sacrum was still attached. The extent of weathering and fracture of the dorsal ridge on the sacrum suggests that this pelvis was in the arroyo prior to the Upper Kill episode. It, too, may have originated in the deeper bonebed.

Two-thirds of the upper bonebed were removed before any additional exposure of the second bone deposit began. The final one-third

Figure 10. Damage to the bonebeds by burrowing gophers was often easily detected during the excavations. Bone was simply gnawed away.

A

B

Figure 11. The nose of a bison skull protrudes from the rib cage of an Upper Kill animal (a). Once the ribs were removed, it was shown that the skull rested within the rib cage (b) of this articulated skeleton.

of the Upper Kill proved difficult to uncover due to the intermingling of the two bonebeds. Confounding the situation was the extensive overlapping of articulated skeletons in this section of the Upper Kill. Three completely articulated skeletons lay one on top of the other as if they had fallen over in domino fashion. One of these skeletons had two point fragments in its chest cavity. A shattered midsection of one projectile point (of Edwards Plateau chert) was found between the right sixth and seventh ribs. A tip from another point (Alibates agatized dolomite) was found alongside the left ninth rib.

Underneath these three was the skeleton of a calf. Abrupt changes in the angle of the vertebrae of the neck (cervicles) and lower back (lumbars) suggested that this animal had been trampled to death (fig. 12). The fragile nature of the young bones hampered extraction attempts. The calf was the lowest skeleton in this section of the bonebed and indicated that the Upper Kill deposits extended west of the underlying bonebed.

In the area of bonebed overlap, elements of the deeper deposit could be segregated from those of the upper one by following the articulations. The thin line of gray sediment identified in the eastern portion of the upper bonebed continued to the western margin. Truncations in this deposit were noticed where it had been transected by gopher tunnels. Any bones dipping through the gray lense were in the deeper bonebed.

An undulation in the upper bonebed was noticed near the western margin. The deposits dipped into what must have been the channel in the arroyo floor. The articulated skeletons of several Upper Kill animals followed the curvature of this ancient channel.

Several of the bones articulated with skeletons from the deeper bonebed had circular fractures on their upper surfaces. These fractures were consistently oval and between 10 and 12 cm in their greatest dimension (fig. 13). The morphology of the fractures indicated that they had occurred while the bone was midway between fresh or green and dry or brittle. From their context it was proposed that the fractures were the result of trampling. Their singular concentration in the area of bonebed overlap indicates that bones from the earlier kill that had not been buried by sediments accruing between kill episodes were trampled by the animals of the Upper Kill. The completely articulated animals in the upper bed and bone with trample fractures in the deeper

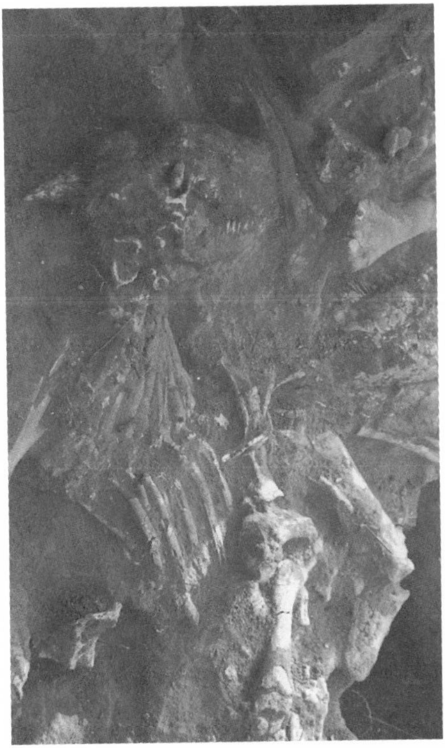

A

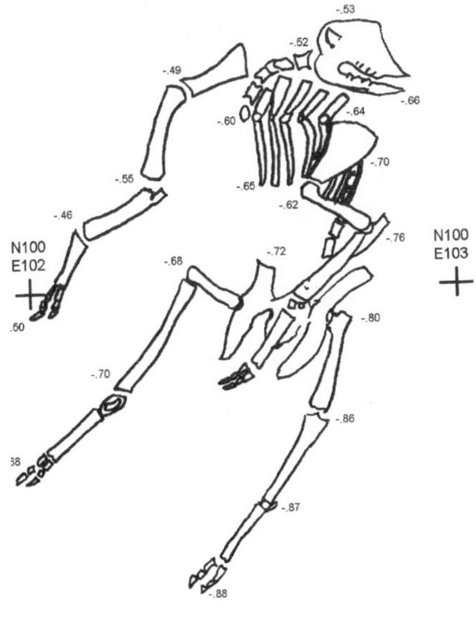

B

Figure 12. Photograph (a) and plan map (b) of the skeleton of a calf thought to have been trampled to death.

bed demonstrate that the Upper Kill was distinct and apart from the deeper one and not a slopewash mantle of a portion of the same bonebed.

Numerous Folsom points, flake knives, resharpening flakes, and fist-sized cobbles were found in the upper bonebed. The projectile points bestowed instant fame to the discovering individual. This was particularly true when the discoverer was one of the Oklahoma Anthropological Society members, but even professional participants were not immune to their effect. The more mundane fist-sized cobbles spurred many discussions. Normally, these artifacts are considered hammerstones that were used to fracture leg bones for marrow removal. Few of the Upper Kill bones were broken in this manner. The cobbles were not a natural component of the gully fill, so they had to have been purposefully brought to the kill site.

After the removal of the upper bonebed, excavations continued downward to expose the deeper bone deposit. This second bonebed was uncovered from south to north and east to west. The greatest separation between the upper and this lower bonebed was found near the center of the excavation block, where the coarse sand deposit was nearly 30 cm thick (figs. 14a, b). Although gopher runs crisscrossed these sands, the only evidence that bone or cultural material was transported from one level to the other is the possible fit of a projectile base from the deeper bonebed to the point tip found in the gopher tunnel above the upper bonebed. Since the tip was found in a filled in gopher tunnel, it is assumed that the base was in situ and that both therefore belong to the deeper deposit.

The deeper bonebed shared many characteristics of the upper one. First, the bones were in good condition. Second, the bonebed consisted almost entirely of fully articulated skeletons. Third, it was not long before several Folsom points and resharpening flakes were uncovered.

Excavation progressed rapidly once the orientation of an articulated skeleton was discerned. In these instances, it was easy to follow one skeletal element until its junction with the next bone and so on. The positioning of the skeletons was similar to that observed in the Upper Kill. Both rear legs were tucked underneath the pelvis to support positioning of the animal on its belly. Front legs were often drawn close to the rib cage in a flexed position. Other skeletons lay on

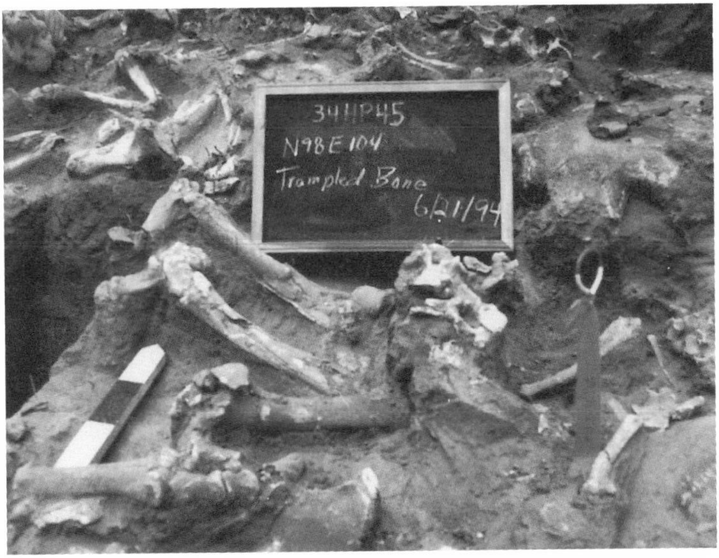

Figure 13. Two rear leg bones (tibii) with circular fractures, attributed to trampling by animals of a subsequent kill episode, were uncovered as excavations progressed into the lower bone levels.

one side with legs either flexed or straight. Legs from one animal often extended over or under a portion of another skeleton.

The skeletons were primarily oriented to the long axis of the ancient arroyo. However, the middle of this bonebed contained skeletons turned perpendicular to the arroyo and others facing opposite those coming up the gully. Apparently the lead animals, upon reaching the arroyo head (and dead end), turned in an attempt to flee back down the gully, but the way was blocked by their followers. The area where the variously facing animals met came to be known as the bison convergence (fig. 15). The skulls of nine fully articulated animals came to rest within a 1.5×2 m area.

Two skulls had large holes in the vault. One hole, entering from the left side, was later found to contain a gopher nest. The hole edges bear gnawing marks, indicating that the origin was due to gophers and not people. The hole in the second skull was in the top of the cranium although off center. No rodent gnaw marks were found. The edges are

Figure 14. The separation between the uppermost bone deposit and next one down is illustrated in these two photographs.

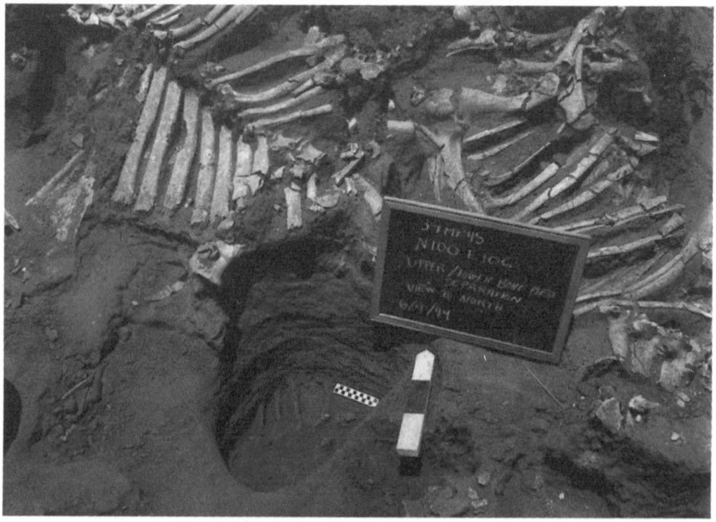

Figure 15. An area of densely packed articulated skeletons became known as the bison convergence. The position of the skeletons indicates that the lead animals tried to turn around when they reached the end of the arroyo trap.

sharp but do not display the encircling fracture lines typical of impact-induced cavities. If the hole were from trampling, then bone fragments should have been contained in the cavity. Such is not the case. This skull may be evidence that the brain was removed by the hunters, but this is not conclusive.

Several projectile points, flake knives, resharpening flakes, and fist-sized cobbles were recovered from the second bonebed. Again, the cobbles appeared out of place. Even fewer of the deeper kill bones were splintered from hammering.

The effects of gophers remained highly visible. In addition to the fossorial assemblage of gophers, snakes, and lizards, the intact, curled skeleton of a young badger was found within the bonebed. Although a burrow was not discernible, the damage to the enveloping bones by the badger's claws indicated that the animal had tunneled into the deposit and died. Even this skeleton was not protected from the ravages of the gophers. The top of the badger's skull had been destroyed by a gopher tunnel.

As with the upper bonebed, the bison bones conformed to the dip of the gully channel located near the western edge of the bone deposit. As noted, the bonebed did not extend as far west as did the Upper Kill.

Excavation of the slump deposits on and into the floodplain continued. A 2-meter-wide trench perpendicular to the bluff face followed the dip in the bedrock that protected the site. The profile created by this trench showed that bone had been continuously eroding from the bluff face and accumulating on the floodplain ever since the last time the river channel had cut against the bedrock (figs. 16a, b). Estimating how long it has been since the river last lapped the base of the bluff was a frequent topic of conversation. Guesses ranged from over 5,000 years ago to under 500 years ago. A dark, highly organic river deposit just above the present water table provided a means to settle the debate. A radiocarbon date obtained from the organics in this zone indicated that the river had last flowed against the bedrock at the base of the site approximately 850 years ago (840 ± 50 BP). All bone and artifacts recovered from the slump excavation had eroded from the site within the last 850 years.

Not surprising, the bones were highly fragmented and weathered after tumbling over 6 m from their original position in the bonebed to rest on the floodplain floor until buried by more sediment eroding from the bluff. Also recovered from the slump were several projectile points, flake tools, resharpening flakes, and fist-sized cobbles. The most exquisite complete Folsom point from the site (and probably from any site) was unearthed from the slump material (fig. 17). As with all the slump bone and artifacts, it is impossible to attribute the material to a specific bonebed. Hence, we could not assign this fine specimen of a Folsom point to a particular bed.

Many Folsom kill sites have associated butchering and processing areas, usually within 100 m of the kill locality (Hill and Hofman 1997; Hofman et al. 1991; Jodry 1987). Considerable effort was spent searching for a camp or processing site near the Cooper kills. An exploratory 1 × 2 m excavation unit opened 26 m upslope of the kill site deposits yielded no cultural material. Coring of the area upslope of the unit, around it, and between the unit and the bonebeds failed to produce evidence of a processing camp. Inspection and

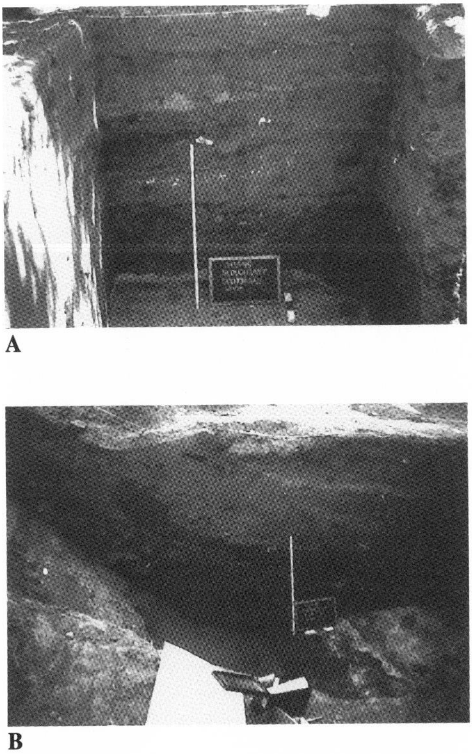

Figure 16. North-south (a) and east-west (b) profiles of the slump excavation detail the incorporation of bones eroded from the kill site into the floodplain deposits.

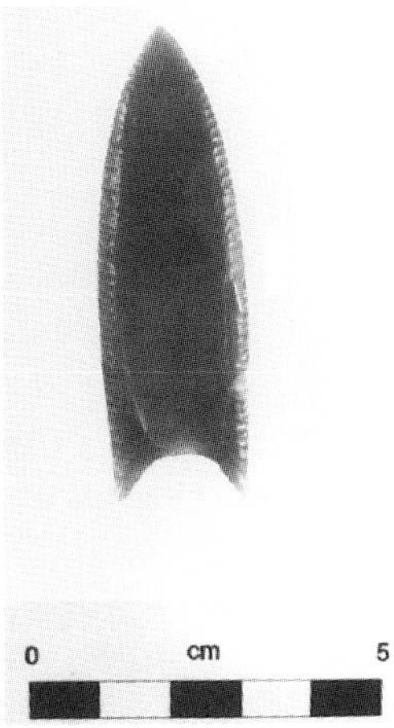

Figure 17. This projectile point is one of the finest examples of Folsom craftsmanship yet recovered from a site.

Figure 18. Screening of all dirt from around the bones was conducted in the shade provided by large trees on the floodplain below the site.

cleaning of the steep banks along the deeply eroded modern gullies within 200 m of the site likewise produced no camp debris. The absence of cultural or bone material demonstrated that whatever was left of the Cooper site was in the small remnant of the ancient arroyo.

As summer temperatures climbed, the shaded slump excavation became a popular spot after the excitement of working in the bonebed waned. All screening was conducted on the floodplain under the large shade trees (fig. 18).

Excitement in the bonebeds, however, was far from over. The deeper bonebed was removed from east to west. As the skeletons of the bison convergence were removed, another layer of articulated skeletons emerged. Bones of these lower skeletons often displayed the large oval fractures seen along the edges of the bison convergence and attributed to trampling. Yet in this lowest bone level, the trampled bone was scattered throughout. The upper surfaces of the bones from the lower articulated skeletons were more weathered than those from the underside of the bison convergence skeletons. The increase in weathered bone and the evidence of trampling indicated that yet another kill had transpired in this ancient arroyo. Continued excavation segregated the lower bonebed into two distinct kill events. The arroyo at Cooper contained three distinct bonebeds! Skeletons now emerging in the arroyo channel were separated from the bison convergence by 5 cm of coarse sandy fill similar to that separating the convergence from the upper bonebed. Again, the presence of articulated skeletons aided the task of segregating the two Lower Kill events.

The excavators in the bonebed usually carried on a fairly constant chatter, some of which occasionally touched on archaeological matters. When one of the excavators grew quiet, this was usually a sign that he or she had discovered a stone tool, probably a projectile point. Often all would stop working and inquire if in fact something had been found. If so, then a flurry of activity employing cameras and blow-by-blow descriptions of the discovery ensued. Afterward, work and the endless drone of conversation resumed.

Such was the situation on July 11 when we were removing the remaining skeletons of the bison convergence and uncovering the lower bonebed. I do not know what the topic of conversation was—probably the road kill report or the latest inane commercial on the radio. I was removing dirt from an articulated leg, the bones of which lay across the eye orbits of a skull. As the forehead of this skull was uncovered, a brilliant red zigzag line was exposed (fig. 19). Noticing that I had dropped from the conversation, the other excavators stopped work and, in anticipation of the inevitable announcement of a discovery and hence a much needed respite, stood and looked my direction.

The zigzag of red stood in stark contrast to the bleached white skull surface and was visible from all areas of the bonebed. To say there was an instant of incredulous awe does not quite describe that moment of discovery. Here, in a gully in northwest Oklahoma, among the bones of an extinct species of bison, was a painted skull. We were at once exhilarated yet meditative. Euphoric over the discovery, we proceeded to document the find to the fullest extent possible. The zigzag line became known as the lightning bolt. Calls were made to the Survey, National Geographic Society, and to Solveig Turpin, expert in prehistoric North American rock art. The remainder of the day was spent in silence, a marked contrast to the usual hubbub. Thoughts turned inward. This find was a great reward for the many

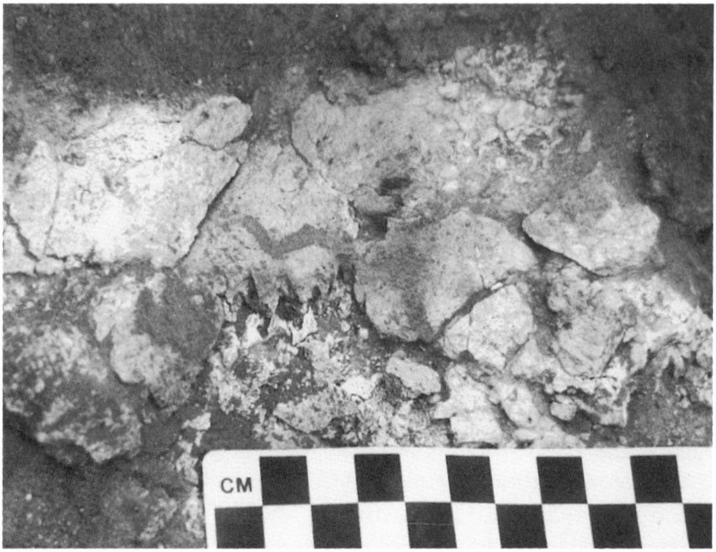

Figure 19. Shown partially excavated is the red zigzag design found on a bison skull underlying the Middle Kill bonebed.

hours of tedious work in the bonebeds. It also made us reflect on all the other skulls unearthed. Did they have something on them that we had missed? Only inspecting them in the lab in Norman would settle that question. And that would have to wait. All the skulls were encased in spray foam.

Dr. Turpin arrived at the site two days after the skull discovery. She corroborated that the design on the skull had been painted and reveled in its preservation. Instructions were proffered about the technique to encapsulate and remove the skull. Suggestions for its analysis were also forthcoming.

Additional cleaning of the skull showed that it had been trampled by bison of the Middle Kill and disturbed by rodent tunneling. A large portion of the right horn core and forehead had been destroyed by gophers. The nasal portion of the skull and the left eye orbit were crushed into tiny fragments. What appeared to be the start of another line of paint disappeared into the trampled mess. A portion of the left maxilla was intact and hinted at the presence of a painted line.

A rodent tunnel passed between the skull and the atlas vertebra. At first, it seemed the gopher had destroyed the atlas, but additional excavation determined that the skull was separated from the atlas and the rest of its articulated skeleton. The skull had apparently been repositioned to look straight down the arroyo in the direction of oncoming animals.

The articulated leg on top of the painted skull was part of an animal killed during the second use of the arroyo. The painted skull was from an animal in the lowest kill. Prior to painting, the skull had been skinned, defleshed, and dried, all processes best left to nature. If correctly interpreted, the trampled bone indicated a three- to five-year interval between kill episodes, so that the elements would have had sufficient time to prepare the skull. A logical sequence is as follows. In anticipation of reuse of the gully, hunters selected a skull from the earlier kill, painted it for use as a talisman, and positioned it facing downslope. Animals herded into the gully for the second kill trampled the painted skull along with any other bones exposed on the surface. Bison skulls, rocks, and other offerings were used in a similar way in preparation for bison kills on the northern plains during early Historic times (Verbicky-Todd 1984).

From the time the painted skull was uncovered until its removal seven days later, it rained in excess of 5 inches on the excavations. Removal of the skeletons from the Middle Kill progressed smoothly. The excavation and extraction of the Lower Kill was also completed without difficulties. As with the other bonebeds, the Lower Kill yielded Folsom points, resharpening flakes, and fist-sized cobbles. Flake knives were missing from the inventory. No other painted skulls were found during the excavation.

Excavation of the Cooper site ceased on July 23, 1994. The final tasks included detailed descriptions of the profiles in the arroyo and filling the slump block trench. A 2 × 2m square containing a portion of the Upper and Middle kills along the northern edge of the arroyo was to be preserved. Unfortunately, this block was vandalized during the two days we were transporting equipment and bone to the Survey. Upon returning to the site, we covered what was left of the block with hog fence and buried it. The floor of the ancient arroyo beneath the Lower Kill was once again empty of bison: a circumstance not seen for over 10,000 years.

The excavation documented three successful bison kills attributable to Folsom people. The animals had been herded into a dead-end arroyo and killed by hunters positioned on the gully rim. Drastic changes in the landscape allowed the ancestral Beaver River to remove all of this old gully except a portion 8 m wide and 6 m long that was protected by a basal layer of sandstone bedrock. The size of the original arroyo and the number of animals killed in each event is unknown, but I estimate that somewhere between 25 and 50% of the deposits were preserved.

CHAPTER 4

Excavation Procedures

The excavation of the Cooper site adhered to the rigorous field techniques of bonebed investigation that have developed over the past twenty-five years. Major advances in bonebed excavation procedures have grown out of the realization that the position and condition of bones within a deposit are the result of multiple processes (Bement 1986, 1994b; Jodry 1987 Johnson 1987; Todd 1987b; Wheat 1972). Although many of these processes are linked to butchering and meat handling techniques, others are the result of natural agencies such as weathering and postdepositional alterations. This realization has led to the development of detailed recording and excavation techniques (Jodry 1987; Johnson 1987; Todd 1987b). The bonebed, once thought to be strictly an artifact of past human behavior, is now considered the result of many factors that must be segregated before human activities can be studied. For this reason, the bones themselves must be preserved for study. Techniques that allow preservation of bone often require extended excavation time to allow hardeners and casing materials to dry and exacting documentation procedures to be conducted. In the end, the additional time spent in the field ensures higher return on data concerning prehistoric carcass handling, butchering practices, and nonhuman agents acting on the postkill assemblages. Great attention was paid to details that help differentiate patterns of human behavior from those of natural or animal agents. Detailed plan maps, including base elevations of bones, and profiles along excavation borders were drawn and documented. Particular attention was paid to the location of rodent disturbances in the bonebeds.

A 2 × 2 m grid was placed over the site area. Each bonebed was completely exposed, photographed, and drawn to scale before any bone was removed. In this fashion, skeletal elements from a single animal could be documented and kept separate from those representing another animal. Strike and dip or, more precisely, the orientation and vertical displacement of long bones were recorded for all isolated bones. Only representative measurements were taken from individual bones within a completely articulated skeleton since an articulated carcass contains bones that are naturally oriented in a number of directions. Perpendicular orientations are usually found between axial skeletal components (skull, vertebral column) and appendicular ones (front and rear legs). The vertical dip within an articulated skeleton can also vary according to the positioning of the skeleton (whether it is lying on its side, back, or belly). In these instances, only the strike and dip of elements lying on the underside of articulated carcasses define the landform morphology of the site at the time of the kill.

Each bone and artifact was given a field number. Articulated segments were assigned a common field number but individual bones within the articulation received a second number during analysis, so that components could be analyzed separately or in aggregate.

Overall, the bones at the Cooper site are well preserved. Chemical consolidants and encasement materials—plaster of Paris and spray foam (Bement 1985)—were used when necessary to remove fractured bone. In an attempt to reduce excavator-induced damage to the bones, bamboo splints and brushes were used where possible. Trowels aided in the removal of large bones and articulations. A special machete was employed to undercut foam-encased skulls at the time of extraction. Occasionally, underlying bones were damaged by removal of overlying specimens.

All dirt removed from the bonebeds was screened through fine-mesh (3 mm) hardware cloth. Additional bulk samples were collected from each bonebed and from intervening sterile layers. In addition, a sample from each bonebed was water screened to establish maximum recovery rates of material. The water screening provided no benefit over dry screening. Hence, the majority of the fill was dry screened.

Documentation of the excavation used both color and black and white photographs, VHS recording, scaled drawings of plan maps and profiles, and a log written daily by the principal investigator. Brian Carter employed hand augering and a truck-mounted bull probe to study the adjacent landscape and soils for clues to the site's setting at the time of the kills.

CHAPTER 5

Dating the Deposits

The age of the Cooper site has been determined by a combination of radiocarbon dating, stratigraphy, index artifacts, and bison species identification. The first assessment was derived from the bones themselves. Upon discovery, it was determined that the bison remains were from animals substantially larger than modern bison. These bones fit the size ranges of either *Bison antiquus* or *B. occidentalis*, both of which are known to predate 5,000 years ago.

The broken Folsom projectile point provided evidence that at least part of the bone deposit was over 10,000 years old. Folsom points have been found in datable contexts at other sites and are assigned to a time range from 10,900 to 10,200 years ago (Haynes et al. 1992). The subsequent discovery of Folsom points in all three kills indicates that all three are between 10,900 and 10,200 years old.

Attempts to place the kill episodes more precisely within the 700-year-long Folsom period have not been successful. Radiocarbon assay of bone yielded a date of 7020 ± 120 years BP (Beta-60260) (table 1). An attempt to date hackberry seeds from the deposits indicated that the seeds were modern intrusions. Further attempts at dating the site used soil samples. Bulk-carbon assay of a dark deposit underlying the lowermost kill episode provided an age of 10,050 ± 210 BP (Beta 75899). A one-sigma span of this age barely places the date within the upper end of the established time frame for Folsom cultures. The possibility of contamination by recent carbon in the bulk-carbon date suggests that this date can only be viewed as a minimum age for the Cooper deposits.

Radiocarbon assays of sediments were able to provide a general time line for the site formational processes following its cultural use. A

Table 1
Radiocarbon Dates

Sample ID	Material	Provenience	Date (yrs BP)
Beta-60260	Bone	Slump surface	7020±120
Beta-74202	Soil	Buried A	1100± 50
Beta-75899	Dirt	Beneath kills	10,050±210
Beta-74205	Gopher fill	Beneath kills	8880±190
Beta-74203	Soil	Slump trench	600± 80
Beta-74204	Soil	Slump trench	840± 50

sample from a buried paleosol directly beneath the eolian sands that mantle the area today yielded an age of 1100 ± 50. This indicates that the paleosol was forming at this time. Subsequent erosion of this horizon was then followed by deposition of the sands. Thus, the windblown deposits are less than 1,100 years old.

CHAPTER 6

Soils and Landscape Features

BRIAN J. CARTER

Preliminary soil and geologic investigations and survey maps have previously been completed for the general study-site area (northern Woodward and southern Harper counties, Oklahoma; Carter et al. 1990; Myers 1959, 1962; Nance et al. 1960; Nance et al. 1963). Cooper site soil and rock descriptions include sedimentary deposits of Permian, Pleistocene, and Holocene age. Tertiary-age sediments are found in the uplands 4 km north of the Cooper site. Rock exposures within the immediate site include Pleistocene alluvium, Holocene eolian sands, and Permian Rush Springs sandstone.

Geologic and soil-forming processes including erosion, sedimentation, humus accumulation, and leaching are inferred by the examination of sediment and soil layers (horizons). The soil and sediments at the site were described to assist in archaeological investigation and discussion. Hydraulically driven soil cores, hand-augered soil cores, and hand-dug soil excavations were made in and near the site. Hand-augered soil cores were described in the floodplain and in a dry gully channel adjacent to the site. Hydraulically driven soil cores were described on the bluff immediately above the site. Soil profile descriptions were also made along the east to west–trending bluff wall within 100 m of the site. Hand-dug soil excavations were described at the site and in a similar bluff position to the east. A hand-dug soil excavation was also placed at the foot of the bluff to describe mass wasting of the bluff face into the adjacent floodplain. Soil and sediment descriptions included particle size analysis (field-determined soil texture), soil color, soil cracking pattern (soil structure), and soil consistency (ability of the soil to resist rupture or crushing). The depth and thickness of soil layers were recorded, along with soil reaction (lime content) and special features for each layer. Such special features included root content, gravel content, lime ($CaCo_3$ precipitates) concentrations, and animal burrows. The soil and sediment layers were named (A horizon = surface layer, B horizon = subsoil layer, C horizon = sediment without soil features) and the type of geologic process that produced the sediment was identified: eolian (wind-deposited sand), alluvium (stream-deposited sand, silt, and clay), and colluvium (sediment produced by gravity along the base of steep bluff walls).

Sediments

Observations along the south-facing wall of the east to west– trending bluff identify three distinct sediment layers. The lowest is the bedrock unit of Permian age (240–290 million years old), consisting of red sandstone with minor components of red shale, and of gray sandstone and shale. The bedrock is weakly consolidated and is difficult to dig with a shovel. The middle sediment unit overlying the bedrock is unconsolidated (easily dug with a shovel) red alluvium. This middle sediment unit contains the bison remains and associated artifacts. The alluvium is produced by a wash of sediments through small arroyos that drain the uplands on the north side of the floodplain. The alluvium occurs both as current arroyo fill along the level of the floodplain and as previous discontinuous remnants, which are lenses approximately 3 to 4 m thick and 10 to 50 m wide along the bluff face. The arroyo sediment remnants on the bluff face are dissected by modern arroyos, which grade to current floodplain level. The alluvium associated with modern arroyos produces small alluvial fans as the arroyos merge with the floodplain. Only large arroyos maintain a defined channel extending to the Beaver River just south of the site. Overlying the alluvium is eolian sand, the uppermost sediment layer. The eolian sand forms a thin (1–2 m) layer which discontinuously covers the alluvium and bedrock.

The ground surface along the bluff and within the uplands above the bluff is eroding. Constructional (stable) surfaces of eolian dunes and alluvial terraces are absent. The surfaces within the floor of modern arroyos receive sediments periodically due to the hillslope water runoff and erosion. Wind erosion and deposition within the bluff area are not currently active. Many trees located on the floodplain serve to block the wind. The uplands contain alluvium from previous levels of the Beaver River and Permian bedrock. Alluvium from ancient rivers and streams extends north of the site to the divide separating the Cimarron from the Beaver drainage basin. The ancient alluvium contains sand, gravels, and cobbles. The lithology is typical "Rocky Mountain outwash," including quartzite, limestone, shale, granite, and sandstone. The ancient alluvium contains lithologies typical for the Ogallala formation and other rock formations found within the western portion of the Beaver and Cimarron drainage basins.

Soils

Soils found at the site represent periods when erosion was interrupted by ground surface stabilization by plant and animal communities. One buried soil is preserved within the dig site. Small areas of soils also exist across the current ground surface. The soil buried beneath the uppermost sediment (eolian sand) is formed in the middle sediment layer (arroyo deposits). The 1100 BP (Beta 74202) soil date represents the time when the soil was buried by windblown sand. The buried soil is well formed and indicates a 2,000- to 3,000-year period of stability before burial. It contains a dark humus-rich surface layer (A horizon) overlying a clay-rich subsoil (Btk-argillic horizon). Below the subsoil are stratified alluvial sediments, which contain bison remains and artifacts. The only other soil in the immediate site area occurs at the current ground surface and forms in eolian sand. The surface soil contains only a slightly darkened surface layer (A horizon), which directly overlies the sand. The lack of subsoil below the surface layer supports the limited period (< 1,100 years) of maximum possible surface stability and soil formation. The thin surface layer is produced by modern erosion, which removes soil materials.

Important surface and buried soils also occur adjacent to and below the site in the Beaver River floodplain. These soils contain bison remains and artifacts eroded from the site by water and incorporated into floodplain soils by flood waters (fig. 20). Three buried soils, each containing only a surface layer (A horizon), are separated by floodplain sediments. The surface soil also contains only an A horizon. Two radiocarbon dates from the upper buried layers (600 and 840 BP [Beta 74203, 74204]) support the relatively young age of the

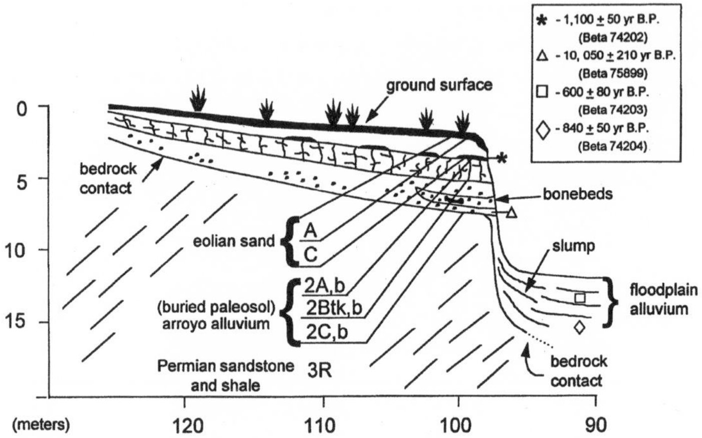

Figure 20. The location of key radiocarbon-dated samples is shown on a general north-south profile of the site and slump deposits.

soils and sediments in the floodplain, and the relatively recent incorporation of bison remains and artifacts into the floodplain.

Painting a Landscape through Time: Landscape Inversion

Using the geologic idea that the present is the key to the past, images of human and geologic events that occurred at the site can be recreated. Several facts are used to support these images. The first critical piece of evidence is that the layers containing the bison remains and human artifacts are similar to modern arroyo sediments. Analysis of the spatial distribution and physical characteristics of the layers produces a bison-kill site occurring within an active arroyo. The Folsom artifacts indicate that the arroyo was active at least during the time span from 10,000 to 11,000 years ago: arroyo sediments separate the three kill events. No soils are found within the conformable arroyo sediments. Lack of soils indicates lack of ground surface stabilization by plant and animal communities. Not until 1100 BP does a soil occur at the top of these truncated arroyo deposits.

For the arroyo to have filled with sediments, it is likely that either the level of the Beaver River channel changed or the hill slopes were denuded of vegetation, or both. An increase in sedimentation was probably caused by a decrease in rainfall and plant cover followed by intense storm runoff. Severe storms and runoff occur in the area today. Greater plant cover today compared to 10,000 to 11,000 years ago limits rapid arroyo aggregation. The three layers containing bison remains and human artifacts could have been deposited by storm events separated by several weeks or up to several years. Lack of soils within the arroyo supports a closely timed (weeks to several years) occurrence of the bison kills. Arroyo deposition stopped by at least 3000 BP. This estimate is based on the sum of the age of the soil surface (1100 BP) and the time it took to form the soil (2000 BP). At 3000 BP or before, the arroyo cut laterally and down in response to undetermined environmental conditions. The lateral and downward incision creates an image of landscape inversion; the sediment once deposited in an arroyo channel is now observed on the bluff wall (fig. 21).

A possible explanation for the lateral movement and incision of the arroyo is the erodability of the underlying sediments. During arroyo sedimentation at 10,000 BP, the arroyo walls consisted of soft (weakly consolidated) Permian bedrock. Erosion in the arroyo removed the soft Permian bedrock. Deposition of sandy loam sediments followed erosion in the arroyo until about 3000 BP. As a new arroyo channel formed and started to remove sediment at the site, two sediment types were now available for removal by erosion: the sandy loam within the old arroyo and the adjacent Permian bedrock. The new arroyo channel formed in the soft Permian bedrock because of the inferior plant-root environment in the bedrock compared to that in the deep arroyo sandy loam. Even though the bedrock is soft, root penetration and soil formation is shallow because of the low porosity of the bedrock compared to the sandy loam arroyo sediment. Compared to the deep sandy loam soil within the old arroyo, the soft Permian bedrock is more susceptible to erosion by running water. Erosion in the arroyo hence removes sediment from the bedrock area rather than from the sandy loam arroyo soil. Lateral migration and incision within the arroyo produces a bluff wall remnant consisting of arroyo sediments. During the last 1,100 years, windblown sand covered the site and floodplain deposits accumulated, incorporating

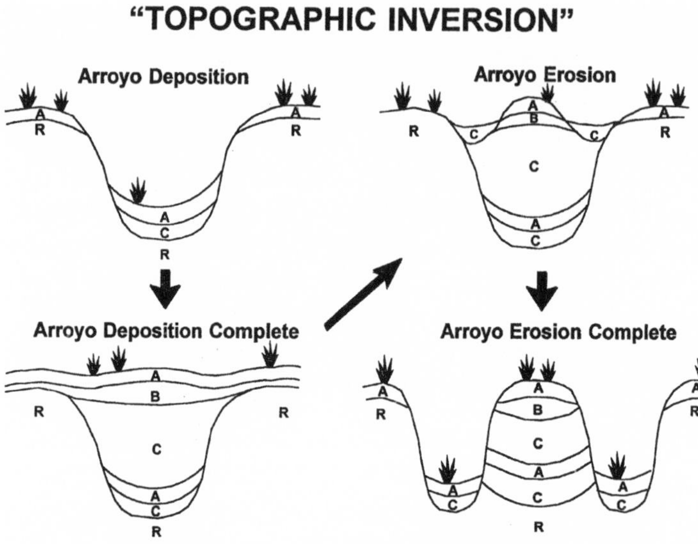

Figure 21. This model of topographic inversion illustrates the sequence of landscape evolution that resulted in the ancient gully bottom being high in the bluff face.

sediments, bison remains, and human artifacts all eroded from the old arroyo.

Comparing Colors: Soil Material versus Paint

The soils and sediments at the site are red, gray, and dark brown. Dark brown colors are associated with buried and surface soil layers that contain humus. Gray colors are associated with bison remains. Decaying bison in contact with soil material changed the soil materials from red to gray. Decomposition of carcass remains by facultative aerobic and anaerobic microorganisms produced gray layers within predominantly red-oxidized sediments above and below the bonebed. The gray colors extend several centimeters away from bone deposits. The gray soil in the periphery of the bones indicates rapid burial of decomposing organic matter and is similar to features identified at the Waugh site (Hofman, Carter, and Hill 1992). Iron oxides coat all the sand, silt, and clay-sized soil particles producing a red color in most of the soil. Only small amounts (0.2–2.0%) of the iron oxides are needed to give the soil a red hue. Most of the soil material is composed of minerals other than iron oxides, including quartz, feldspars, calcite, kaolinite, hydrous mica, and smectite.

The paint found on the bison skull is distinctly different than the surrounding soil material and sediments. This paint contains a majority of iron oxides and hydroxides. The iron minerals impart to the paint an intense red color when compared to adjacent soil material. Concentrations of iron oxides and hydroxides do occur in the area and are found in sandstones and shales. Iron oxides were probably collected from these local rock-source concentrations and used as paint. The alternative source requires the separation of iron oxides from soil material, which is difficult; the required technology was probably not known to the Folsom culture.

CHAPTER 7

Description and Analysis of Recovered Materials

One of the most difficult descriptors of the Cooper site bonebeds to portray is their size. With animal numbers in the twenties for each kill episode, one would think that the kill area would be huge and that the remnants of each would decrease with depth, the ancient gully being V-shaped in cross section. Indeed, although an area 6 × 8 m (18 × 24 ft) was excavated, the lower bonebed is contained in an area of only 3.5 × 4 m (10 × 12 ft). The Middle Kill encompasses 5.5 × 4 m (16.5 × 12 ft) and the Upper Kill approximately 6 × 4 m (18 × 12 ft). But the overall area concerned is not large. For reference, the drive lane in a basketball court is roughly 5 × 4 m (15 × 12 ft) (fig. 22): each kill remnant is approximately the size of a basketball drive lane.

Originally each kill was substantially larger than the remnant uncovered. The meandering channel of the Beaver River and the erosion caused by downcutting of a modern gully on the eastern side of the site removed an estimated 50 to 75% of each bonebed. Even if only 50% of each kill were missing, the herd sizes would approach fifty animals per kill.

The following description of the site materials progresses from top to bottom, following the sequence of discovery and excavation.

Upper Kill

The Upper bison bonebed (fig. 23) occupied an area 6 m from east to west by 4 m from north to south (fig. 24). The southern edge was truncated by the Beaver River. Similarly, the eastern edge was defined by a modern gully. The western and northern perimeter followed the edges of the ancient arroyo. The bones along the northern and western

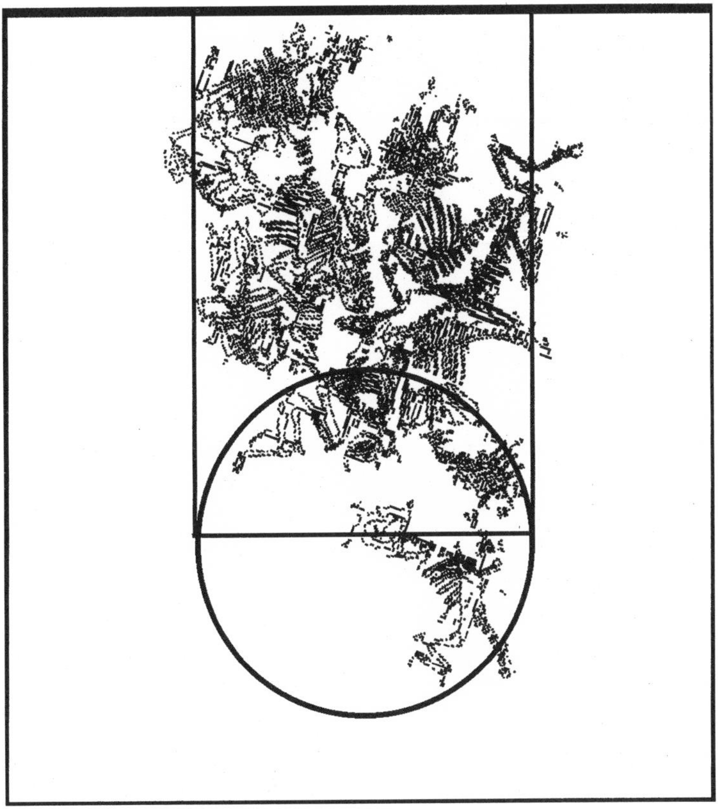

Figure 22. In an attempt to portray the size of the bonebed remnants, skeletons of the bison convergence of the Middle Kill are placed within the drive lane of a basketball court.

edges inclined sharply, marking the steeper slopes of the gully head. The bones along the side and head of the gully had average dip of 40 and 50% respectively, compared to 15% in the gully bottom. The long axis of the ancient arroyo is oriented 20 degrees east of north and the majority of its terminus (knick point) was removed by the modern gully flanking the eastern edge of the site.

Figure 23. Excavations uncover the Upper Kill bonebed remnant.

Bone Analysis

A total of 972 identifiable bison bone elements was recovered from the Upper Kill deposits. This number is actually higher (ca. 1,450) because some elements, such as ribs and vertebrae, were analyzed as a unit. Only 63 bones (6.5%) were not articulated with at least one other element when uncovered. Some of the isolated elements were overlying the upslope articulations, suggesting that they were redeposited downslope from the knick point during burial by gully infilling. The others are remnants from skeletons that had eroded from the bluff face or had been removed by the side gully. Within the main excavation area, complete skeletons were articulated.

A minimum number of twenty-nine individuals (MNI) was determined from the count of individual elements sorted by age, side, and articulation categories. MNI by age indicates that these twenty-nine individuals were three calves (group I), two yearlings (group II), six two-year-olds (group III), five three-year-olds (group IV), five four-year-olds (group V), three five-year-olds (group VI), three six-year-olds (group VII), and two animals ages seven years old or older (group VIII). None of the animals was older than ten years. The eldest individuals still retained teeth with sufficient enamel for an estimated five additional years of natural life. (Age determination detail is given in the appendix.)

SEASONALITY. The tooth eruption and wear criteria employed to age the animals also provide a means to determine the season of death. Modern bison have an annual birthing pulse in which the majority of calves are born in a two-week period. On the southern

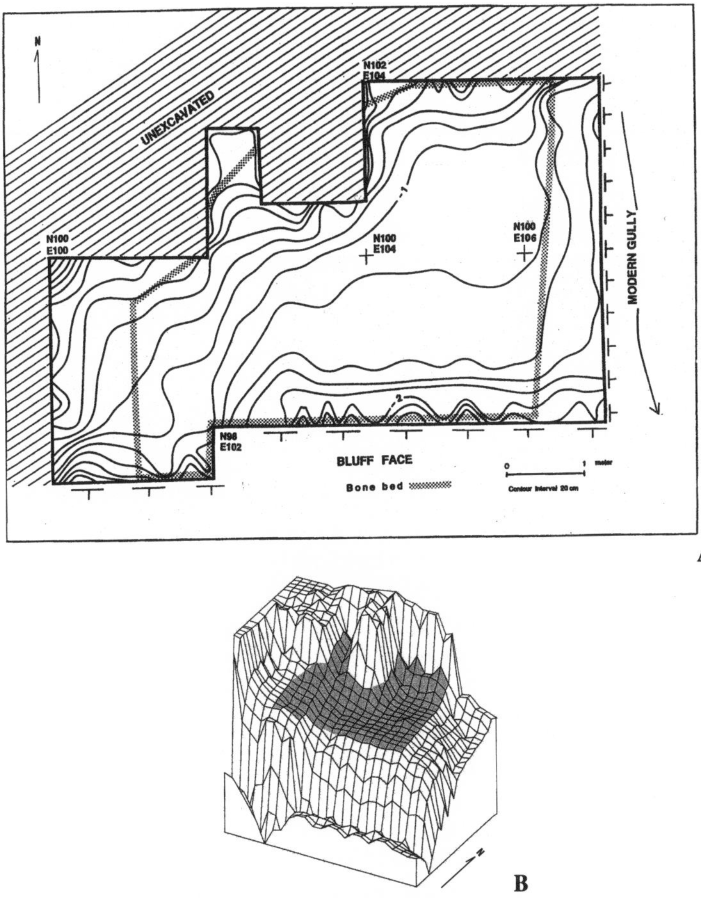

Figure 24. Contour (a) and three-dimensional (b) maps of the Upper Kill remnant were generated from the elevation taken from the underside of the bison skeletons.

plains, this peak extends from the end of April through the beginning of May, approximately three weeks earlier than for northern plains herds. We assume that during Folsom times the bison had a similar date for the calving pulse. The tooth eruption and wear pattern in bison has an accuracy of plus or minus one month. This is sufficient to allow determination of the season of death by combining age and birthing pulse. The Upper Kill animals have tooth eruption and wear patterns indicating an age of n + 0.3 years age. The calves are 0.3 years old, followed by yearlings at 1.3, etc. The age cohorts are approximately four months (0.3 years) beyond the calving peak. If the calving peak occurred in late April or early May, the season of death is four months later, in late August or early September.

DIRECT EVIDENCE OF BUTCHERING. The bonebed is the result of a successful hunt. Following the kill event, the hunters assumed the task of butchering the animals. Killing and butchering provide opportunities for human modification of the bison skeletons, including damage from projectile points, marks left from skinning and butchering, and breakage patterns typical of butchering techniques. Subsequent to the human modification, the bones were exposed to weather, animal alteration, and a suite of factors that act on bones before and after they are buried. Many of these taphonomic processes affect the surface of the bones, obliterating the evidence of butchering. For this reason, what is known about the butchering of the animals is a small remnant of what actually occurred.

CUT MARKS. Direct evidence of butchering in the Upper Kill consists of cut marks on five bones: one humerus from a seven-plus-year-old; one pelvis from a five-year-old; three ribs from a seven-plus-year-old and two from animals of indeterminate age; and two tibiae with possible cut marks, one from a two-year-old and one from a five-year-old (fig. 25a; table 2). Confirmation of the true nature of these marks awaits special analysis using the scanning electron microscope.

SPIRAL FRACTURES. Green bone spiral or helical breaks were found on five elements: one femur, two humeri, one scapula, and one tibia (fig. 25b; table 3). In addition, several thoracic vertebrae have breaks thought to be associated with the butchering process.

Surface Factors

Other damage to the bones can be attributed to noncultural factors including weathering, root etching, rodent gnawing, carnivore gnawing, overburden pressure, possible trampling, and indeterminate causes (Hill 1979a, b; Hill and Behrensmeyer 1985).

WEATHERING. Degree of weathering is a measure of the condition of the surface of a bone as it undergoes changes brought about by

A

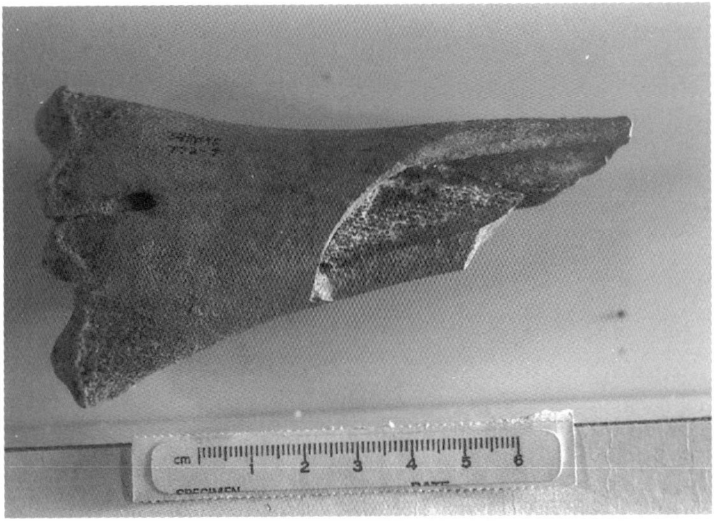

B

Figure 25. Bones with cut marks (a) and green bone spiral fractures (b) provide evidence that the animals were butchered.

Table 2
Upper Kill Cut Marks

Element	N	Absent	Present
1st phalanx	125	125	0
2nd phalanx	111	111	0
3rd phalanx	76	76	0
Astragalus	37	37	0
Cervical vertebrae	32	32	0
Calcaneus	38	38	0
Caudal vertebrae	7	7	0
Femur	36	36	0
Humerus	34	33	1
Lumbar vertebrae	18	18	0
Metacarpal	32	32	0
Metatarsal	42	42	0
Naviculo-cuboid	38	38	0
Patella	22	22	0
Pelvis	20	19	1
Radius	31	31	0
Ribs	65	62	3
Sacrum	15	15	0
Scapula	34	34	0
Skull	19	19	0
Sternal ribs	2	2	0
Sternum	10	10	0
Thoracic vertebrae	55	55	0
Tibia	40	38	2
Ulna	33	33	0
Total	972	965	7
%	100	99.28	0.72

exposure to the ravages of nature, particularly exposure to sun and wind. Behrensmeyer (1978) devised a system that ranks the weathering stage by identifying key changes observable on the surface of the bone. This system has been modified by Todd (1987b) to include a nonweathered stage. The ranking varies from 0 (nonweathered) through level 6 (complete rendering of the bone to a pile of splinters). Intervening levels include degrees of degreasing or drying, cracking, splitting, and splintering. The relative level of weathering is correlated to the length of time the bones lay on the surface prior to burial. Some subsurface weathering can take place, but this is usually minor compared with preburial weathering.

Table 3
Upper Kill Spiral Fractures

Element	N	Absent	Present
1st phalanx	125	125	0
2nd phalanx	111	111	0
3rd phalanx	76	76	0
Astragalus	37	37	0
Cervical vertebrae	32	32	0
Calcaneus	38	38	0
Caudal vertebrae	7	7	0
Femur	36	35	1
Humerus	34	32	2
Lumbar vertebrae	18	18	0
Metacarpal	32	32	0
Metatarsal	42	42	0
Naviculo-cuboid	38	38	0
Patella	22	22	0
Pelvis	20	20	0
Radius	31	31	0
Ribs	65	63	2
Sacrum	15	15	0
Scapula	34	33	1
Skull	19	19	0
Sternal ribs	2	2	0
Sternum	10	10	0
Thoracic vertebrae	55	55	0
Tibia	40	39	1
Ulna	33	33	0
Total	972	965	7
%	100	99.28	0.72

The degree of weathering displayed by the Upper Kill bones consisted of 35% with no weathering (level 0), 24% level 1, 39% level 2, and 2% level 3 (table 4). No bones displayed advanced weathering stages 4 through 6, indicating that the bones were probably buried fairly rapidly, accounting for their excellent state of preservation. In addition, the weathering was confined to the upper surface, indicating that the bones were not subjected to forces rolling them to expose the other surfaces to weathering conditions. This situation is consistent with the recovery of numerous completely articulated skeletons.

CARNIVORE CHEWING. The large amount of waste carnage left after a successful kill attracts the attention of scavengers such as foxes,

Table 4
Upper Kill Weathering

Element	N	Ranking			
		0	1	2	3
1st phalanx	125	52	25	47	1
2nd phalanx	111	49	25	32	5
3rd phalanx	76	21	19	30	6
Astragalus	37	15	10	11	1
Cervical vertebrae	32	5	9	18	0
Calcaneus	38	13	10	15	0
Caudal vertebrae	7	3	2	1	1
Femur	36	13	7	16	0
Humerus	34	9	5	19	1
Lumbar vertebrae	18	6	8	4	0
Metacarpal	32	9	5	18	0
Metatarsal	42	13	11	17	1
Naviculo-cuboid	38	15	10	13	0
Patella	22	10	4	8	0
Pelvis	20	7	5	8	0
Radius	31	10	1	18	2
Ribs	65	18	20	26	1
Sacrum	15	5	5	5	0
Scapula	34	15	3	16	0
Skull	19	19	0	0	0
Sternal ribs	2	2	0	0	0
Sternum	10	5	2	3	0
Thoracic vertebrae	55	5	25	24	1
Tibia	40	11	14	14	1
Ulna	33	9	7	16	1
Total	972	339	232	379	22
%	100	34.88	23.99	38.99	2.26

coyotes, and wolves. The amount of damage attributed to scavengers is affected by such factors as accessibility to the kill area, quickness of burial, proximity of human camps, time of the year, and weather conditions. Carnivores can have various effects on the skeletal remains. First, they can dismember and transport carcass components away from the kill. Second, they can destroy parts of bones left in place or moved minimal distances from the main concentration. The variable of carnivore damage is used to determine the amount of nonhuman disarticulation, transport, and damage that may have contributed to the condition of the bone accumulation prior to burial. Carnivore tooth marks and the pattern of bone alteration are telltale signs that carnivores have scavenged a kill site (Haynes 1980, 1982, 1983). Carnivore teeth leave circular punctures and broad grooves in the soft ends of bones. Extensive chewing produces bone cylinders with one end or both scooped out (Binford 1978).

Carnivore damage was ranked from a low of 0 to a high of 3. A ranking of 0 indicates that no carnivore marks were observed on the bone. One indicates that carnivore damage consisted of a few tooth punctures or grooves, 2 implies that one-half of one end was chewed off, and 3 means complete removal of one or both ends.

The Upper Kill bones gave few signs of scavenging, with 99% of the bones displaying no evidence of carnivore damage (table 5). The remaining 1% is equally divided between rankings of 1 and 2. The deposit contained no level 3 bone cylinders. The almost complete lack of such damage to the Upper Kill elements indicates either that carnivore activity in the vicinity of the kill was low or that some factor prevented scavenging of the kill spoils. This topic receives further consideration later in this chapter.

CRUSHING. Crushing of bones can be attributed to a number of factors, including trampling by other animals at the time of a kill, later movement of animals over the kill remains, or the weight of overburden. Crushing was ranked according to the extent of damage to a bone: 0 means no evidence of crushing, 1 represents a small area of crushing, 2 indicates that 25% of the bone was crushed, and 3 means 50% or more of the bone was crushed (table 6).

Less than 0.4% of the elements were ranked at 3, 8% at 2, and 2% at 1. Over 89% of the bones were not crushed at all. The crushed skull, rib cage, pelvis, and long bones of a completely articulated calf skeleton suggest that it was trampled to death during the Upper Kill. The seventh cervical vertebra was snapped back, laying the neck and head over the thoracic vertebrae, and the first lumbar was snapped anteriorly, laying the pelvis and rear legs under the sternum. Crushing of this skeleton is attributed to the hooves and bodies of the larger animals that came to rest on top of this young animal.

Subsurface Factors

ROOT ETCHING. This occurs after burial, when the roots of surface plants dissolve the bone surface. The soil depth necessary for

Table 5
Upper Kill Carnivore Chewing

Element	N	Ranking		
		0	1	2
1st phalanx	125	125	0	0
2nd phalanx	111	109	1	1
3rd phalanx	76	76	0	0
Astragalus	37	37	0	0
Cervical vertebrae	32	31	0	1
Calcaneus	38	38	0	0
Caudal vertebrae	7	7	0	0
Femur	36	35	1	0
Humerus	34	33	1	0
Lumbar vertebrae	18	18	0	0
Metacarpal	32	32	0	0
Metatarsal	42	42	0	0
Naviculo-cuboid	38	38	0	0
Patella	22	22	0	0
Pelvis	20	19	0	1
Radius	31	31	0	0
Ribs	65	63	1	1
Sacrum	15	15	0	0
Scapula	34	34	0	0
Skull	19	19	0	0
Sternal ribs	2	2	0	0
Sternum	10	10	0	0
Thoracic vertebrae	55	53	1	1
Tibia	40	38	0	0
Ulna	33	33	0	0
Total	972	962	5	5
%	100	98.97	0.51	0.51

etching to occur is not known, nor have the plants responsible for the etching been identified. Root etching was a ranked variable with 0 representing no evidence of etching, 1 meaning less than 5% of a 3 cm^2 area of the surface was etched, 2 for 25% of a 3 cm^2 area etched, and 3 for 50% or more of a 3 cm^2 area etched. Since etching can remove other marks on the surface of a bone, such as cut marks, this variable provides a measure of the intactness of the bone surface and the probability that cut marks and other modifications might have been erased.

The Upper Kill bones were moderately etched, with 26% having a ranking of 0, 35% a 1, 34% a 2, and 5% a 3 (table 7). Although

Table 6
Upper Kill Crushing

Element	N	Ranking			
		0	1	2	3
1st phalanx	125	121	1	3	0
2nd phalanx	111	111	0	0	0
3rd phalanx	76	75	0	1	0
Astragalus	37	37	0	0	0
Cervical vertebrae	32	24	3	5	0
Calcaneus	38	37	0	1	0
Caudal vertebrae	7	5	2	0	0
Femur	36	31	0	5	0
Humerus	34	27	0	7	0
Lumbar vertebrae	18	14	2	2	0
Metacarpal	32	31	0	1	0
Metatarsal	42	42	0	0	0
Naviculo-cuboid	38	37	0	1	0
Patella	22	21	1	0	0
Pelvis	20	16	0	3	1
Radius	31	29	1	1	0
Ribs	65	49	5	11	0
Sacrum	15	14	1	0	0
Scapula	34	21	0	12	1
Skull	19	19	0	0	0
Sternal ribs	2	2	0	0	0
Sternum	10	9	1	0	0
Thoracic vertebrae	55	35	2	18	0
Tibia	40	34	2	4	0
Ulna	33	26	2	3	2
Total	972	867	23	78	4
%	100	89.20	2.37	8.02	0.41

extensive etching was found on only 5% of the bones, the relatively large percentage of bones with rankings of 2 and 1 (69%) probably contributes to the low number of cut marks observed on the Upper Kill bones.

RODENT GNAWING. Marks left by rodent teeth are distinctively different from those made by carnivores. Rodents gnaw with flat incisors that produce broad, planar tooth marks, whereas carnivores gnaw with canines, or more likely carnasials, pointed or rounded teeth that leave concave rather than planar marks.

Ranking rodent gnawing according to extent of damage to the bone, a 0 meant that no gnawing was seen on the element. Deter-

Table 7
Upper Kill Root Etching

Element	N	Ranking			
		0	1	2	3
1st phalanx	125	29	54	35	7
2nd phalanx	111	43	52	14	2
3rd phalanx	76	43	26	5	2
Astragalus	37	8	10	16	3
Cervical vertebrae	32	6	13	13	0
Calcaneus	38	8	16	10	4
Caudal vertebrae	7	3	2	2	0
Femur	36	5	6	18	7
Humerus	34	5	5	21	3
Lumbar vertebrae	18	2	10	6	0
Metacarpal	32	3	8	18	3
Metatarsal	42	5	10	23	4
Naviculo-cuboid	38	5	21	11	1
Patella	22	10	8	4	0
Pelvis	20	2	7	11	0
Radius	31	3	6	20	2
Ribs	65	16	22	25	2
Sacrum	15	5	5	3	2
Scapula	34	10	9	15	0
Skull	19	19	0	0	0
Sternal ribs	2	2	0	0	0
Sternum	10	7	3	0	0
Thoracic vertebrae	55	5	22	28	0
Tibia	40	5	8	22	5
Ulna	33	5	13	14	1
Total	972	254	336	334	48
%	100	25.13	34.57	34.36	4.94

minations of 1, 2, or 3 indicated that rodent gnawing covered less than 10%, 10–30%, or more than 30% of the bone surface, respectively.

Some 72% of the Upper Kill bones had no evidence of rodent gnawing (table 8), with 16% displaying level 1 gnawing and 11% level 2. Just 1% exhibited the extensive gnawing indicative of rank 3. The typical planar mark (fig. 26a) of the flat occlusal surface of the incisor is often accompanied by a more chiseled mark where the animal turned its head slightly to the side and clamped onto the bone with the side of the tooth (fig. 26b). These latter marks can be confused with the V-shaped marks produced by stone tools, but their context with the typical tooth marks belies their source.

Table 8
Upper Kill Rodent Gnawing

Element	N	Ranking			
		0	1	2	3
1st phalanx	125	88	25	12	0
2nd phalanx	111	79	24	8	0
3rd phalanx	76	63	4	7	2
Astragalus	37	28	5	2	2
Cervical vertebrae	32	25	4	3	0
Calcaneus	38	27	6	3	2
Caudal vertebrae	7	6	0	1	0
Femur	36	25	5	6	0
Humerus	34	18	10	5	1
Lumbar vertebrae	18	16	2	0	0
Metacarpal	32	19	10	3	0
Metatarsal	42	22	12	8	0
Naviculo-cuboid	38	28	8	2	0
Patella	22	18	4	0	0
Pelvis	20	18	1	1	0
Radius	31	17	8	5	1
Ribs	65	40	12	12	1
Sacrum	15	14	0	1	0
Scapula	34	26	1	7	0
Skull	19	19	0	0	0
Sternal ribs	2	2	0	0	0
Sternum	10	10	0	0	0
Thoracic vertebrae	55	46	3	6	0
Tibia	40	21	12	6	1
Ulna	33	23	4	6	0
Total	972	698	160	104	10
%	100	71.81	16.46	10.70	1.03

In addition to rodent gnaw marks, many of these bones have been scratched by the claws of tunneling rodents (figs. 26c, d). These marks have a distinctive half-circle pattern of parallel grooves produced by the claws on the animal's foot. The bone surface exposed in a rodent run often was highly polished (fig. 26e). Apparently, the dirt-laden fur on the gopher's underbelly worked to polish the bone in high-traffic areas.

Rodent gnaw marks are included in the subsurface damage category because most if not all of them on the Upper Kill bones were produced by gophers tunneling through the sandy deposits. Upon encountering a bone, the rodent had the options of tunneling around the obstacle or gnawing and clawing its way through.

A B C D E

Figure 26. Bone attributed to gophers included gnawing (a, b), clawing (c, d), and trafficking (e).

Gopher tunnels provided an avenue for other animals as well as other destructive forces. Snake and lizard skeletons were found in a number of the old burrows. Gopher runs provided subsurface avenues to other conditions that generally are limited to the surface. The ventral surface of the centrum of one lumbar vertebra (BN609) in an articulated segment that included the pelvis through the twelfth thoracic vertebra was burned. Fire, probably from a surface grass fire, must have swept down a rodent burrow and scorched the bone area exposed in the run. None of the surrounding soil or the other bones in the articulation show signs of fire.

SKID MARKS. In loose sediment where overburden is shallow and the matrix is sandy, the mere pressure exerted by standing can produce striated and planed bone surfaces. Termed "skid marks," these marks are often associated with trampling damage when surface bones can slide over a coarse sandy matrix (Behrensmeyer, Gordon, and Yanagi 1986). The resultant skid on the underside of the bone is caused by the incision of angular sand grains into it. Similar marks can be produced by the excavators of a site as they stand on sediments containing bones. The slight shifting of sand grains underfoot can produce skidlike marks. Skid damage was ranked on a scale from 0 to 3, with 0 being no evidence of skidding, 1 a single occurrence of skidding, 2 less than 5 occurrences, and 3 indicating 5 or more skid areas.

Almost 99% of the Upper Kill bones received a ranking of 0 for skid marks (table 9). The remaining 1% was divided between a ranking of 1 (0.8%) and 2 (0.3%). None of the Upper Kill bones was rated 3. The low level of skid marks indicates that little trampling or damage affected the bones while they were exposed or buried under shallow sandy soils.

Pathologies

Several anomalies were noted during the inspection and measurement of skeletal elements. Bones with surfaces that appeared remodeled, lumped, or more porous than usual were listed as pathologies. Most of the pathologies noted were related to healed fractures or to slight infections probably associated with fractures.

Only 10 (1%) of the 972 bones in the Upper Kill were found to have a pathology (table 10). Healed fractures were found on two first

Table 9
Upper Kill Trampling Skid Marks

Element	N	Ranking		
		0	1	2
1st phalanx	125	123	0	2
2nd phalanx	111	110	1	1
3rd phalanx	76	75	1	0
Astragalus	37	37	0	0
Cervical vertebrae	32	32	0	0
Calcaneus	38	38	0	0
Caudal vertebrae	7	7	0	0
Femur	36	36	0	0
Humerus	34	33	1	0
Lumbar vertebrae	18	18	0	0
Metacarpal	32	32	0	0
Metatarsal	42	41	1	0
Naviculo-cuboid	38	38	0	0
Patella	22	22	0	0
Pelvis	20	20	0	0
Radius	31	30	1	0
Ribs	65	62	2	1
Sacrum	15	15	0	0
Scapula	34	34	0	0
Skull	19	19	0	0
Sternal ribs	2	2	0	0
Sternum	10	10	0	0
Thoracic vertebrae	55	54	1	0
Tibia	40	40	0	0
Ulna	33	33	0	0
Total	972	961	8	3
%	100	98.87	0.82	0.31

phalanges, one third phalanx, one metatarsal, two ribs, one thoracic vertebra, and one tibia. Areas of localized infection were found on one humerus and one patella.

Interpretive Analyses

One of the goals of the bison skeletal analysis is to link the bison bone assemblage to the people who conducted the kill, in the hope that some aspect of the decision-making process confronting the hunters and members of their group is reflected in what remains at the site.

Table 10
Upper Kill Pathologies

Element	N	Absent	Present
1st phalanx	125	123	2
2nd phalanx	111	111	0
3rd phalanx	76	75	1
Astragalus	37	37	0
Cervical vertebrae	32	32	0
Calcaneus	38	38	0
Caudal vertebrae	7	7	0
Femur	36	36	0
Humerus	34	33	1
Lumbar vertebrae	18	18	0
Metacarpal	32	32	0
Metatarsal	42	41	1
Naviculo-cuboid	38	38	0
Patella	22	21	1
Pelvis	20	19	1
Radius	31	31	0
Ribs	65	63	2
Sacrum	15	15	0
Scapula	34	34	0
Skull	19	19	0
Sternal ribs	2	2	0
Sternum	10	10	0
Thoracic vertebrae	55	54	1
Tibia	40	39	1
Ulna	33	33	0
Total	972	962	10
%	100	98.97	1.03

Since the bison bones are the most substantial component of the Cooper site, interpretive hints were coaxed from the pile of bones, the tools, and the context.

One analytical technique relates the various animal body parts, as represented by the skeletal elements, to the various actions of either people or noncultural agencies such as those in the aforegoing discussion. The basic data block for this analysis is the bison bone and its associated meat/tool/fat/hide component. On the one hand, a bone has a preservation component dictated by its shape, size, density, and thickness. On the other hand, a bone has food value defined by the muscle, fat, marrow, and grease attached to or contained within it. A third dimension is sometimes applicable if the bone has a raw-material component used in the manufacture of bone tools. This third dimension is not widely applicable during the Folsom time period and will not be considered here except for bone tools made to be used in the immediate task of butchering the kill.

MINIMUM ANIMAL UNIT. The basic data consists of the bone or minimum animal unit (MAU). The MAU can include the combined elements of an entire leg, two or more elements of a leg (such as the femur/patella/tibia), a single element (such as the humerus), half of an element (proximal tibia, distal tibia, etc.), or an identifiable fragment of an element (Morlan 1994), such as the cranial surface of the proximal tibia. For most Paleoindian bison kills, the MAU is rarely reduced beyond the level of half an element (Todd 1987a).

The minimum animal unit is determined by dividing the total number of portions of a particular element found by the number of that element occurring in a bison skeleton (Binford 1978). For example, if a site produced 34 proximal tibiae fragments, the MAU for that element portion would be 17 (34 divided by the number of proximal tibiae in a bison skeleton, 2, equals 17). This computation is repeated for each element portion recovered from a site. The determination of MAU ignores further subdivision based on element side or age. For analytical purposes, the MAU is converted to a percentage using the greatest MAU as 100%.

The MAU for the Upper Kill at Cooper is presented in table 11. The metatarsal provides the greatest MAU at 21 and thus is set at 100% and used to figure the percentage of the other element portions. In and of itself, the MAU is not very useful as an inferential technique to understand prehistoric hunters. However, when compared with the preservational aspects of the bone as represented by its density and the useful aspects of the bone as represented by its associated muscle, fat, and grease, the MAU provides an interpretive tool.

DENSITY. The differential effect of natural factors is related to variation in the density of the bone (Binford and Bertram 1977). Extreme weathering conditions remove thin-walled, light bones before dense-walled, heavy bones. Thus, density-mediated preservation can mold the general composition of a bonebed. The density of various bones or bone portions has been figured for caribou (Binford 1978),

Table 11
Upper Kill Minimum Animal Unit, Density, and Food Utility Index

Element	N	MAU	%MAU	Bone Density	Food Utility
1st phalanx	125	15.6			
2nd phalanx	111	13.8			
3rd phalanx	76	9.5			
Astragalus	37	18.5	88.10	32	30
Calcaneus	38	19	90.48	33	30
Femur	36	18	85.71	6	100
Humerus	34	17	80.95	10	28.4
Metacarpal	32	16	76.19	29	6
Metatarsal	42	21	100.00	21.5	15.9
Naviculo-cuboid	38	19	90.48	18	30
Pelvis	20	20	95.24	24	39.8
Radius	31	15.5	73.81	15	19.7
Sacrum	15	15	71.43	3	39.8
Scapula	34	17	80.95	20	28.4
Skull	19	19	90.48		10.4
Tibia	40	20	95.24	12	58.1
Ulna	33	16.5	78.57	31	19.7
Spearman's rho				0.25	0.12

deer (Lyman 1982, 1984), and bison (Kreutzer 1992, 1996). Density values for the bison element portions identified in the Upper Kill are presented in table 11. If the bone preserved in the Upper Kill is dictated by the density of the element portions, then plotting the density values against the MAU values should produce a positive correlation. If preservation-mediated factors are not responsible for the bones in the Upper Kill, then there should not be a correlation between the MAU(%) and density values. The Spearman's rho statistic indicates that there is no correlation between the MAU(%) and the bone density values (Sr = 0.25).

FOOD UTILITY INDEX. The other factor of interpretive value plots the MAU(%) against the food value of the element portion. The food value associated with each element portion has been defined for bison (Emerson 1993) and is presented in table 11. These values include the total food utility of meat, marrow, fat, and grease associated with a skeletal element. Plotting the MAU(%) against the food value assumes that important meat, fat, marrow, and grease portions of an animal will be transported away from the kill site for further processing and consumption at a camp site. Therefore, the kill site should be deficient in the bones with the highest food values. If food value is the deciding factor for the presence or absence of an element portion in the Upper Kill deposits, then a positive correlation should be seen between the MAU(%) and the food utility index. If food value is not the determinant factor, then there should be no correlation between the MAU(%) and food utility index. The Spearman's rank order analysis between MAU(%) and food utility index yields no correlation between the MAU(%) and food value (Sr = 0.12) in the bison bone portions from the Upper Kill at Cooper.

Not surprisingly, neither the bone density nor the food value of the bison element portions explains the pattern of bone preservation in the Upper Kill at the Cooper site. As noted, the bone deposit is composed primarily of completely articulated bison skeletons, indicating that the skeletal elements were not being transported away from the kill site. Yet, the presence of cut marks, spiral fractures, other bone damage, and stone butchering tools with resharpening flakes indicates that the animals were utilized and not abandoned. The butchering practice that results in abandonment of the skeletal elements is known as muscle stripping or filleting. Depending on which muscle masses are stripped, this technique is referred to as a "gourmet" strategy in butchering (Binford 1978) because only the choicest meat portions of each carcass are filleted from the bones. The bones and skeleton remain intact. Many of the techniques developed for bonebed analysis are dependent on the removal of bones from, or to, the site (Binford 1978); many of these analyses are rendered moot by the completeness of the skeletons at Cooper.

In apparent contrast to this pattern of skeletal articulation is a single skull that was found inside the chest cavity of an articulated skeleton. The skull was from a 2.3 year old. The mandibles were missing, as were the nasals. Both horn cores were intact. The skull was placed with the base on the lower rib cage and the nose against the upper rib cage of a skeleton resting on its left side (figs. 11a, b). From its position, it appears that the skull was used to prop open the chest cavity after the entrails were removed. The purpose of this action was probably to accelerate cooling of the carcass, thus avoiding rapid decay due to body heat. A similar action employing a stick is common among big game hunters today.

The fact that the skull consisted only of a partial cranium, devoid of mandibles and nasals, suggests that the skull was not from a recent kill. Since the pattern of skull treatment evident from the other animals in the Upper Kill was to leave the mandibles and nasals attached, the skull was probably scavenged from a Middle Kill animal that had been partially exposed along the edge of the arroyo floor. Use of the skull in this manner suggests an idiosyncratic but expedient decision by one of the butchers.

Upper Kill Lithic Assemblage

PROJECTILE POINTS. A total of thirteen complete or fragmented projectile points was recovered from the Upper Kill deposits (some of these are illustrated in fig. 27). The points and fragments were directly associated with the bison carcasses and, in several cases, the point was in the chest cavity of an articulated animal. The size and shape of the Upper Kill points fall within the ranges ascribed to the Folsom type (table 12). Length of complete or near complete points ranges from a maximum of 42.2 mm to a minimum of 28.0 mm, with width and thickness ranges from 22.6 mm to 17.0 mm and 4.2 mm to 3.0 mm, respectively.

Five (38%) of the points are complete or near complete. The remaining projectiles are represented by fragments: three (23%) tips, one (8%) distal two-thirds of a point, two (15%) midsections, and two (15%) edge fragments. No basal fragments were found. The lack of bases suggests that the spear shafts or foreshafts were retrieved.

Ten of the thirteen points are made from Alibates and two are made from Edwards Plateau chert. The remaining point is made from Niobrara jasper. Five of the projectile points, including four of Alibates and one of Edwards Plateau chert, bear no evidence of being reworked. Another five, including three Alibates, one Edwards, and the single Niobrara point, had previously been fractured and reworked prior to use at Cooper. Both edge fragments and one of the two midsections are too fractured to discern if they had been previously reworked.

Ten (77%) of the points are fluted on both surfaces. One of the reworked Alibates points retains evidence of only one flute. The channel scar on the opposite face may have been present on the original point but been lost upon subsequent breakage and reworking. Two fragments are too fractured to tell if the points were fluted or not.

Impact damage to the projectile points is indicated by the broken tips, edges, and midsections. Additional damage is exhibited along the edges and tips of some of the more complete points (fig. 27, points D, G, and HH). The nature of the fractures suggests these points struck bone. The jagged edges on point D may have resulted from the point ricocheting between two ribs before penetrating the chest cavity.

FLAKE TOOLS. In addition to projectile points, the Upper Kill yielded tools that fit into the category of flake knives. These specimens are made on large flakes struck from either bifacial or blade cores. These flake blanks could potentially be made into one of a number of tools, depending on the task at hand. The functional aspect, knives, is partially defined by the context of their discovery: the bonebed. Characteristics of tool shape and edge treatment further define the functional category of knife. Little or no shaping was necessary to create a sharp edge. The natural edge was sharp enough for any cutting tasks. However, maintaining a sharp edge required retouch, which was accomplished in a unifacial manner using either soft hammer percussion or pressure flaking (Brosowske and Bement 1997).

The Upper Kill assemblage contains four flake knives. A fifth knife is made on a flute or channel flake. Since the number of implements is small, each specimen is described in detail.

Flake tool A is made on an irregular bladelike Alibates flake 99.8 mm long, 36.9 mm wide, and 11.1 mm thick (fig. 27). Flake scars on the dorsal surface indicate that the flake was not a true blade, and the platform angle, in relation to the ventral surface, is 110 degrees. The longest edge of this tri-edged tool is straight to slightly recurved. Two-thirds of the edge has been resharpened at least once; the remaining one-third exhibits nibbling from use. The edge adjacent to the platform is damaged on both ventral and dorsal surfaces from use in a knifelike fashion. The edge opposite the platform has a broad, squared projection formed by the removal of small pressure flakes. The projection and edge have minute flakes removed from dorsal and ventral surfaces as a result of use.

Table 12
Upper Kill Projectile Points

ID	Length	Width	Thickness	Flute Thickness	Portion	Material	No. of Flutes	Reworked
D	42.2	22.6	3.9	1.2	Complete	Alibates	2	N
E	20.5	18.0	3.8	2.1	Tip	Alibates	2	N
F	18.0	15.6	2.3	1.3	Tip	Aalibates	2	Y
G	31.6	19.8	4.2	2.3	Complete	Niobrara	2	Y
J	28.0	19.1	3.1	1.9	Complete	Edwards	2	Y
M	35.6	20.8	3.7	2.5	Distal ⅔	Alibates	2	N
N					Edge	Alibates	2	
O					Midsection	Alibates		
P	30.3	20.6	3.9	2.6	Complete	Alibates	1	Y
Q	43.2	21.8	3.8	2.9	Midsection	Edwards	2	N
X	14.2	17.0	3.2	1.8	Tip	Alibates	2	N
GG					Edge	Alibates		
HH	32.1	17.0	3.0	2.3	Complete	Alibates	2	Y

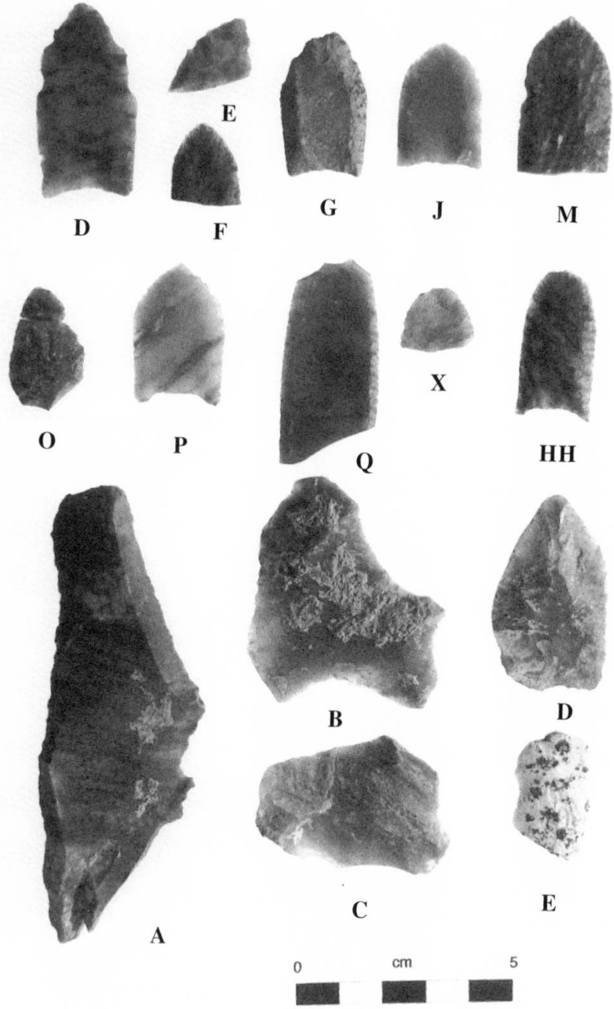

Figure 27. These projectile points (two rows above) and flake tools (two rows below) were recovered from the Upper Kill remnant. Letters correspond to specimen identifications in table 12 and the text.

Flake tool B (fig. 27) is also made of Alibates. This tool is 54.0 mm long, 44.5 mm wide, and 5.4 mm thick. The multifaceted platform has an angle of 90 degrees in relation to the ventral surface of the flake. The two edges converging at the platform show signs of use; the other edges appear unused. No evidence of intentional retouch is present. One use edge is convex and the other is concave.

Flake tool C (fig. 27), made of Alibates or possibly Day Creek dolomite, is 35.0 mm long, 44.4 mm wide, and 8.2 mm thick, with a multifaceted and heavily battered platform. The platform angle is 105 degrees. The straight lateral edge is heavily worn after resharpening; the other lateral edge has an irregular shape, although straight portions were used. The edge opposite the platform is snapped.

Flake tool D (fig. 27) is made of translucent brown Edwards Plateau chert and is 42.9 mm long, 26.5 mm wide, and 3.5 mm thick. The platform is multifaceted and at an angle of 110 degrees in relation to the ventral surface. Both convex lateral edges were utilized. The edge opposite the platform has a small portion of use associated with the corner where it joins the lateral edge.

The final flake tool, E, from the Upper Kill is made on a channel flake midsection of gray Edwards Plateau chert (fig. 27). The fragment is 26.5 mm long, 17.6 mm wide, and 2.4 mm thick. The longer lateral edge has been normalized by use. No sign of use is present on the other edge or on either end. A black residue of an as yet unidentified material dots the dorsal surface.

RESHARPENING FLAKES. Evidence that the flake knives were used on the animals is found in the recovery of resharpening debris. This debris consists of small flakes and flake fragments removed from the dulled edges in order to reconstitute a sharp edge. Out of a total of forty-six pieces of shatter from the Upper Kill, forty-five are attributed to resharpening of knives. The remaining piece is a small fragment of projectile point.

Twenty-six of the resharpening flakes retained a portion of the tool's edge. This portion is also the striking platform where force was applied to remove the flake and thus resharpen the tool. The morphology of the edge remnant on the striking platform tells much about the use and origin of the flake. Since all of the flake knives recovered from the Upper Kill had edges shaped by removal of flakes from one surface (unifacial) it follows that the remnant tool edge on the resharpening flakes should also bear evidence of unifacial flaking. The platform should consist of a portion of the flat side or underside of the tool and should thus consist of a single facet. Twenty-five of the twenty-six resharpening flakes have single-faceted platforms.

In all cases, the edge remnant bears evidence of heavy use. Polish and striations on the remnant edge indicate that the tool was dull and could not adequately perform the desired task without refurbishing of the working edge. Preliminary usewear analysis revealed wear types (polish and damage) attributable to green hide and meat cutting.

In stone type, the resharpening flakes mirror the types of the knives. The majority are Alibates (n = 41) and the rest are Edwards Plateau chert (n = 4).

FIST-SIZED COBBLES. Eleven large river cobbles were recovered from the Upper Kill bonebed (fig. 28). These cobbles range in size from 9.2 cm long, 6.4 cm wide, 5.1 cm thick, and 381 g in weight to 23.5 cm long, 15.1 cm wide, 11.4 cm thick, and 4,300 g in weight (table 13). They are the size of a hammerstone and are easily grasped in the hand. All are examples of stone types common in the large gravels that cap the river divides. Included in this collection are cobbles of limestone, sandstone, petrified wood, Day Creek dolomite, and quartzite.

The presence of such cobbles in a bonebed is usually associated with the task of breaking open thick bones for the removal of marrow. Few of the bones in the Upper Kill, however, bear evidence of this behavior. An alternative explanation is that the stones were used to aid in the removal of the hides (Frison 1991). Stones such as these could be employed to pound hides from carcasses.

Summary of Upper Kill

The high number of articulated skeletons suggested at first glance that these animals had not been butchered. A group of fourteen similar skeletons in the center of the bonebed at the Lipscomb site (Todd, Hofman, and Schultz 1990) was attributed to overkill, in which more animals were killed than were needed or could be processed. The Upper Kill at Cooper seemed to present the same situation. However, as excavations progressed, it became clear that the animals had been subjected to at least some level of carcass handling. First, the pelvi of some skeletons were positioned with the legs folded underneath,

Figure 28. Several cobbles were found in the Upper Kill. While similar cobbles are thought to have been used to break bones during processing, these may have been used to pound the hide from the carcasses.

suggesting that the animals had been propped up on their bellies. Several of the carcasses had fallen over in domino fashion. Second, skeletons outnumbered projectile points, indicating that the hunters had recovered many of their spear tips. Those left behind consisted

Table 13
Upper Kill Unmodified Cobbles

ID	Length (cm)	Width (cm)	Thickness (cm)	Weight (g)	Material
305	11.2	6.3	6.3	573	Limestone
370	10.2	3.9	3.6	188	Petrified wood
402	11.4	10.1	6.2	727	Sandstone
403	13.0	9.7	7.0	1,235	Quartzite
423	10.0	6.0	5.5	438	Limestone
427	9.2	6.4	5.1	381	Quartzite
607	12.5	9.2	5.5	695	Day Creek
608	23.5	15.1	11.4	4,300	Sandstone
653	23.3	17.4	7.5	3,600	Limestone
658	15.6	9.8	9.1	1,820	Limestone
659	13.2	9.3	8.9	1,090	Quartzite

mainly of fragmented tips and edges, the larger basal portions had been retrieved with their shafts.

Flake knives, resharpening flakes, and fist-sized cobbles comprised an assemblage of butchering tools that saw use in the bonebed, but the nature and extent of that use cannot be quantified. The distribution of projectile points, tools, and resharpening flakes indicates that the hunters and processors moved extensively among the animals (fig. 29). The cut marks on the bones are consistent with the butchering tool assemblage. Cut marks are located in areas that usually support large amounts of muscle, such as the humerus and pelvis. Even the ribs are blanketed by flesh that must be removed before a mark can be left on the bone. The green bone fracture on one humerus also indicated that the meat had been removed from this element before it was broken. However, in this case, the humerus was not still articulated with any skeleton. All evidence supported the proposition that these animals had been butchered to some degree, which minimally included stripping some large muscle masses from articulated carcasses.

Middle Kill

Approximately 25 cm beneath the Upper Kill, bones from an earlier bison kill episode (fig. 30) covered an area approximately 5.5 m from east to west by 4 m from north to south (fig. 31). The western edge of

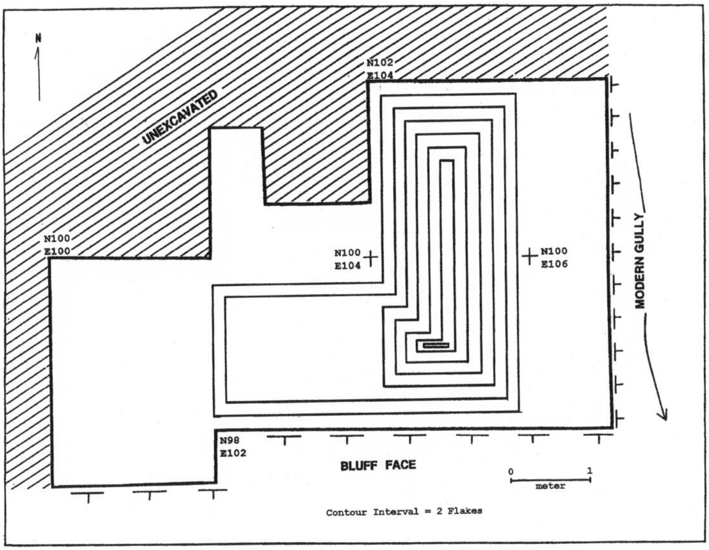

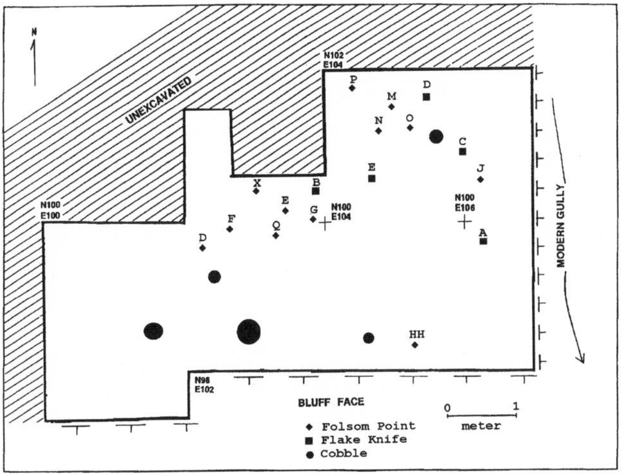

Figure 29. The distribution plots of projectile points, tools, cobbles, and re-sharpening flakes indicate that Folsom skinners and butchers were active in the Upper Kill.

Figure 30. Excavation in the Middle Kill bonebed remnant uncovered a concentration of fully articulated skeletons.

the bonebed, however, was shifted approximately 50 cm to the east due to the slope of the original arroyo wall. Erosion caused by the modern arroyo along the eastern edge allowed an extension of the preserved bonebed an additional 50 cm east beyond that seen in the Upper Kill. A similar shift along the southern edge of the deposits is related to the slope of the erosional bank onto the Beaver River floodplain.

The western edge of the Middle bone deposit intermingles with the Upper Kill. Separation of the two along this fringe relied on plotting entire skeletons as they dipped to the east and also on the identification of trampled bones. The trampled bones exhibited roughly oval fractures about the size of a bison's hoof (fig. 13). Such fractures could only occur if the bones had been exposed at the time of the later or Upper Kill. The occurrence of fractures due to trampling along articulated legs that dipped into the Middle Kill layer allowed

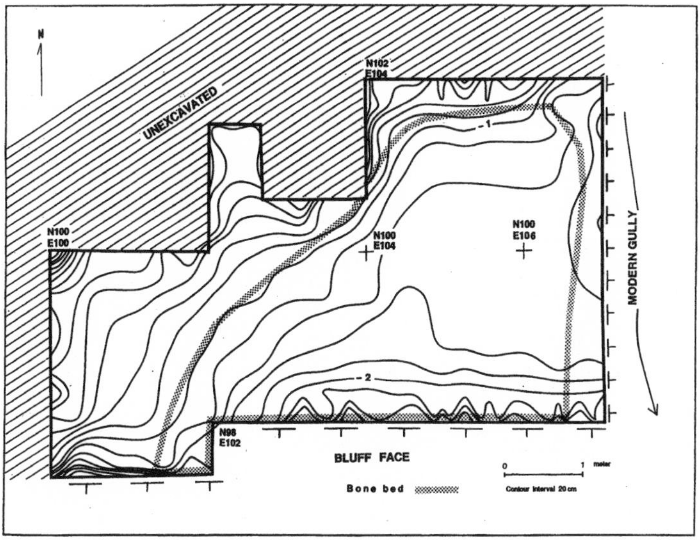

A

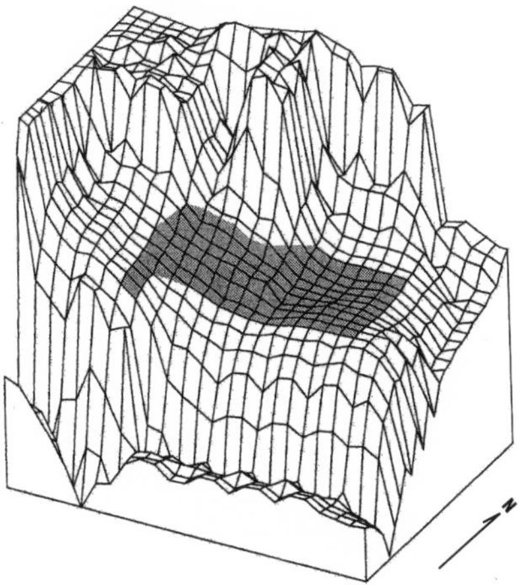

B

Figure 31. Contour (a) and three-dimensional (b) maps of the arroyo bottom at the time of the Middle Kill were generated from bone elevations.

separation of the Upper and Middle kills along the western fringes where the two overlapped.

As with the Upper Kill layer, the bones along the western and northern edges dipped at higher rates than those in the center of the bonebed. Slopes varied from 35% and 45% along the western and northern fringes to 10% in the center of the bone deposits.

Bone Analysis

A total of 707 elements or element groups were recovered from the excavation of the Middle Kill. The actual number of identified bones, including individual ribs and vertebrae, is over 1,200. Of the 707 individually coded elements, only 12 (1.7%) were not part of an articulated segment or complete skeleton.

An MNI of twenty-nine animals was calculated based on element counts, age, side, and articulations. Age distribution of these individuals is one calf (group I), five yearlings (group II), nine two-year-olds (group III), seven three-year-olds (group IV), four four-year-olds (group V), and three five-plus-year-olds (group VI, VII, or VIII). No advanced-age individuals were recovered. The three animals five years old or older could not be aged beyond this general category due to the lack of skulls and mandibles. However, none of the skeletal elements expressed the characteristics of extreme age (such as lipping of articular surfaces) seen in the samples from the other bonebeds. The high number of immature individuals in this bonebed is striking: the Middle Kill contains a nursery herd. Were the rest of the animals in the kill this young or is this the product of sampling error? This question will never be answered.

SEASONALITY. The season of death of these animals is set at late summer or early fall. Based on tooth eruption and wear patterns, their age consistently equals n + 0.3 years old. Thus, each age cohort is approximately four months beyond the birthing pulse that occurs from late April through early May.

BONE WITH IMPACT DAMAGE. The right sixth rib of a three-year-old bears the scar of a projectile point entry wound (fig. 32). The projectile point penetrated the lateral surface of the rib near the posterior margin. The lateral surface forward of the impact was upthrust. The projectile penetrated the bone, fracturing and pushing

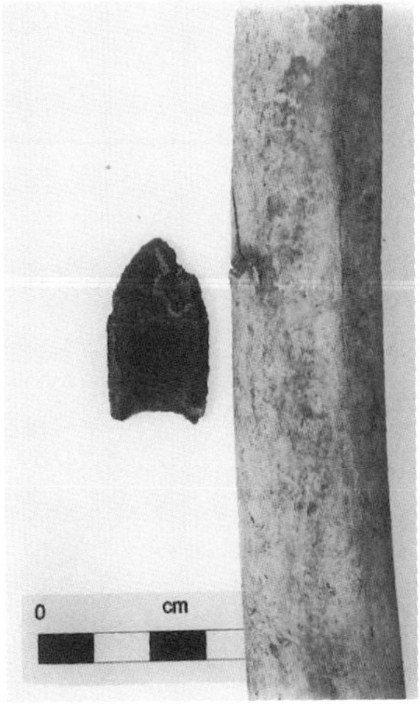

Figure 32. This rib from a Middle Kill animal displays impact damage from a projectile point. The projectile point exhibiting impact damage came from inside the rib cage of this animal and is thought to be the point that caused the damage.

the medial surface. A portion of the point made of the dark gray to black chert from the Edwards Plateau remained embedded in the impact slice. The rest apparently glanced off the edge of the rib and continued into the chest cavity. An edge-damaged projectile point (point U) of Owl Creek chert was recovered from the underside of this articulated skeleton (fig. 32). The damaged edge conforms to the morphology of the point fragment embedded in the rib. If this is the projectile point, then the spear did in fact continue into the chest cavity after ricocheting off the rib. This projectile point is the equivalent of the "smoking gun" for the demise of this individual.

CUT MARKS. Direct evidence of butchering is found on the bones in the distribution of cut marks produced by the sharp edges of stone tools. A total of fourteen definite cut marks was found (table 14). The

Table 14
Middle Kill Cut Marks

Element	N	Absent	Present
1st phalanx	93	93	0
2nd phalanx	84	84	0
3rd phalanx	65	65	0
Astragalus	28	28	0
Cervical vertebrae	15	15	0
Calcaneus	28	28	0
Caudal vertebrae	2	2	0
Femur	32	32	0
Humerus	30	29	1
Lumbar vertebrae	15	14	1
Metacarpal	29	29	0
Metatarsal	29	29	0
Naviculo-cuboid	26	26	0
Patella	16	16	0
Pelvis	18	18	0
Radius	33	33	0
Ribs	29	19	10
Sacrum	10	10	0
Scapula	29	29	0
Skull	16	16	0
Sternum	4	4	0
Thoracic vertebrae	17	15	2
Tibia	32	32	0
Ulna	27	27	0
Total	707	693	14
%	100	98.02	1.98

highest occurrence was on ribs (10 with cuts), followed by thoracic vertebrae (2 with cuts). Cuts were also found on a single lumbar vertebra and a humerus. While the distribution of cuts suggests that the front quarters and spine were targeted for butchering, it must be remembered that the fourteen cut bones comprise only 2% of the total bone analyzed from the Middle Kill. Thus, the dominant pattern is that no cut marks are found on the bones. Cut marks were found on the bones of individuals from 1.3 to over 5.3 years old, indicating that there was no selection based on age (table 15). This is not surprising given the young age of the animals in this sample. Furthermore, this supports the contention that all animals were butchered to some degree.

SPIRAL FRACTURES. Spiral fractures are often associated with the butchering of animals. The Middle Kill bonebed contained two

Table 15
Age of Individuals with Cut Marks from the Middle Kill

Bone Number	Element	Side	Age
768	Ribs	Left	3.3
768	Ribs	Right	3.3
806	T. vertebrae		2.3
761	Ribs	Right	1.3
677	Ribs	Right	3.3
677	T. vertebrae		3.3
759	Humerus	Left	2.3
712	Ribs	Right	5+
758	Ribs	Right	4.3
758	L. vertebrae		4.3
740	Ribs	Left	4.3
695	Ribs	Right	3.3
695	Ribs	Left	3.3
686	Ribs	Left	3–4

metatarsals with spiral fractures. In addition, ribs and thoracic vertebrae were sometimes broken. The total of only four elements or element groups with fractures out of 707 elements (less than 0.6%) suggests that bone breaking was not part of the butchering task (table 16).

Surface Factors

The bones of the Middle Kill display many of the taphonomic characteristics described in the Upper Kill sample. Again, these postkill factors served to limit the evidence of human actions.

WEATHERING. For 54% of the Middle Kill bones there is no evidence of weathering (table 17). Another 19% have slight weathering characteristics (level 1), 26% have level 2 weathering, and only 1% have level 3 weathering. None of the bones exhibit the cracking and splintering associated with advanced stages of weathering. Weathering was restricted to the upper side of the bone, indicating that the elements had not rolled bones to expose the undersides.

CARNIVORE CHEWING. With the exception of a single ulna, the Middle Kill assemblage was devoid of signs of carnivore scavenging (table 18). This paucity is consistent with the presence of numerous fully articulated skeletons in the Middle Kill deposits. The factors responsible for keeping the scavengers at bay are not known. It

Table 16
Middle Kill Spiral Fractures

Element	N	Absent	Present
1st phalanx	93	93	0
2nd phalanx	84	84	0
3rd phalanx	65	65	0
Astragalus	28	28	0
Cervical vertebrae	15	15	0
Calcaneus	28	28	0
Caudal vertebrae	2	2	0
Femur	32	32	0
Humerus	30	30	0
Lumbar vertebrae	15	15	0
Metacarpal	29	29	0
Metatarsal	29	27	2
Naviculo-cuboid	26	26	0
Patella	16	16	0
Pelvis	18	18	0
Radius	33	33	0
Ribs	29	28	1
Sacrum	10	10	0
Scapula	29	29	0
Skull	16	16	0
Sternum	4	4	0
Thoracic vertebrae	17	16	1
Tibia	32	32	0
Ulna	27	27	0
Total	707	703	4
%	100	99.43	0.57

is probable that some level of scavenging took place, but that little evidence of the activity was preserved.

CRUSHING. Almost 79% of the Middle Kill bones were not crushed (table 19). Of the remaining 21%, 5% received a ranking of 1, 15% a ranking of 2, and 1% a ranking of 3. The higher number showing level 2 crushing is attributed to trampling of the elements along the lateral edges of the bone deposit by the animals of the Upper Kill.

Subsurface Factors

ROOT ETCHING. Just under 53% of the Middle Kill bones show no root etching. Approximately 33% have a ranking of 1, 14% a

Table 17
Middle Kill Weathering

Element	N	Ranking			
		0	1	2	3
1st phalanx	93	53	13	26	1
2nd phalanx	84	54	12	17	1
3rd phalanx	65	33	7	24	1
Astragalus	28	18	8	2	0
Cervical vertebrae	15	9	3	2	1
Calcaneus	28	11	10	7	0
Caudal vertebrae	2	2	0	0	0
Femur	32	23	2	7	0
Humerus	30	14	5	11	0
Lumbar vertebrae	15	8	4	3	0
Metacarpal	29	8	8	13	0
Metatarsal	29	5	12	12	0
Naviculo-cuboid	26	14	8	4	0
Patella	16	9	6	1	0
Pelvis	18	10	4	4	0
Radius	33	15	7	11	0
Ribs	29	20	4	4	1
Sacrum	10	2	2	6	0
Scapula	29	17	4	8	0
Skull	16	16	0	0	0
Sternum	4	3	0	1	0
Thoracic vertebrae	17	10	5	1	1
Tibia	32	17	8	7	0
Ulna	27	12	4	10	1
Total	707	383	136	181	7
%	100	54.17	19.24	25.60	0.99

ranking of 2, and 0.6% a ranking of 3 (table 20). Root etching was limited to the upper surface of the bones. Also, within a complete skeleton, etching was most often found on the elements on the upward side of the carcass. The upper portion of the carcass proved to be a fairly impenetrable barrier to roots.

RODENT GNAWING. Less than 18% of the Middle Kill assemblage has been damaged by rodent gnawing. This total consists of 11% level 1, 6% level 2, and less than 0.6% level 3 (table 21). The rodent damage is a combination of gnaw and scratch marks attributed to gophers burrowing through the bonebed deposits. Gnawing marks include the planar as well as V-shaped tooth marks noted in the Upper Kill assemblage.

Table 18
Middle Kill Carnivore Chewing

Element	N	Ranking	
		0	1
1st phalanx	93	93	0
2nd phalanx	84	84	0
3rd phalanx	65	65	0
Astragalus	28	28	0
Cervical vertebrae	15	15	0
Calcaneus	28	28	0
Caudal vertebrae	2	2	0
Femur	32	32	0
Humerus	30	30	0
Lumbar vertebrae	15	15	0
Metacarpal	29	29	0
Metatarsal	29	29	0
Naviculo-cuboid	26	26	0
Patella	16	16	0
Pelvis	18	18	0
Radius	33	33	0
Ribs	29	29	0
Sacrum	10	10	0
Scapula	29	29	0
Skull	16	16	0
Sternum	4	4	0
Thoracic vertebrae	17	17	0
Tibia	32	32	0
Ulna	27	26	1
Total	707	706	4
%	100	99.86	0.14

SKID MARKS. Over 95.6% of the Middle Kill bones are free from skid marks (table 22). The remaining 4.6% are distributed between rankings 1 and 2 with 3.8% and 0.6%, respectively. The majority of the skid marks are found on elements near the edges of the bonebed where trampling by the Upper Kill herd occurred.

Pathologies

Seven (1%) of the Middle Kill bones display characteristics associated with pathologies (table 23). Healed fractures were found on two first phalanges and two ribs. Porous and remodeled bone suggestive of

Table 19
Middle Kill Crushing

Element	N	Ranking			
		0	1	2	3
1st phalanx	93	87	1	4	1
2nd phalanx	84	84	0	0	0
3rd phalanx	65	62	0	3	0
Astragalus	28	28	0	0	0
Cervical vertebrae	15	4	5	6	0
Calcaneus	28	26	0	1	1
Caudal vertebrae	2	0	2	0	0
Femur	32	21	4	6	1
Humerus	30	19	2	9	0
Lumbar vertebrae	15	8	0	7	0
Metacarpal	29	26	0	3	0
Metatarsal	29	26	1	2	0
Naviculo-cuboid	26	23	0	2	1
Patella	16	15	1	0	0
Pelvis	18	8	1	8	1
Radius	33	23	1	7	2
Ribs	29	7	6	16	0
Sacrum	10	5	3	2	0
Scapula	29	16	1	11	1
Skull	16	16	0	0	0
Sternum	4	2	1	1	0
Thoracic vertebrae	17	5	3	9	0
Tibia	32	26	1	5	0
Ulna	27	18	2	7	0
Total	707	555	35	109	8
%	100	78.50	4.95	15.42	1.13

healed infections were found on two humeri and one pelvis. The low level of pathologies mirrors that observed in the Upper Kill assemblage.

Interpretive Analyses

In keeping with current trends in bonebed analysis, the analytical techniques comparing the MAU(%) to bone density values and food utility rankings are presented for the Middle Kill (table 24). The large number of completely articulated skeletons bespeaks the limited usefulness of this analysis; however, for comparative purposes with other kill sites, the results are presented. It comes as no surprise that there is

Table 20
Middle Kill Root Etching

Element	N	Ranking			
		0	1	2	3
1st phalanx	93	54	30	9	0
2nd phalanx	84	58	23	3	0
3rd phalanx	65	56	9	0	0
Astragalus	28	15	12	1	0
Cervical vertebrae	15	4	9	2	0
Calcaneus	28	17	6	5	0
Caudal vertebrae	2	0	2	0	0
Femur	32	9	14	9	0
Humerus	30	5	13	11	1
Lumbar vertebrae	15	5	7	3	0
Metacarpal	29	16	7	6	0
Metatarsal	29	17	10	2	0
Naviculo-cuboid	26	14	10	2	0
Patella	16	12	4	0	0
Pelvis	18	7	5	5	1
Radius	33	15	13	4	1
Ribs	29	7	11	11	0
Sacrum	10	4	2	4	0
Scapula	29	9	14	5	1
Skull	16	16	0	0	0
Sternum	4	2	2	0	0
Thoracic vertebrae	17	5	10	2	0
Tibia	32	8	14	10	0
Ulna	27	18	7	2	0
Total	707	373	234	96	4
%	100	52.76	33.10	13.58	0.56

no correlation between the MAU(%) and bone density rankings (Spearman's rho = 0.012). Likewise, there is no correlation between the MAU(%) and the food utility ranking (Spearman's rho = 0.18).

Middle Kill Lithic Assemblage

PROJECTILE POINTS. Seven complete or fractured projectile points were recovered in direct association with the bison bones of the Middle Kill (fig. 33). Two fragments (specimens I and C) are from the same projectile point. The distal end was found in a rodent run above the Upper Kill. The proximal end was recovered among the bones of

Table 21
Middle Kill Rodent Gnawing

Element	N	Ranking			
		0	1	2	3
1st phalanx	93	84	7	2	0
2nd phalanx	84	74	9	1	0
3rd phalanx	65	62	2	1	0
Astragalus	28	23	5	0	0
Cervical vertebrae	15	11	3	1	0
Calcaneus	28	22	3	2	1
Caudal vertebrae	2	2	0	0	0
Femur	32	25	5	2	0
Humerus	30	25	3	2	0
Lumbar vertebrae	15	12	2	1	0
Metacarpal	29	21	3	5	0
Metatarsal	29	22	4	2	1
Naviculo-cuboid	26	25	0	1	0
Patella	16	13	1	2	0
Pelvis	18	14	2	2	0
Radius	33	24	6	3	0
Ribs	29	15	8	6	0
Sacrum	10	9	1	0	0
Scapula	29	24	1	2	2
Skull	16	16	0	0	0
Sternum	4	4	0	0	0
Thoracic vertebrae	17	13	4	0	0
Tibia	32	26	3	3	0
Ulna	27	18	6	3	0
Total	707	584	78	41	4
%	100	82.60	11.03	5.80	0.57

the Middle Kill. A small sliver—the midsection of this point—was not recovered during excavation. However, the distinctive nature of the channel flaking on the base portion is also found on the distal fragment, indicating that they are from the same point. These two fragments, once conjoined, constitute the largest projectile point from this kill. The resultant length would be in excess of 52 mm (table 25). The smallest complete point from the Middle Kill is 20.8 mm long. Width and thickness maximums and minimums for this assemblage range from 22.2 to 15.3 mm and from 4.0 mm to 3.0 mm, respectively.

In addition to the refitted projectile point fragments, the Middle Kill yielded six complete or nearly complete points. Damage to these

Table 22
Middle Kill Trampling Skid Marks

Element	N	Ranking		
		0	1	2
1st phalanx	93	89	3	1
2nd phalanx	84	84	0	0
3rd phalanx	65	65	0	0
Astragalus	28	28	0	0
Cervical vertebrae	15	15	0	0
Calcaneus	28	27	1	0
Caudal vertebrae	2	2	0	0
Femur	32	32	0	0
Humerus	30	24	6	0
Lumbar vertebrae	15	15	0	0
Metacarpal	29	29	0	0
Metatarsal	29	26	3	0
Naviculo-cuboid	26	26	0	0
Patella	16	16	0	0
Pelvis	18	18	0	0
Radius	33	30	3	0
Ribs	29	24	3	2
Sacrum	10	9	1	0
Scapula	29	26	2	1
Skull	16	16	0	0
Sternum	4	4	0	0
Thoracic vertebrae	17	13	4	0
Tibia	32	31	1	0
Ulna	27	27	0	0
Total	707	676	27	4
%	100	95.62	3.82	0.56

specimens ranges from a missing basal ear to irregular edge crushing, both attributed to impacts with hard substances, probably bone.

All seven points from the Middle Kill are made from cherts from Central Texas. Three points are gray to brown Edwards Plateau cherts. The remaining four are a black or dark gray variety of Edward's chert known as Owl Creek. The source area for Owl Creek chert is north of Fort Hood, Texas, along the Flint Creek and Preacher's Creek drainages and possibly on the divide between Owl and Henson creeks (Frederick and Ringstaff 1994). Although other sources of black chert are known (Banks 1984, 1990), under long wave ultraviolet light the Owl Creek variety has a distinctive dark brown refractivity that

Table 23
Middle Kill Pathologies

Element	N	Absent	Present
1st phalanx	93	91	2
2nd phalanx	84	84	0
3rd phalanx	65	65	0
Astragalus	28	28	0
Cervical vertebrae	15	15	0
Calcaneus	28	28	0
Caudal vertebrae	2	2	0
Femur	32	32	0
Humerus	30	28	2
Lumbar vertebrae	15	15	0
Metacarpal	29	29	0
Metatarsal	29	29	0
Naviculo-cuboid	26	26	0
Patella	16	16	0
Pelvis	18	17	1
Radius	33	33	0
Ribs	29	27	2
Sacrum	10	10	0
Scapula	29	29	0
Skull	16	16	0
Sternum	4	4	0
Thoracic vertebrae	17	17	0
Tibia	32	32	0
Ulna	27	27	0
Total	707	700	7
%	100	99.00	1.00

matches the refraction of the Cooper projectile points. Small white inclusions in the dark chert are another identifying characteristic. Larger inclusions of lighter gray color often refract the orange color typical of Edward Plateau chert.

Six of the seven points are fluted on both surfaces. The other (specimen U) is made of Owl Creek chert and is fluted on only one side. The channel flake scar on the fluted side bears ripple marks originating from both base and tip, indicating the simultaneous removal of flutes from both ends. One lateral edge of this specimen is shattered; the result of hitting a rib that retained the edge portion. This single-fluted point was reworked prior to use in the Middle Kill. Four other points had been reworked. Thus, five (71%) of the Middle Kill

Table 24
Middle Kill Minimum Animal Unit, Density, and Food Utility Index

Element	N	MAU	%MAU	Bone Density	Food Utility
1st phalanx	93	11.6			
2nd phalanx	84	10.4			
3rd phalanx	65	8.1			
Astragalus	28	14	77.78	32	30
Calcaneus	28	14	77.78	33	30
Femur	32	16	88.89	6	100
Humerus	30	15.5	86.11	10	28.4
Metacarpal	29	14.5	80.56	29	6
Metatarsal	29	14.5	80.56	21.5	15.9
Naviculo-cuboid	26	13	72.22	18	30
Pelvis	18	18	100.00	24	39.8
Radius	33	16.5	91.67	15	19.7
Sacrum	10	10	60.61	3	39.8
Scapula	29	14.5	80.56	20	28.4
Skull	16	16	88.89		10.4
Tibia	32	16	88.89	12	58.1
Ulna	27	13.5	75.00	31	19.7
Spearman's rho				0.012	0.18

projectiles had been reworked. Ripple marks on the flute scars on both surfaces of specimen S show that the point was turned around, the base becoming the point and vica versa. Such reversal of ends usually resulted when a point was badly fractured during use. Of the remaining two nonreworked specimens, one is made of Owl Creek and the other of translucent brown Edwards Plateau chert.

FLAKE TOOLS. Two flake tools were recovered from the Middle Kill deposits (fig. 33). The first (flake tool H) is a secondary flake midsection of Ogallala quartzite. It is 25.9 mm long, 30.1 mm wide, and 6.3 mm thick. Both the platform and termination are missing. One lateral edge is dull from use. The other edge appears unused.

Flake tool I is a radial fracture tool made on a uniface of Owl Creek chert. The specimen is 22.6 mm long, 31.4 mm wide, and 5.5 mm thick. Snap fractures created two sharp beaks similar to that seen at the intersection of two burins. One of these beaks and the sharp edges of the fractures show signs of use. The small segment of the unifacial edge of the original tool shows heavy use.

Table 25
Middle Kill Projectile Points

ID	Length	Width	Thickness	Flute Thickness	Portion	Material	No. of Flutes	Reworked
I	14.0	21.3	3.3	1.8	Proximal	Edwards	2	N
R	46.2	21.0	3.2	2.2	Complete	Owl Creek	2	N
S	26.2	17.1	3.0	1.7	Complete	Edwards	2	Y
U	32.2	18.4	3.1	2.2	Complete	Owl Creek	1	Y
V	31.6	22.2	3.0	2.5	Complete	Edwards	2	Y
Y	35.4	18.7	4.0	2.3	Complete	Owl Creek	2	Y
Z	20.8	15.3	3.1	2.2	Complete	Owl Creek	2	Y
C	38.6	22.1	3.8	1.2	Distal	Edwards	2	N

Figure 33. These projectile points and flake knives and this single cobble were found in the Middle Kill.

RESHARPENING FLAKES. In many instances, the resharpening flakes from the Middle and Lower kills could not be segregated by kill. Rodent disturbance and the close stacking of the two episodes precluded confident sorting. Those flakes known to be with the Lower Kill are discussed in the description of the Lower Kill. The remaining flakes are summarized here.

A total of forty-six resharpening flakes and three projectile point shatter fragments were recovered. Of these, twenty-nine retained a portion of the tool edge and striking platform. Twenty-five flakes have single-faceted platforms and four have multiple-faceted platforms. The dominance of single-faceted platforms conforms to the pattern seen in the Upper Kill assemblage and indicates that most of the resharpened tools were unifaces. Usewear analysis of the edge remnants indicates that the tools were used on green hide and meat. The majority (n = 34) of the resharpening flakes were made of Edwards Plateau chert followed by Alibates (n = 10) and an unidentified chert (n = 2).

FIST-SIZED COBBLE. A single fist-sized quartzite cobble was recovered from the Middle Kill bonebed (fig. 33). It is 9.2 cm long, 8.1 cm wide, 5.7 cm thick, and weighs 467 g. The cobble exhibits no evidence of pounding or other use, and its use in the bonebed remains unknown.

Middle Kill Summary

The heads of a large number of articulated skeletons converged at a point in the middle of the excavation area that became known as the bison convergence. Each carcass had apparently been propped up on its belly with its hind legs turned in underneath to supply support. In this position, a large number of animals could be worked on at the same time in a confined area. Once butchering was complete, the carcasses were either pushed over or left to fall over on their own. They cascaded in domino fashion, each skeleton lying partially on top of the next.

The level of carcass handling has been reconstructed from the artifact and bone analyses. Few projectile points were found within the bison skeletons and those were small fragments of tips and edges of points that broke upon impact. The larger remnants had been removed.

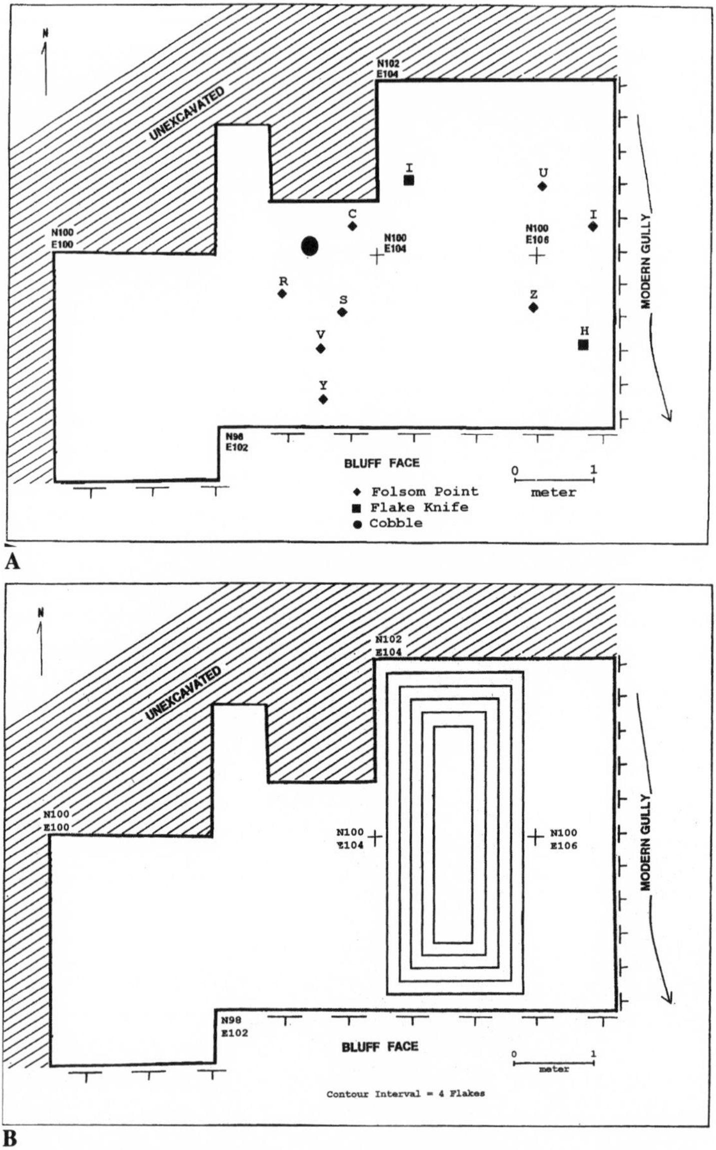

Figure 34. The distribution of projectile points, knives, cobble, and resharpening flakes indicate that Folsom hunters butchered the densely packed carcasses of the Middle Kill.

Thus, at the very least, the hunters had moved among the animals to retrieve their spears. In contrast, more complete projectiles were found in the skeletons along the steep arroyo wall that bordered the western edge of the kill (fig. 34a). But even here, the number of projectiles is far below the number of bison carcasses, indicating that many points were retrieved. The flake knives and numerous resharpening flakes recovered from around and under the toppled skeletons were used to skin and butcher the animals (figs. 34a, b).

Analysis of the bones yielded direct evidence of butchering in the form of cut marks on the bones from the bison convergence and on other animals. A few butchering fractures have been identified. All these lines of evidence lead to the conclusion that the animals in the Middle Kill were skinned and butchered.

THE PAINTED SKULL. Underlying the bones of the Middle Kill was a skull from the Lower Kill that had a red zigzag lightning bolt design painted on its frontals (fig. 19). The extent of painting is not known. The skull had been removed from articulation with a skeleton from the Lower Kill and placed at the head of the arroyo prior to the Middle Kill. Animals from the Middle Kill trampled the skull, rendering it into hundreds of small pieces. The skull was further ravaged by gopher tunneling. The significance of the painted skull is discussed in chapter 9.

Lower Kill

Upon removal of several of the articulated skeletons in the Middle Kill layer, it was discovered that underlying skeletons often had elements fractured in the same manner as those attributed to trampling in the Middle Kill. Because of their location in the center of the ancient arroyo (where the Middle Kill was separated from the Upper by over 25 cm) and the vertical position beneath the Middle Kill, it was concluded that a third or Lower Kill episode was contained in the gully. Limited separation of the Lower Kill from the Middle Kill was found along a segment of a narrow channel at the western edge of the bones. The presence of trampled bones and limited stratigraphic separation of the deposits suggests that the two kills transpired within a relatively short time.

Figure 35. Last to be removed during excavation of the Lower Kill bonebed remnant was this articulated skeleton.

The Lower Kill contains a minimum of twenty mostly articulated skeletons (fig. 35) from mature cows, calves, and juvenile bison. The horizontal extent of the bone deposit is 4 m from east to west by 3 m from north to south (fig. 36). Unlike in the Upper and Middle kills, the bones in the Lower Kill consistently slope at 15% except where they dip into a shallow channel that runs along the west edge of the Lower Kill deposit.

Bone Analysis

A total of 444 identifiable elements and element groups was recovered from the Lower Kill remnant; This total increases to approximately 900 if the ribs and vertebrae are counted individually. Only six (1.4%) of the 444 coded elements were not articulated with other bones or complete skeletons. Many of the articulations were probably part of

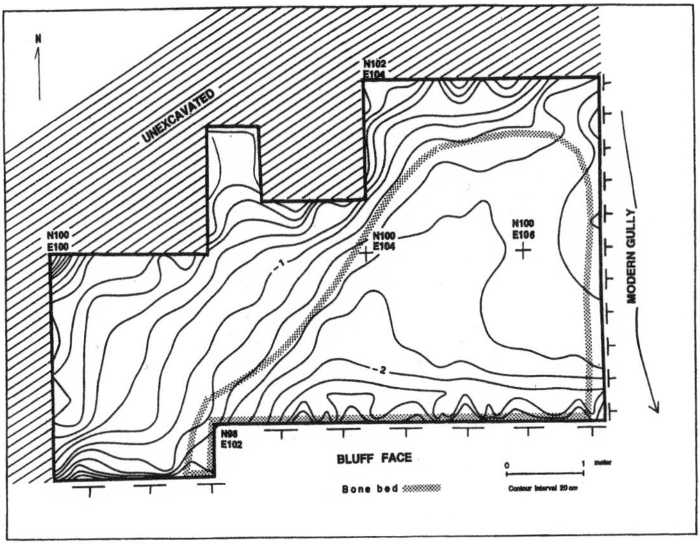

A

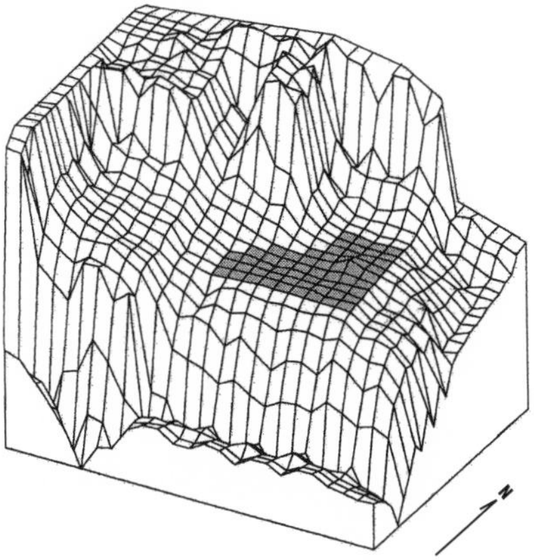

B

Figure 36. Contour (a) and three-dimensional (b) maps of the Lower Kill were generated from elevations and distributions of the skeletal remains.

Figure 37. Fragments of the tip of a projectile point are embedded in the surface of this rib from the Lower Kill.

complete skeletons, but the modern gully to the east and the Beaver River to the south had substantially eroded the bonebed, removing many body parts.

The age distribution of the Lower Kill MNI of twenty individuals is: one calf (group I), one yearling (group II), five two-year-olds (group III), six three-year-olds (group IV), two four-year-olds (group V), three five-year-olds (group VI), and two seven-year-olds (group VIII). No six-year-olds or individuals older than seven years old were recovered in the Lower Kill deposit.

SEASONALITY. The tooth eruption and wear patterns indicate that the animals had lived 0.3 years beyond the birthing peak. Assuming a calving pulse from late April to early May, their season of death was at the end of summer (late August) or early fall (September).

BONE WITH IMPACT DAMAGE. A seventh rib from a seven-year-old individual displays the compression morphology of a projectile point impact on its lateral surface (fig. 37). Fragments of the projectile's tip are lodged inside the impact scar. The implement was

Table 26
Lower Kill Cut Marks

Element	N	Absent	Present
1st phalanx	50	50	0
2nd phalanx	50	50	0
3rd phalanx	49	49	0
Astragalus	10	10	0
Cervical vertebrae	10	10	0
Calcaneus	11	11	0
Caudal vertebrae	3	3	0
Femur	21	20	1
Humerus	23	22	1
Lumbar vertebrae	13	13	0
Metacarpal	18	18	0
Metatarsal	15	15	0
Naviculo-cuboid	10	10	0
Patella	8	8	0
Pelvis	13	13	0
Radius	24	24	0
Ribs	16	15	1
Sacrum	6	6	0
Scapula	23	23	0
Skull	14	14	0
Sternum	4	4	0
Thoracic vertebrae	15	14	1
Tibia	17	16	1
Ulna	21	20	1
Total	444	438	6
%	100	98.65	1.35

made of gray Edwards Plateau chert. This is direct evidence for the intentional dispatching of these animals.

CUT MARKS. Direct evidence of butchering is found in the distribution of cut marks on the bones. A total of six (1.4%) specimens had cut marks (table 26): a femur, humerus, rib, thoracic vertebra, tibia, and an ulna.

SPIRAL FRACTURES. A single scapula out of the 444 bones from the Lower Kill displayed a green bone spiral fracture (table 27). Scapulae are not typically fractured intentionally since they contain little marrow. Perhaps the fracture is related to projectile point impact or simply occurred during the milling about of the kill. In addition, several thoracic vertebrae were broken, probably a result of butchering.

Table 27
Lower Kill Spiral Fractures

Element	N	Absent	Present
1st phalanx	50	50	0
2nd phalanx	50	50	0
3rd phalanx	49	49	0
Astragalus	10	10	0
Cervical vertebrae	10	10	0
Calcaneus	11	11	0
Caudal vertebrae	3	3	0
Femur	21	21	0
Humerus	23	23	0
Lumbar vertebrae	13	13	0
Metacarpal	18	18	0
Metatarsal	15	15	0
Naviculo-cuboid	10	10	0
Patella	8	8	0
Pelvis	13	13	0
Radius	24	24	0
Ribs	16	16	0
Sacrum	6	6	0
Scapula	23	22	1
Skull	14	14	0
Sternum	4	4	0
Thoracic vertebrae	15	15	0
Tibia	17	17	0
Ulna	21	21	0
Total	444	443	1
%	100	99.77	0.23

Surface Factors

WEATHERING. A little over 51% of the Lower Kill bones display no weathering (table 28). Of the remaining 49%, 28% were at level 1, 19% at level 2, and 2% at level 3. Weathering was limited to the top of bones, indicating that they remained stationary while they lay on the surface.

CARNIVORE CHEWING. There was no evidence of carnivore scavenging on 98.6% of the Lower Kill bones (table 29). Of the remaining bones, 0.9% were at the 1 ranking and only 0.5% was at the 2 level. No bones displayed extensive (level 3) carnivore damage. Punctures and grooves were found on a humerus, metacarpal, patella, rib, third phalanx,

Table 28
Lower Kill Weathering

Element	N	Ranking			
		0	1	2	3
1st phalanx	50	30	17	3	0
2nd phalanx	50	34	13	3	0
3rd phalanx	49	33	7	8	1
Astragalus	10	5	2	2	1
Cervical vertebrae	10	3	3	4	0
Calcaneus	11	5	3	2	1
Caudal vertebrae	3	2	1	0	0
Femur	21	10	7	3	1
Humerus	23	14	5	4	0
Lumbar vertebrae	13	4	6	3	0
Metacarpal	18	6	6	4	2
Metatarsal	15	3	5	7	0
Naviculo-cuboid	10	6	2	1	1
Patella	8	3	3	2	0
Pelvis	13	7	4	2	0
Radius	24	5	12	7	0
Ribs	16	7	4	5	0
Sacrum	6	2	1	2	1
Scapula	23	10	7	6	0
Skull	14	14	0	0	0
Sternum	4	2	1	1	0
Thoracic vertebrae	15	7	4	4	0
Tibia	17	4	9	4	0
Ulna	21	11	4	6	0
Total	444	227	126	83	8
%	100	51.13	28.38	18.69	1.80

and an ulna. This scant evidence of carnivore scavenging repeats the condition of bones in the Middle and Upper kill assemblages.

CRUSHING. Some 16.5% of the Lower Kill assemblage displayed evidence of crushing. Of this, 4% was at level 1 rating, 10% at level 2, and 2.5% at level 3 (table 30). The most extensive crushing was found on the skulls, which were apparently trampled by animals of the Middle Kill. The crushed bones in the Lower Kill were more evenly distributed across the bonebed than was the case in the Middle Kill, where the periphery was more trampled. This distribution indicates that many of the bones of the Lower Kill were only partially buried at the time of the Middle Kill.

Table 29
Lower Kill Carnivore Chewing

Element	N	Ranking		
		0	1	2
1st phalanx	50	50	0	0
2nd phalanx	50	50	0	0
3rd phalanx	49	48	0	1
Astragalus	10	10	0	0
Cervical vertebrae	10	10	0	0
Calcaneus	11	11	0	0
Caudal vertebrae	3	3	0	0
Femur	21	21	0	0
Humerus	23	22	1	0
Lumbar vertebrae	13	13	0	0
Metacarpal	18	17	1	0
Metatarsal	15	15	0	0
Naviculo-cuboid	10	10	0	0
Patella	8	7	1	0
Pelvis	13	13	0	0
Radius	24	24	0	0
Ribs	16	15	1	0
Sacrum	6	6	0	0
Scapula	23	23	0	0
Skull	14	14	0	0
Sternum	4	4	0	0
Thoracic vertebrae	15	15	0	0
Tibia	17	17	0	0
Ulna	21	20	0	1
Total	444	438	4	2
%	100	98.65	0.90	0.45

Subsurface Factors

ROOT ETCHING. Signs of root etching are not visible on 43% of the Lower Kill assemblage (table 31). Evidence of level 1 root etching occurs on 45.5% of the bones, and level 2 and level 3 are at 11% and 0.2% respectively.

RODENT GNAWING. Only 14% of the bones were rodent gnawed and most of these (10.8%)were at level 1 gnawing (table 32). Less than 3% were at level 2 and only a single bone (0.2%) received a level 3 ranking. The close vertical proximity between the Lower and Middle kills left little space for the vertical movement of the gophers.

Table 30
Lower Kill Crushing

Element	N	Ranking			
		0	1	2	3
1st phalanx	50	50	0	0	0
2nd phalanx	50	49	1	0	0
3rd phalanx	49	47	1	1	0
Astragalus	10	10	0	0	0
Cervical vertebrae	10	6	0	4	0
Calcaneus	11	9	2	0	0
Caudal vertebrae	3	2	0	1	0
Femur	21	17	3	1	0
Humerus	23	18	1	3	1
Lumbar vertebrae	13	9	0	4	0
Metacarpal	18	18	0	0	0
Metatarsal	15	12	1	2	0
Naviculo-cuboid	10	9	1	0	0
Patella	8	8	0	0	0
Pelvis	13	9	2	2	0
Radius	24	17	2	5	0
Ribs	16	8	0	7	1
Sacrum	6	6	0	0	0
Scapula	23	20	0	3	0
Skull	14	5	0	0	9
Sternum	4	4	0	0	0
Thoracic vertebrae	15	8	1	6	0
Tibia	17	13	1	3	0
Ulna	21	17	2	2	0
Total	444	371	18	44	11
%	100	83.56	4.05	9.91	2.48

SKID MARKS. Only ten bones had skid marks on them (table 33), a skid mark percentage comparable to that found on the Middle Kill bones. The relatively small size of this kill deposit precludes drawing meaningful inferences about the distribution of skid marks across the bonebed.

Pathologies

Fractures in the Lower Kill bone assemblage affected a vertebra, ribs, and an ulna (table 34). Infections were evident on a femur and humerus. Four thoracic vertebrae, all from a seven-year-old individual, display the lipping associated with arthritis.

Table 31
Lower Kill Root Etching

Element	N	Ranking			
		0	1	2	3
1st phalanx	50	20	27	2	1
2nd phalanx	50	24	24	2	0
3rd phalanx	49	37	12	0	0
Astragalus	10	1	8	1	0
Cervical vertebrae	10	5	2	3	0
Calcaneus	11	5	5	1	0
Caudal vertebrae	3	2	1	0	0
Femur	21	2	15	4	0
Humerus	23	6	11	6	0
Lumbar vertebrae	13	4	8	1	0
Metacarpal	18	9	5	4	0
Metatarsal	15	5	8	2	0
Naviculo-cuboid	10	3	7	0	0
Patella	8	1	7	0	0
Pelvis	13	6	6	1	0
Radius	24	11	9	4	0
Ribs	16	5	9	2	0
Sacrum	6	3	2	1	0
Scapula	23	9	10	4	0
Skull	14	13	1	0	0
Sternum	4	2	2	0	0
Thoracic vertebrae	15	5	6	4	0
Tibia	17	4	8	5	0
Ulna	21	9	9	3	0
Total	444	191	202	50	1
%	100	43.02	45.50	11.26	0.22

Interpretive Analyses

Cross plots of the MAU(%) with bone density ranking and food utility ranking indicate no correlation between these variables (table 35). Hence, the Lower Kill bone assemblage was not affected by transport decisions or density-mediated preservational factors.

Lower Kill Lithic Assemblage

PROJECTILE POINTS. Excavation of the Lower Kill deposits produced seven projectile points associated with the bison remains

Table 32
Lower Kill Rodent Gnawing

Element	N	Ranking			
		0	1	2	3
1st phalanx	50	44	5	1	0
2nd phalanx	50	42	7	1	0
3rd phalanx	49	48	1	0	0
Astragalus	10	10	0	0	0
Cervical vertebrae	10	9	1	0	0
Calcaneus	11	11	0	0	0
Caudal vertebrae	3	3	0	0	0
Femur	21	17	4	0	0
Humerus	23	19	2	2	0
Lumbar vertebrae	13	11	2	0	0
Metacarpal	18	18	0	0	0
Metatarsal	15	10	2	3	0
Naviculo-cuboid	10	10	0	0	0
Patella	8	8	0	0	0
Pelvis	13	7	5	1	0
Radius	24	18	4	2	0
Ribs	16	9	6	1	0
Sacrum	6	5	1	0	0
Scapula	23	20	2	0	1
Skull	14	14	0	0	0
Sternum	4	4	0	0	0
Thoracic vertebrae	15	12	3	0	0
Tibia	17	14	3	0	0
Ulna	21	19	0	2	0
Total	444	382	48	13	1
%	100	86.04	10.81	2.93	0.22

(fig. 38). Only two specimens are complete (table 36): point T is 37.2 mm long, 18.6 mm wide, and 4.0 mm thick, and point BB is 48 mm long, 24.7 mm wide, and 4.6 mm thick. The remaining five specimens are fragments: two tips, one edge, one midsection, and the proximal two- thirds of a large projectile point (specimen CC). The distal end of specimen CC was removed by an impact fracture. One of the basal ears also broke. Fragments of the shattered tip are probably classified as debitage from this kill.

Point BB also experienced extensive impact damage. The various parts of this point were recovered and the implement can be refitted.

Table 33
Lower Kill Trampling Skid Marks

Element	N	Ranking	
		0	1
1st phalanx	50	49	1
2nd phalanx	50	50	0
3rd phalanx	49	49	0
Astragalus	10	10	0
Cervical vertebrae	10	10	0
Calcaneus	11	11	0
Caudal vertebrae	3	3	0
Femur	21	21	0
Humerus	23	23	1
Lumbar vertebrae	13	13	0
Metacarpal	18	16	2
Metatarsal	15	13	2
Naviculo-cuboid	10	9	1
Patella	8	8	0
Pelvis	13	13	0
Radius	24	22	2
Ribs	16	16	1
Sacrum	6	5	1
Scapula	23	23	0
Skull	14	14	9
Sternum	4	4	0
Thoracic vertebrae	15	14	1
Tibia	17	17	0
Ulna	21	21	0
Total	444	434	10
%	100	97.75	2.25

Five of the Lower Kill Folsom points are fluted; two are not. The unfluted points are made from Alibates and Owl Creek chert. Two of the fluted points are made from Alibates, one from Owl Creek, and two from gray or brown Edwards Plateau chert.

Specimen AA is a fluted preform of Alibates that functioned as a projectile point. This point was recovered from inside the chest cavity of skeleton BN763 and bears extensive impact damage on the tip and proximal end. Of the seven points from the Lower Kill, three show no evidence of reworking, three are indeterminate, and one is reworked (table 36).

Table 34
Lower Kill Pathologies

Element	N	Absent	Present
1st phalanx	50	50	0
2nd phalanx	50	50	0
3rd phalanx	49	49	0
Astragalus	10	10	0
Cervical vertebrae	10	10	0
Calcaneus	11	11	0
Caudal vertebrae	3	3	0
Femur	21	20	1
Humerus	23	22	1
Lumbar vertebrae	13	12	1
Metacarpal	18	18	0
Metatarsal	15	15	0
Naviculo-cuboid	10	10	0
Patella	8	8	0
Pelvis	13	13	0
Radius	24	24	0
Ribs	16	14	2
Sacrum	6	6	0
Scapula	23	23	0
Skull	14	14	0
Sternum	4	4	0
Thoracic vertebrae	15	11	4
Tibia	17	17	0
Ulna	21	20	1
Total	444	434	10
%	100	97.75	2.25

FLAKE TOOLS. No flake tools were recovered from the Lower Kill deposits. The presence of resharpening flakes, however, indicates that such tools were used in the butchery of the animals.

RESHARPENING FLAKES. As mentioned in the discussion of resharpening flakes from the Middle Kill, it was impossible to divide all the flakes according to kill. However, twenty-six flakes and one projectile point piece are clearly attributable to the Lower Kill. Of these, only eight retain remnants of the old edge. Seven of the eight have single-faceted platforms and the remaining one has a multifaceted platform. Usewear is consistent with the tasks of cutting green hide and meat. Edwards Plateau chert dominates (89%) the resharpening flake assemblage.

Table 35
Lower Kill Minimum Animal Unit, Density, and Food Utility Index

Element	N	MAU	%MAU	Bone Density	Food Utility
1st phalanx	50	6.3			
2nd phalanx	50	6.3			
3rd phalanx	49	6.1			
Astragalus	10	5	35.71	32	30
Calcaneus	11	5.5	39.29	33	30
Femur	21	10.5	75.00	6	100
Humerus	23	11.5	82.14	10	28.4
Metacarpal	18	9	64.29	29	6.0
Metatarsal	15	7.5	53.57	21.5	15.9
Naviculo-cuboid	10	5	35.71	18	30
Pelvis	13	13	92.86	24	39.8
Radius	24	12	85.71	15	19.7
Sacrum	6	6	42.86	3	39.8
Scapula	23	11.5	82.14	20	28.4
Skull	14	14	100.00		10.4
Tibia	17	8.5	60.71	12	58.1
Ulna	21	10.5	75.00	31	19.7
Spearman's rho				0.18	0.04

FIST-SIZED COBBLE. The Lower Kill bonebed yielded a single fist-sized cobble similar to those found in the Upper and Middle kills (fig. 38). This limestone cobble is 11.5 cm long, 8.0 cm wide, 4.3 cm thick, and weighs 508 g. Its function is not readily apparent as there is no definite use damage.

Lower Kill Summary

The Lower Kill bonebed was dominated by articulated skeletons. And, once again, the recovered number of projectile points was insufficient to kill the number of animals in the arroyo. No flake knives were recovered; however, resharpening flakes indicate that knives made predominantly of Edwards Plateau chert were used. A single fist-sized cobble was in the bonebed. Evidence for the butchering of the animals is found in the presence of cut marks, damage to bones, removal of projectile points, and the distribution of butchering tools and resharpening flakes (figs. 39a, b).

Table 36
Lower Kill Projectile Points

ID	Length	Width	Thickness	Flute Thickness	Portion	Material	No. of Flutes	Reworked
T	37.2	18.6	4.0		Complete	Alibates	0	Y
W					Tip	Edwards		
AA	39.4	25.5	5.0	3.1	Midsection	Alibates	2	Preform
BB	30.6	21.9	3.6		Complete	Owl Creek	0	N
CC	48.0	24.7	4.6	2.9	Proximal	Owl Creek	2	N
DD					Tip	Edwards	2	
EE					Edge	Alibates	2	

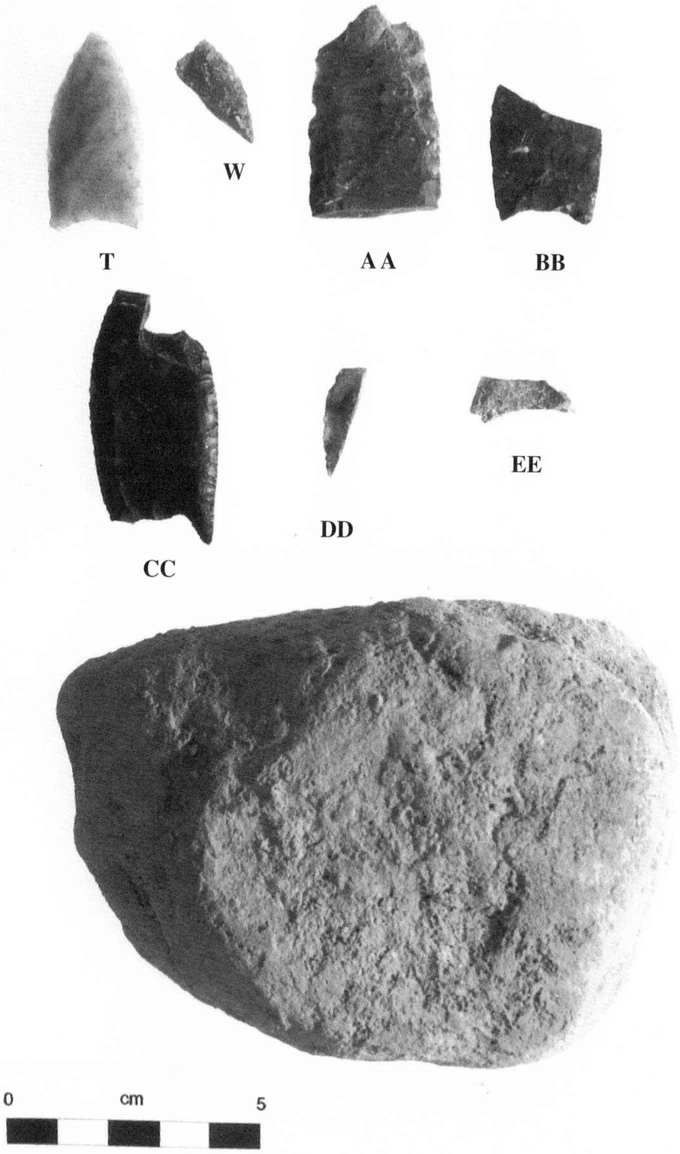

Figure 38. These projectile points and one cobble were recovered from the Lower Kill deposits.

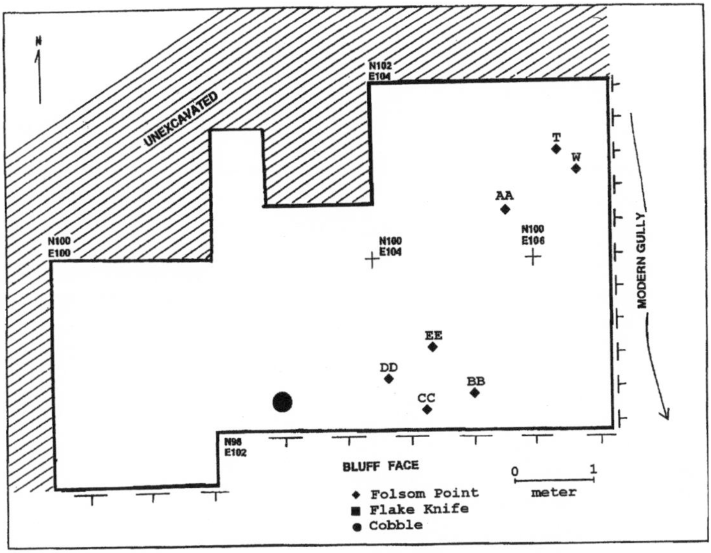

A

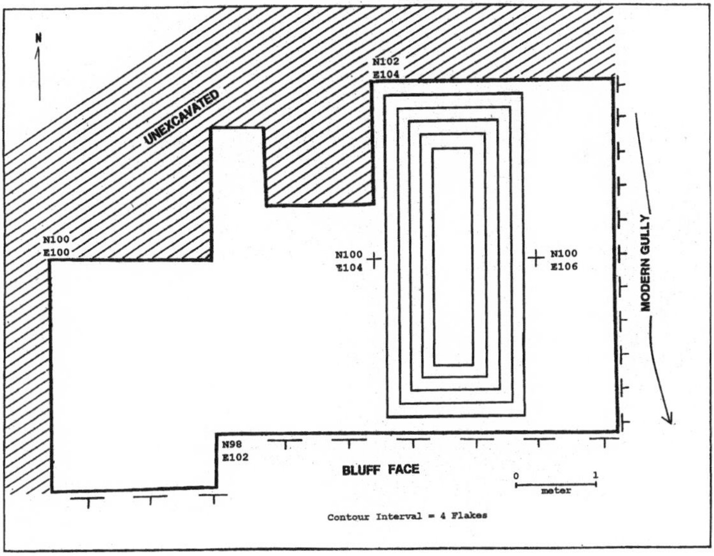

B

Figure 39. Distribution maps of projectile points, cobble, and resharpening flakes lend evidence that the hunters processed these animals.

Slump Block

The modern gully that truncates the eastern edge of the site contained little bison bone. The slope of this gully exposed each of the bonebeds to some degree but none extensively. However, the same cannot be said for the vertical face left along the south edge of the site by the Beaver River. A steep, sloping slump block or collapse of the bone-bearing sediments of the ancient arroyo extended from the truncated bluff face onto the Beaver River floodplain. This eroded material, known as the slump block, was excavated to recover the numerous bones and artifacts it contained. A drop of approximately 6 m separates the bone-bearing layers from the modern floodplain surface. The vertical face or bluff line was formed by the lateral widening of the floodplain by the meandering of the river channel. An exposure of red sandstone bedrock at the bottom of this bluff resisted the lateral widening of the floodplain; the river channel was unable to penetrate the bedrock. The ancient arroyo deposits above this bedrock bench were spared simply because the river could not continue its lateral migration.

Excavation of the slump material to and beneath the modern floodplain indicated that the bedrock exposure is one stairstep bench of the floodplain margin. The bedrock slopes southward into the floodplain. A trench, extending from the bluff face southward 5 m, provided a glimpse of the sediments that have aggraded since the last time the river channel eroded the bluff face. The majority of the floodplain deposits overlying the sloping bedrock bench to the south consisted of colluvial sands, gravels, bones, and artifacts from the Cooper site vicinity. Ponded sediments directly above the bedrock bench are probably channel fill, as the channel retreated to the south. A radiocarbon date for this sediment of 840 ± 50 years BP (Beta 74204) provides a date for the last time the river channel followed the bluff face. A total of 2.5 m of colluvial and aeolian deposits have accumulated on the bedrock bench over the past 840 years. Slump blocks containing bones and artifacts from all three kill episodes were intermixed in the floodplain deposits. The slump deposits yielded the bones of at least thirty-three bison, six projectile points, four large flake tools, six resharpening flakes, and two fist-sized cobbles (fig. 40).

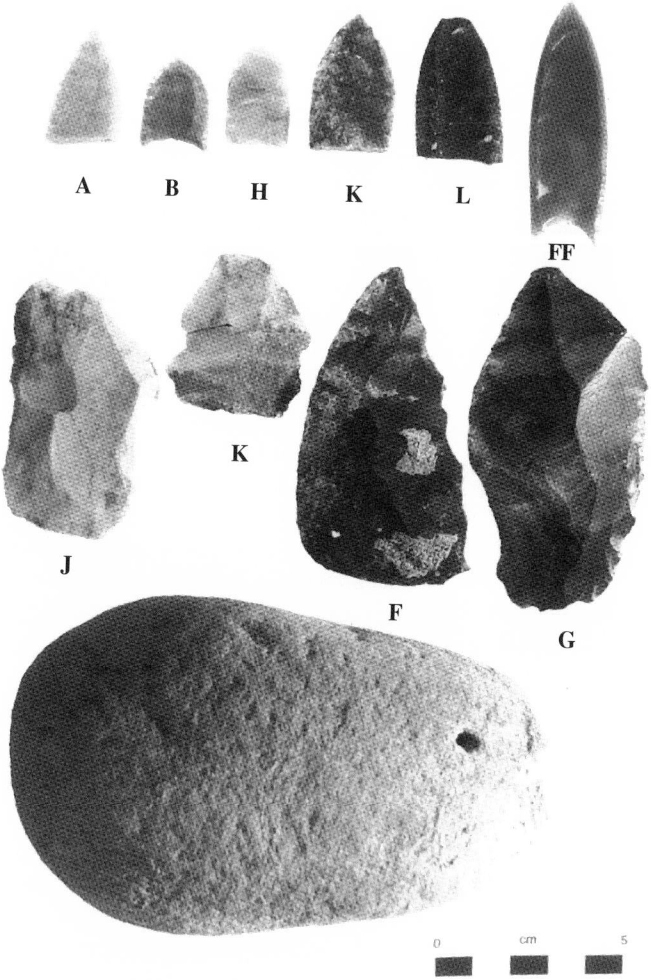

Figure 40. Projectile points, knives, and a cobble were found during excavation of the slump block deposits.

Slump Bison Bones

The bones contained in the slump material include representatives of every element of the bison skeleton. Minimum number of individuals

Table 37
Select Slump Bone Counts and Minimum Number of Individuals

Element	N	Left	Right	Unsided	MNI
Patella	32	18	13	4	18
Radial carpal	39	13	22	4	22
Ulnar carpal	39	20	17	2	20
Inter. carpal	40	21	17	2	21
2 + 3 carpal	37	16	21	0	21
4th carpal	43	24	18	1	24
Malleous	34	17	16	1	17
2 + 3 Tarsal	58	23	33	2	33
Naviculo-cuboid	56	24	32	2	32
Astragalus	58	31	27	0	31
Calcaneus	37	20	16	1	20

from the slump as a whole is set at thirty-three based on the number of right 2 + 3 tarsals with counts of thirty-two and thirty-one right naviculo-cuboids and left astraguli, respectively (table 37). Front and rear leg elements have similar counts.

The bones ranged from complete elements to highly fractured pieces that contrast with the good condition of the bones in the primary contexts, where skeletal elements were often still articulated and complete. The breakage is a result of reworking of the bonebeds by erosional processes—weathering, sediment abrasion, tumbling vertically for 6 m and then up to 5 m horizontally. Reexposure to the air also allowed renewed scavenger activity. Many of the bones from the slump block bear recent tooth marks from rodent gnawing.

The condition of the bone does not, in itself signal that the deposits are secondary. Many of the taphonomic agencies at work (rodent and carnivore gnawing, weathering) have also been identified in primary contexts at other sites, particularly those where the carcasses have been disarticulated and extensively processed such as at Stewart's Cattle Guard (Jodry and Stanford 1992) and Lubbock Lake (Johnson 1987).

Slump Lithics

PROJECTILE POINTS. Six projectile points were recovered from the slump excavation (fig. 40; table 38). Half are made from

Table 38
Slump Block Projectile Points

ID	Length	Width	Thickness	Flute Thickness	Portion	Material	No. of Flutes	Reworked
A	31.0	20.0	3.8	2.2	Tip	Alibates	2	N
B	23.6	18.3	3.5	2.2	Complete	Edwards	2	Y
H	28.0	16.6	3.5	1.6	Complete	Alibates	2	Y
K	36.0	21.5	5.0	3.3	Distal	Alibates	2	N
L	39.2	22.6	4.0	3.1	Distal	Owl Creek	2	N
FF	63.6	21.0	3.2	2.7	Complete	Edwards	2	N

Alibates and half are Edwards Plateau cherts. One of the Edwards Plateau chert points is made from the Owl Creek variety.

The largest complete Folsom point from the Cooper site came from the slump deposits. This point, specimen FF, is 63.6 mm long, 21.0 mm wide, and 3.2 mm thick (table 38). One of the smallest points from the site also came from the slump: specimen B is 23.6 mm long, 18.3 mm wide, and 3.5 mm thick. Three points are complete, two consist of the distal half, and one is the distal tip. All six specimens are fluted on both surfaces. Four of the six Folsom points are not reworked and two are reworked.

Since these points came out of the slump deposits, their primary context is not known. Based on material type, the single Owl Creek specimen could be from either the Middle or Lower kill, both of which produced Owl Creek projectile points. The Alibates points could be from either the Upper or Lower kills, and the gray and brown Edwards points could be from any of the three kill deposits.

FLAKE TOOLS. Four flake tools were recovered from the slump deposits (fig. 40). The first, flake tool J, made of Alibates, is 65.2 mm long, 38.2 mm wide, and 5.1 mm thick. The platform is multifaceted and is set at an angle of 110 degrees in relation to the ventral surface. The entire perimeter of the flake has been used and the edges have been resharpened. All retouch is found on the dorsal surface. However, nibbling flakes from use are prevalent on the ventral surface, particularly along the edge opposite the platform.

Flake tool K, made of Day Creek chert, was broken in two during excavation. The platform is multifaceted and is set at an angle of 95 degrees in relation to the ventral surface. The lateral edges adjacent to the platform are worn from use. The other edges bear no sign of use and the distal end of the flake is broken. There are no resharpening flakes removed from this tool.

Flake tool F is made on a large flake of Owl Creek chert. The tool is 77.9 mm long, 44.2 mm wide, and 10.2 mm thick. Most of a multifaceted striking platform is shattered, leaving only a small segment. The flake terminates in a sweeping hinge fracture that shows no sign of use or alteration. One lateral edge is covered by white patina, indicating either cortex or older flake scarring. The use edge is the opposite lateral edge. It is convex and has been resharpened many times.

The final flake tool, G, also made on a large flake of Owl Creek chert, is 84.4 mm long, 45.7 mm wide, and 8.9 mm thick. The platform is heavily lipped and oriented 115 degrees in relation to the ventral surface. Termination of the flake is hinged. With the exception of the hinge, all edges were utilized and resharpened at least once. One lateral edge is predominantly straight. The other consists of a convex portion leading distally into a broad concavity. Retouch is limited to the dorsal surface on all edges. Fine nibbling can be found on the ventral surface along most edges.

RESHARPENING FLAKES. Six resharpening flakes were recovered from the slump block. Edge remnants are preserved on four of the six flakes. All platforms are single-faceted, indicating that the flakes were struck from unifacially flaked knives. Three of the flakes are made of Alibates and two of Edwards Plateau chert, and one is Ogallala quartzite.

FIST-SIZED COBBLES. The slump block produced two fist-sized limestone cobbles (fig. 40). One is 12.5 cm long, 8.4 cm wide, 6.0 cm thick, and weighs 728 g; the other is 11.5 cm long, 7.0 cm wide, 3.8 cm thick, and weighs 498 g. Both exhibit damage from pounding on one end.

Slump Block Summary

Excavation into the deposits below the vertical face created by the Beaver River yielded bones and artifacts that had eroded from each kill. All bone and artifact classes found in the undisturbed bonebeds were represented in this mixed deposit. Unfortunately, no means was found to associate the displaced materials with their original kill layer. Investigation of the slump material increased the number of artifacts attributable to Folsom hunting technology, providing a larger sample for analysis. It also provided a glimpse of the character of displaced site deposits as might be found at other kill sites.

Summary of Excavations

The excavations revealed the presence of three Folsom-age bison kills in a single arroyo adjacent to the Beaver River floodplain. Each kill contained the remains of a predominantly cow-calf herd trapped and killed after being maneuvered up the gully from the floodplain. Cut marks on the bones and recovery of resharpening flakes and broken spear points indicate that meat was stripped from the animals within the arroyo, leaving articulated skeletons to be buried by gully fill. Scant evidence was found to indicate that scavengers had entered the gully and altered the abandoned skeletons. In the next chapter the three kill episodes are compared and contrasted to set the stage for reconstructing Folsom activity in this region of the southern plains.

CHAPTER 8

Inter-Kill Comparisons

The Cooper site provides the opportunity to compare and contrast three Folsom-age bison kills from the same landscape feature. Similarities between the three kills can be used to define patterns in Folsom hunting, butchering, and decision making. Differences between the kills illustrate the variability inherent in cultural systems brought about by idiosyncratic behavior; the changing situational factors; and the effects of preservation. The similarities and differences among the three kills are presented in the same sequence of topics as is used to describe each kill.

Original Size of Kills

The original size of each kill remains unknown. The Beaver River and modern gully action saw to that. However, the size of each remnant was predicated on the shape of the original arroyo and the processes affecting gully filling and erosion. The profile of the lower segment of the ancient gully indicates that the arroyo had steep, expanding side walls. Thus, within the area excavated, the Lower Kill was restricted to a small space, the Middle Kill had slightly more floor area, and the Upper Kill had the most room. Movement up the arroyo was halted by the position of the knick point or gully head. In terms of our modern excavation grid, the knick point at the time of the Lower Kill was apparently along the N101 m grid line. By the time of the Middle Kill, the knick point was at N101.5 m. The upslope progression of the headcut was greatest at the time of the Upper Kill, when it reached the N102.25 m grid line.

The slope of the floor inclined sharply along the west wall and end of the arroyo. At the point where the modern gully cut into the eastern edge of the bonebeds, the floor remained fairly flat, indicating that the eastern wall of the arroyo was still some distance away. At least one-fourth of the width of each bonebed is thought to be missing because of the modern gully. The original length of the bonebeds within the arroyo is difficult to postulate. Recovery of lower leg bones along the bluff edge and the remains of at least thirty-three animals in the slump deposits suggest that a considerable area of each kill was lost. For this reason, it is suggested that an additional one-fourth of each kill was lost to the river.

Elevation changes between the kills reflect the extent of arroyo filling between kill episodes. As the gully filled, the floor area increased due to the widening of the arroyo walls and progression of the knick point. The Middle Kill is 40 cm higher than the Lower Kill. The floor of the arroyo at the time of the Upper Kill was 80 cm above that of the Middle Kill or 1.2 m above the Lower Kill floor. The top of the Lower Kill was exposed at the time of the Middle Kill, resulting in the trampling damage observed on many of the skeletal remains, particularly the skulls. Sufficient gully fill surrounded the Middle Kill bones to protect all but those along the western margin from trampling by animals of the Upper Kill.

Gully sediments covering all three kills consisted of sand-size particles washed in from upslope. The sediment underlying each bonebed was gray, the result of gleying from the microbial action on the bison organic remains.

Comparisons of Bison Remains

Bone counts for the kills are 972, 707, and 444 from Upper to Lower. The decrease in bone count with depth can be attributed to the size of the kill remnant preserved in what remained of the ancient arroyo. These numbers reflect elements that were measured and entered into a computer database and not the exact number of identifiable elements from each kill. The ribs and vertebrae were treated en masse and thus are grossly underrepresented.

Surprisingly few bones were not part of an articulated segment. The Upper Kill had the greatest number of isolated elements, but even here they represent only 6.5% of the assemblage. Middle and Lower kill percentages of isolated elements are 1.7% and 1.4%, respectively.

Obviously the pattern in all three kills is for articulations. The highest number of isolated elements was recovered from the margins of the excavation and in proximity to the steep bluff face that truncates the bonebeds or to the modern gully on the east side of the bonebeds. Thus, even these elements may have been part of articulations that were removed by erosion.

MNI

The Upper, Middle, and Lower kill remnants yielded MNI counts of twenty-nine, twenty-nine, and twenty bison, respectively, numbers that may represent less than half of the original herd size. All three bonebeds are the result of successful kills of bison herds with age distribution consistent with that of nursery herds, containing only cows and immature individuals (fig. 41).

Seasonality

Seasonality indicators place all three kills in the late summer or early fall, 0.3 years after the calving pulse and immediately after the proposed midsummer bison rut. By this time, the mature bulls would have been finished servicing the females and would have left the main herds. Thus at the end of summer, two herd types would be present, one consisting of cows and immature animals of both sexes and the other containing mature bulls. Either herd type could be hunted, although it has been argued that the bulls, at the end of the rut, are in worse physical shape than the cows (Speth 1983). Given a choice, hunters might have preferred cow-calf herds because of their superior condition. Also, mature bulls are more difficult to handle than cows. Cow-calf herds may be easier to manipulate and kill than the less cooperative and potentially more dangerous bulls.

Point Impacts

Two bones damaged by projectile points have been identified in the bonebeds. Both are rib midshaft fragments from the sixth or seventh rib, sliced on the lateral surface. One, BN808 from the Lower Kill, displays an impact scar where the projectile point penetrated only the

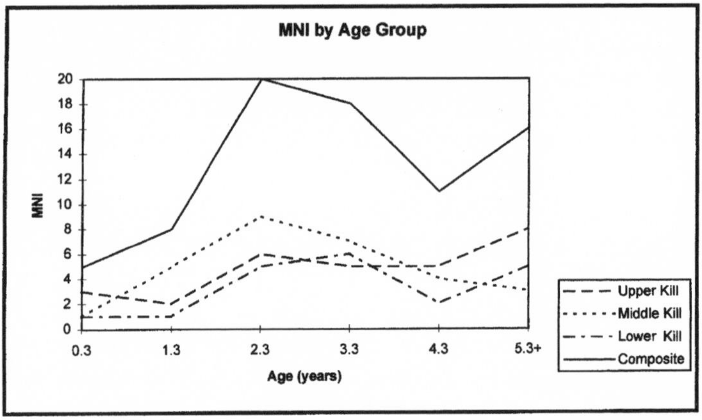

Figure 41. This graphic displays the number of individuals by age and by kill from the Cooper site.

surface of the bone, embedding the fractured tip. The second, BN677 from the Middle Kill, is similar although the projectile point penetrated much deeper. Again, the fragmented tip was left in the bone. Not only do the impacts display typical breakage patterns for projectile points, but each retains a fragment of the projectile embedded in the recess. The impact found in the Middle Kill indicates that the projectile came downward into the rib at an angle of 45 degrees, which suggests that the hunters were positioned on the rim of the arroyo above the animals. These scars are definite proof that the bison herds at Cooper were speared by the Folsom hunters.

Discussion of Preburial Factors

Any cultural alterations to the bison carcasses and, in particular, to the skeletal elements, consisted of the dispatching, skinning, and butchering of the animals during and immediately after the kills. Once the people abandoned the kill area, the agents of scavenging and weathering set in. These taphonomic forces have the potential to erase any patterning or evidence of cultural alteration of the kill site. However, at the Cooper site, the postkill, preburial agents inflicted little damage to the carcasses. Trampling marks helped segregate Lower Kill animals from the Middle Kill animals. The alternating layers of weathered, unweathered, and weathered bone provided further proof that two kill events preceded the Upper Kill.

Cut Marks

Cut marks were few in all three kills (Upper = 0.7%, Middle = 1.9%, Lower = 1.3%). Low numbers of cut marks are typical in Paleoindian bone assemblages even when the carcasses have been extensively disarticulated (Todd 1987a). Often the destructive agents of weathering and various subsurface factors erase such marks from bone surfaces. But cut marks are relevant to the topic of carcass utilization. The high number of completely articulated skeletons from each of the three kills suggests that numerous animals were abandoned untouched. The presence of cut marks and other breaks associated with butchering provides evidence that the carcasses were utilized. The type of bone that was cut or broken and the location of the damage indicate that muscle was removed from these animals (table 39): in all instances, the cuts and breaks occur on bone covered by a layer of flesh and not exposed to the knife used to skin the animal. Furthermore, if skinning was accomplished principally by pounding the skin from the carcass (as is suggested by the fist-sized cobbles), even fewer cuts would be produced.

The interpretation of cut marks and impacts beyond their indication of either hide removal or butchering patterns is problematic. A single mark does not easily translate into a quantity of meat or into expenditure of energy. After all, the cut mark is an unintentional by-product—glancing across the hard bone surface dulls the edge of a stone knife and, as such, is best avoided. The presence of a cut mark on the shaft of a femur indicates that the large muscle masses of the thigh were being removed.

A potentially useful task might be to compare the location of cuts and other butchering damage with the distribution of prime meat masses or highly valued carcass sections. This type of analysis is similar in focus to the correlation of bones to food utility ratings. In this instance, however, the bone is not removed from the site, but marks on the bone would indicate areas of the carcass targeted for filleting. Emerson (1993), in addition to her total products model,

Table 39
Elements with Butchering Marks and Associated Food Utility Ranking

Elements with Cuts	Food Utility Index
Upper Kill	
Pelvis	34.7
Tibia	57.7
Humerus	27.5
Ribs	62.3
Middle Kill	
Humerus	27.5
Ribs	62.3
Thoracic vertebrae	47.4
Lumbar vertebrae	45.1
Lower Kill	
Femur	100.0
Tibia	57.7
Humerus	27.5
Ulna	19.1
Ribs	62.3
Thoracic vertebrae	47.4

calculated the food utility ranking without the dry bone weight. This food utility index measures the caloric yield of the skeletal fat, muscle protein, intramuscular fat, and other dietary products associated with a particular skeletal element. In butchering techniques employing muscle stripping or filleting, the bone is left behind. At Cooper, where the carcasses were not quartered or cut into components prior to muscle stripping, indications of filleting would rely on the occasional cut or butcher mark on the bones. If the location of the marks corresponds to the carcass areas with the highest food utility indices, then gourmet-type butchering could be indicated.

The distribution of possible butchering marks from the three Cooper kills indeed occurs on the skeletal elements with the highest food utility indices (table 39). If entire skeletons were being stripped of usable products, all bones would have similar opportunities for misdirected knife strokes that might leave cut marks. However, since the cut marks only occur on select elements with high food utility indices, it is argued that only the choicest carcass components were removed from the Cooper animals.

Spiral Fractures

All three kills have spirally fractured bones that number less than 1% of the total assemblage. This low level underscores the intact condition of the long bones and that marrow extraction or expedient tool production was not important. Having said this, the Upper Kill produced five fractured bones, while the Middle and Lower kills had only one such bone each. The higher number of spiral fractures in the Upper Kill parallels the higher number of fist-sized cobbles from that level.

A single humerus from the Upper Kill displays a typical green bone fracture (fig. 42). A blow to the anterior medial surface of the distal shaft initiated the fracture. The fracture line arced around the shaft and terminated with a hinge break. The shaft edges show no use as a tool. The proximal portion was not recovered. As with the case of the cut marks, the spiral fractured bones are associated with the highest food utility ratings, further supporting the indications that the Cooper hunters were gourmet butchers.

Weathering

The Middle Kill contained the greatest percentage of nonweathered bones (54%), followed by the Lower Kill (51%) and the Upper Kill (35%). Factors contributing to these differences in weathering include size of the arroyo floor, quantity of colluvial material entering the arroyo, and extent of disarticulation of the skeletons. The first two factors affect the length of time it takes to bury the bones (rate of deposition), while the last factor is a product of the condition of the carcasses prior to burial. If the quantity of rainfall and downslope movement of sediment is held constant, then the area to be covered determines the depth of sedimentation over a period of time. Since the Upper Kill occupies a proportionately larger area in the arroyo bottom than either the Middle or Lower kill, the sediment buildup above it would have amounted to less over the same period of time. This means that it would have taken longer to bury the Upper Kill bones, which would thus have been exposed to weathering conditions for more time.

The effect that the degree of disarticulation has on the extent of weathering is related to the type of articulation. In a totally articulated carcass lying on its side, the bone surfaces on the upper side of the

Figure 42. Characteristics of the break on this humerus from the Upper Kill are indicative of a green bone spiral fracture.

skeleton are exposed to weathering agents the longest. The lower side bones are buried first and also are protected from some weathering by the upper side bones. The amount of muscle and hide clinging to the carcass likewise affects the amount of weathering, and additional contributing factors include the extent of rolling or movement of the bones by water, gravity, wind, scavengers, and other forces.

The Cooper bones are only slightly weathered. No advanced-stage weathering was noted on any of the bones of the three kills, indicating that the processes burying the bones acted rapidly. Geomorphologic analysis (Carter and Bement 1995) suggests that once the ancient arroyo began filling, there was no hiatus or erosion of the deposits until sometime in the Holocene (as indicated by the buried paleosol dated to 1100 BP). The amount of fill that accumulated between kill episodes could have been deposited within one or two wet seasons. Up to 15 cm of sandy gully fill was deposited at the mouth of arroyos during the two months of excavation in 1994. Thus surface weathering may have been limited to a one- to three-year time span.

Additional weathering of the bonebed began with the erosion and truncation of the deposits by the Beaver River and by the modern arroyo on the east side. This modern erosion exposed bone portions as the sediment collapsed from the resulting bluff face and arroyo wall. Advanced levels of weathering were found on the bones recovered from the slump block deposits below the site. But even here, some bones were in exceptional condition. Most of these fell from the primary deposits encased in sediment and were not subjected to weathering conditions.

The weathering of recently exposed bone was witnessed during the excavations. A tornadic system pelted the site with marble- to baseball-sized hail. The damage to the bones ranged from splintering to classic dry bone impact fractures.

Carnivore Chewing

Surprisingly, all three bonebeds lack carnivore damage. The percentages of carnivore-chewed bones range from less than 0.2% in the Middle Kill to a high of 1.4% in the Lower Kill. Less than 1.1% of the bones in the Upper Kill had carnivore damage. It is difficult to account for this apparent lack of interest by scavenging animals in what should have been mass quantities of decaying animal remains. Perhaps the time of year (end of summer) was too hot and the carcasses were reduced to skeletons by maggots. Or perhaps at this time of year carnivores were not seeking carrion to supplement fresher foods. The possibility remains that other now-lost areas of each bonebed were subjected to higher levels of carnivore damage than the upper portion of the arroyo, where access may have been restricted. If large amounts of meat were available, the carnivores, like the humans, might have selected meat over bones—gourmet scavenging, if you will. Also, we are mainly concerned with scavenging activity that leaves marks on bones. Some scavengers, such as vultures and various insects, leave little or no mark on the skeletal remains. So, scavenging may have occurred but at a level too low to be archaeologically visible.

Crushing

Crushing is a result of a number of factors that are often difficult to segregate. Above-ground factors include trampling by animals during the kill episode and trampling of the bones by subsequent hunting or animal movement through the gully. Buried bones can also be crushed by subsequent animal trampling and the weight of overburden sediments. The Cooper kills were ultimately buried under 2 m of sediment. The weight of this overburden is sufficient to crush hollow bones, such as skulls, and porous bone segments, including the proximal humerus and distal femur. Eleven percent of the Upper Kill bone assemblage exhibited evidence of crushing. Higher incidences were seen in the Middle Kill (21.5%) and Lower Kill (16.5%) bonebeds. The increase in crushed bones in the Middle and Lower Kills is partially attributed to trampling by the animals of subsequent kills. Bones crushed in this manner had breaks with characteristics intermediate between green bone and dry bone fractures (Bonnichsen and Sorg 1989; Fiorillo 1989). These intermediate fracture types suggest that two to five years elapsed between kill events. Attributing the crushing to trampling is supported by the distribution of crushed bones in areas of overlap with the bones of a subsequent kill. In the Middle Kill, trampled bones were found along the west wall and arroyo head where the Upper Kill bonebed overlapped the Middle Kill. For the Lower Kill, the trampled bones were more evenly distributed across the floor of the gully. Bones along the western wall were protected from trampling by gully wall collapse that buried them.

Postburial Factors

Root Etching

Various levels of root etching were found on over 73% of the Upper Kill, over 47% of the Middle Kill, and over 57% of the Lower Kill bone assemblages. High incidences of root etching are not uncommon in sandy soils where roots can easily penetrate to great depths and growth of grasses and dense vegetation is common. Most of the root etching at Cooper occurred on the upper surfaces of bones, indicating that the bones had not shifted position since initial burial. The same cannot be said for the bones from the slump block deposit, where root etching could be found on all surfaces of the bones, indicating the secondary nature of the deposits. Root etching varied from slight patches of root scars to extensive root scarring and even root penetration and fracturing of bones. The majority of the root etching, however, consisted of small patches of root scars.

Damage by Burrowing Animals

Active, abandoned, and filled gopher runs were visible in the site sediments. Old tunnels could be tracked across the bonebeds as they twisted around some bones while penetrating others. Nearly 30% of the Upper Kill bones had evidence of gopher gnawing, clawing, or polish. This percentage drops for both the Middle Kill (18%) and Lower Kill (14%). The reduction in gopher damage in the Middle and Lower Kills is attributed to the density of bones in these closely packed bonebeds. Penetration of these bonebeds, however was possible. One annoying habit of the gophers was to remove the horn cores from almost all the skulls in each kill level. The gopher tunnels were visible alongside the skulls and through the horn cores. Consequently, we have few skulls with intact horn cores. The extent of the damage to skulls is demonstrated by one skull in the Middle Kill (BN695) that served as a rodent den, the tunnel entering the brain case.

The gophers could penetrate any bone, regardless of the thickness of its walls. Upon encountering a thick-walled bone, the animal would claw at it, making semicircular, parallel scratches. If the element had a protrusion or sharp corner, the animal would gnaw this off. In some cases of extremely thick bone, the gopher would turn its head slightly and gnaw with the corner of the incisors, creating a broad, V-shaped bite (fig. 26b). An unusual mark left by these creatures was termed the "gopher belly rub" during excavations. On occasion, while following a gopher run across the bonebed, we noticed that where the run crossed a bone that had not presented a barrier to the animal, the surface of this bone, exposed in the run, would be highly polished. Under magnification, this polish appears as a mass of fine scratches, apparently the result of sand grains in the fur of the gopher underbelly (fig. 26e). Had the old runs not been detectable in the deposits, the origin of this polish might have gone unexplained. The co-occurence of gnawing, sideways gnawing, clawing, and polish establish the gopher as the cause of this suite of damage.

On a larger scale, damage on bones of the Middle Kill along the western edge and bluff face can be attributed to a badger. A badger skeleton was found in an area surrounded by bison bone displaying claw marks similar to those described for the gophers but considerably larger. The badger had apparently tunneled into the bonebed and created a den. Again, had the badger skeleton not been found in situ, the origin of the larger claw marks might have been difficult to discern.

Trampling Skid

The relatively friable nature and coarse grain of the sandy deposits surrounding the bison bones makes these deposits susceptible to slight movement from pressures applied from above. Hence, bones under shallow sediment layers could shift slightly from the weight of animals or people walking over them. The resultant damage to the bones is caused by the sliding or skidding of the bone on the sand, or the sand sliding over the bone. In either case, the bone surface becomes etched by the large grains of sand. Furrows created by the sand grains parallel the direction of movement. Similar damage can be obtained by rubbing a piece of sandpaper over a bone surface. Broad areas of resistance in the deposits produce a skid surface composed of striations from the sand grains on flattened, polished areas.

Such trampling skids can be created by episodes such as the gully kill events or can be the result of walking on bones still buried under a thin mantle of sand. To reduce the latter possibility, the excavators wore light shoes or went barefoot while in the bonebed. The majority of the skid marks can thus be attributed to trampling of buried bone during subsequent use of the arroyo for bison kills.

Only 1.1% of the Upper Kill bones had trampling skid marks. Percentages of skid-marked bones in the Middle and Lower kills are 4.3% and 2.3%, respectively. The differences between the various levels are slight.

Interpretation of Subsurface Factors

The Cooper bonebeds were buried for some 10,000 years. During that time, various agents of destruction etched, gnawed, clawed, and trampled the bones. These destructive factors leave marks on bones that can be identified and, to some extent, quantified, so that human modification can be differentiated from nonhuman (natural) alteration to the carcasses. Much of the postburial action on the bones affects the surface and potentially could erase any of the human-induced marks. In this regard, root etching and rodent gnawing are the two most destructive agents in all three kill deposits. In essence, taphonomic factors have had 10,000 years to alter or erase the marks made by the Paleoindian hunters and butchers over the course of only several days. Rodent gnawing, scratching, and polishing, combined with the skid marks, not only remove evidence of human modification but also produce marks that can mimic those left by stone tools. Only macroscopic and microscopic inspection of the bone assemblages allows identification and segregation of the various marks. Overall, the Cooper bones from all three kills are in surprisingly good shape, especially considering that they were buried in sandy deposits. The excellent preservation is probably due to the combined factors of concentration of bones in the deposits, large scale articulations that served as barriers to certain destructive agents, and relatively quick burial of the kills.

Comparisons of MAU(%), Density, and Food Utility

A comparison between the minimum animal unit (MAU%), bone density ranking of elements, and the food utility index of elements is a key to determining if natural preservational factors (density) or cultural factors (food utility) affect the composition of the bone assemblage. In all three kills, there were no correlations between the bones contained in the site and either their resistance to destructive forces (density) or the food value of attached muscle, fat, or grease. Each bonebed contained bones with low and high density values as well as low and high food values. This analysis underscores the fact that all three kills contain the full suite of skeletal elements—that bone has neither been lost due to taphonomic factors nor has bone been transported away from the site as part of butchering practices. Butchering in all three kills at Cooper appears to represent gourmet meat-stripping practice.

Projectile Points

Thirty-three projectile points or projectile point fragments were distributed between the three kills and the slump: thirteen in the Upper Kill, seven in the Middle Kill, seven in the Lower Kill, and six in the secondary deposits at the base of the bluff. With few exceptions, the projectile points from all three kills conform to the Folsom type. Variations in size, material type, and number of flutes reflect vagaries attributed to Folsom technology, resharpening, and mobility patterns, as discussed further in chapter 9. As a group, the thirty-three specimens are one of the largest collections of Folsom points from a single site on the southern plains. Other southern plains Folsom sites include Blackwater Draw, Lipscomb, Elida, Folsom, Lake Theo, and Lubbock Lake, with projectile point counts of 53, 28, 18, 16, 14, and 9 respectively (Harrison and Killen 1978; Harrison and Smith 1975; Hester 1962; Hofman 1991; Hofman, Carter, and Hill 1990; Howard 1935; Johnson 1987; Renaud 1931; Warnica 1961; Wormington 1957). Thus the Cooper site provides an exceptionally large sample for study. Topics of particular merit include manufacture technology, resharpening/maintenance technology, raw material utilization, hafting technology, and discard patterns.

Manufacture Technology

The technology to manufacture a Folsom point is specific and has received considerable attention by archaeologists (Bradley 1993; Frison and Bradley 1980; Tunnell 1977). Kill sites rarely produce evidence of the sequence of manufacture but rather provide examples of the finished product or what is left of it after use. Manufacturing debris has been found in processing camps associated with kills (Jodry 1987), hunting camps (Judge 1973; Amick 1996), and at lithic workshops near quarries (Tunnell 1977; Root and Emerson 1994; Root et al. 1995). The redundancy of manufacturing tasks found at each of these site types indicates that Folsom point production was an ongoing, yet staged, process. In other words, few sites evidence the full range of point production. The initial steps of raw material acquisition and roughing out a preform were conducted at a quarry area. Evidence of the subsequent stages of refining the preform and finishing projectile points is found at other sites. The implication is that Folsom hunters transported flakes and blanks that could be made into projectile points wherever they went. The finished point, however, was not fashioned until it was needed. In this way, the raw material was not committed to a single tool form (that of the point) but could be used to make any number of tools.

Resharpening and Maintenance

The staging of projectile point manufacture allows newly produced projectile points to be added to an assemblage containing battered and reworked points. A wide range of variability in projectile point size provides information on the potential use-life of hunting equipment.

The combined assemblages at Cooper contain projectile points ranging from long, slender specimens—representing new additions—to short, stubby points indicative of several resharpening events. The intact specimens illustrate the characteristics sought in a newly manufactured projectile. Conversely, the heavily reworked specimens illustrate a tool at the end of its uselife. Other points in the assemblages show the intermediate stages as projectile points move from pristine to discard. Point Z (fig. 43) is an example of a depleted projectile point at the end of its uselife. Total length is 20.8 mm, the hafting portion is 12.7 mm, and the tip is 8.1 mm. These measurements represent the minimum acceptable size of a Folsom projectile point.

At the other extreme is point FF, which is 63.6 mm long and has a haft length of 49.6 mm and a tip 14.0 mm long (fig. 43). The difference in length between the newly made point (14.0 mm) and the reworked one (8.1 mm) illustrates the conservative nature of the resharpening technology. A resharpening technique that requires only 8.1 mm of overall length to place a usable tip on a point ensures a longer uselife for a specimen than a technique that utilizes 14.0 mm of length.

When considered separately, the projectile point assemblages from each kill display considerable variation in the size and number of reworked specimens. The average length among Upper Kill projectile

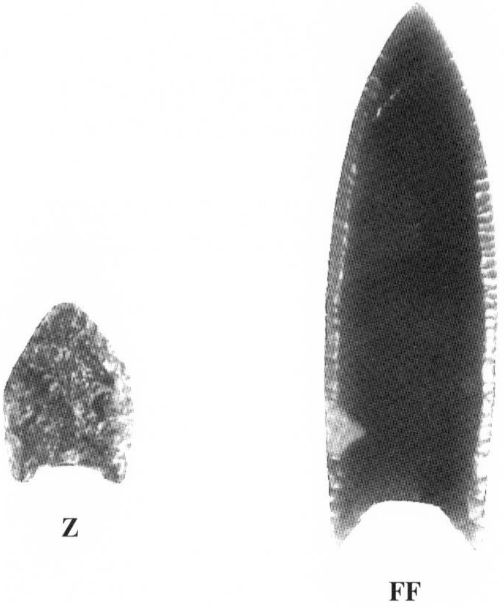

Figure 43. Both extensively reworked (Z) and newly fashioned (FF) projectile points were found at the site, indicating that projectile point refurbishing was a component of Folsom lithic technology.

points is 32.4 mm, and 50% have been reworked. The Middle Kill projectile point average length is 31.5 mm and 71% are reworked. Lower Kill projectile points have a mean length of 33.9 mm and 25% have been reworked. A ratio of these two variables, called the "retooling index," has been proposed by Hofman (1992) to indicate the condition of the lithic stores possessed by a Folsom group. The index suggests a scenario in which as Folsom hunters move through a series of kill episodes, projectile points are lost or broken and replacement points are made from the supply of raw material on hand since the last stop at a quarry site. As the lithic stores are consumed, the projectile points become shorter and more points are reworked rather than discarded, in an attempt to curb that consumption. Eventually, a stop at a quarry will be needed to replenish the toolstone coffers. The relationship between point length and number of reworked points, then, is a measure of the lithic stores on hand. The retooling index for

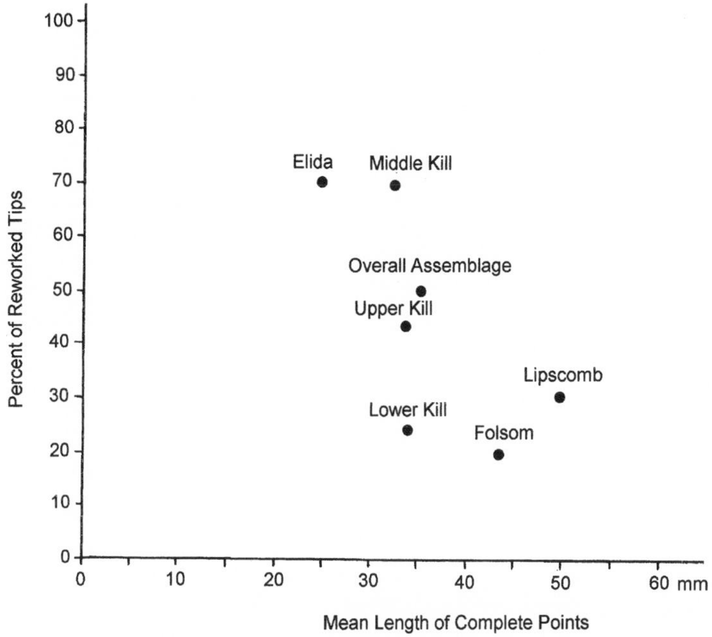

Figure 44. This plot of the retooling index for the three kills and composite from Cooper, Elida, Lipscomb, and Folsom illustrates the variability between Folsom projectile point assemblages.

the three kills at Cooper ranges from that of a spent assemblage in the Middle Kill to a replenished assemblage in the Lower Kill (Bement 1995) (fig. 44). The Upper Kill assemblage is midway between the other two.

Raw Material Utilization

Differences are seen in the use of raw material types in the projectile point component of the three lithic assemblages. The Upper Kill is dominated by points made from Alibates (n = 10, 77%); the remaining points are made of Edwards Plateau chert (n = 2, 15%) and Niobrara (n = 1, 8%). In the Middle Kill, all seven projectile points are made from Edwards Plateau chert. And in the Lower Kill, Edwards Plateau chert points and Alibates points are nearly equal (Edwards = 4, 57%, Alibates = 3, 43%). The differential use of raw material may relate to the areas traversed by each group or to aggregation of more than one group for the kills, topics addressed further in chapter 9.

Of particular interest is the presence of the Owl Creek variety of Edwards Plateau chert in the Middle and Lower kills. This dark gray to black chert has a fairly limited source area along Owl Creek in north-central Texas (Frederick and Ringstaff 1994), and this is its first demonstrated use by Folsom hunters. Since the excavations at Cooper, a single Folsom point made from Owl Creek chert has been identified from a surface collection (the Tindle Collection) from Cedar Creek in west-central Oklahoma. It is anticipated that more examples of this material will surface once archaeologists become familiar with its characteristics.

Discard Patterns

The projectile points recovered from the three kill episodes at the Cooper site were either lost or purposefully abandoned by the Folsom hunters. For those specimens represented by either a tip or edge fragment, it is clear that the remainder of the projectile was retrieved from the kill and transported elsewhere. In these cases, the base or proximal section of the projectile was probably still in the spear shaft and was taken to camp to be reworked or discarded. The more complete projectile points either became dislodged from their hafts and were lost in the animal entrails, or the shaft or foreshaft of the spear broke and was abandoned at the site.

Many of the projectile points left in the bonebeds were still in the condition they had been in before the kills took place. If these projectiles were not lost in the kill debris, then some as yet unrecognized criterion was used to determine their fate.

The presence at kill sites of complete, beautifully crafted points (fig. 27, F, P; fig. 33, S, Z; Fig. 38, T) has led some researchers to speculate that they were intentional offerings left at a site by hunters (Frison and Bradley 1980; Frison 1996). Such a point was found at Cooper in the slump deposits. Was this point left with the painted skull? Was it an offering associated with one of the other kills? We will never know. It is possible that this point just happened to escape damage from collision with a bone. Other points (figs. 27, 33, 38) at the site are of similar high quality workmanship but, because of impacts with bones or other objects, did not survive in pristine form. Relegating the beautiful complete projectile points to the realm of ritual offering may, in some circumstances, overlook a more direct, mundane explanation that the point was simply lost. This does not negate the possibility that the fluting of Folsom points was associated with rituals (Frison and Bradley 1980).

Inter-Assemblage Comparison of Flake Knives

The lithic assemblages from the three kills are dominated by projectile points and resharpening flakes. Flake knives constitute a small portion of these assemblages. The number of butchering tools is highest in the Upper Kill, followed by the Middle and then the Lower kills. The reduction in number of butchering tools corresponds to the shrinkage in size of the bonebed deposits in the Middle and Lower kills.

The recovery of resharpening flakes from the Lower Kill indicates that tools were once present. Unfortunately, all attempts to refit resharpening flakes recovered from the kill deposits to tools from the slump have met with failure. Tools made from the black Owl Creek chert recovered from the slump deposits probably originated in the Middle or Lower kill, since this raw material was absent from the Upper Kill assemblage. Unfortunately, the twenty-five Owl Creek resharpening flakes from excavations do not fit onto either of the two Owl Creek tools from the slump. A similar situation exists for the Alibates resharpening flakes and tools.

Important parallels are seen in the resharpened tools from all contexts. All edges are dull, indicating that the tools were either discarded when the task was complete or lost during use. Low magnification (70×) scrutiny of the worn edges shows patches of polish reminiscent of meat polish (Frison 1979; Hayden 1979; Keeley 1980; Keeley and Newcomer 1977; Newcomer and Keeley 1979; Odell 1975, 1990; Odell and Odel-Vereecken 1980; Vaughan 1985).

Another common condition of the tools is the high degree of smoothness on the striking platform edges. The wear or smoothing is seen around the entire circumference of the striking platform, indicating post–flake removal smoothing. Some of this smoothing and also similar treatment of the flake scar ridges on the dorsal surface may be the result of prehistoric transport damage. In transport, tools kept in a bag receive polish from rubbing each other and the walls of the container.

Comparison of Resharpening Flakes

Resharpening flakes were consistently found around the skeletons in each of the three bonebeds. Roughly 55% of the flakes retained a portion of the old worn edge on the platform. Of these, 91% were removed from unifaces and 9% from bifaces. Usewear on all edge remnants indicates that the parent tools were used to cut green hide and muscle (Brosowske and Bement 1997). In no instances could the flakes be fitted onto any of the tools recovered from the bonebeds or slump. This situation is not surprising, given that most of the tools underwent several resharpening episodes. The resharpening flakes are, however, made from the same general material types as the tools. Slight differences in the stone colors and banding indicate that at least six Alibates and five Edwards Plateau chert tools were resharpened (Brosowske and Bement 1997). In addition, a single tool made from Ogallala quartzite and one from an unidentified chert were present at the site.

All flake tools recovered from the three kills were unifacially flaked. However, several of the resharpening flakes were struck from bifacially flaked tools. This suggests that several bifacial knives were used in the butchering of the bison but were then transported away from the kill site, lost, or perhaps discarded and later washed away by the ancient Beaver River.

Comparison of Fist-Sized Cobbles

One aspect of the lithic assemblage that differentiates the Upper Kill from the other two is the disproportionate number of fist-sized cobbles. Fist-sized cobbles are a typical component of Folsom kill site assemblages and thus are not, in and of themselves, unusual (Jodry and Stanford 1992). However, their increased frequency in the Upper Kill (n = 11), compared to the Middle (n = 1) or Lower kills (n = 1), suggests that some differences existed in the butchering techniques employed by these groups. While the number of spiral-fractured bones is highest in the Upper Kill, as a percentage of the bone assemblage this number is not proportionately different than that seen in the other kills (Upper = 0.7%, Middle = 0.3%, Lower = 0.2%). Perhaps the stones were used to pound the hide from the carcass and not for breaking open bones for marrow extraction (Frison 1991).

Conclusion

The inter-kill comparisons reveal more similarities than differences among the three bonebeds. Perhaps the most striking similarities are found in the high number of articulated skeletons resulting from selective butchering of individuals; the coinciding seasonality in late summer or early fall; low incidence of scavenger activity; and redundancies in stone tool assemblages. Further, all three kills utilized the same arroyo, represent the work of Folsom hunters, and consist primarily of nursery herds containing mature cows and juveniles and calves of both sexes. None of the kills contains evidence of a nearby camp or processing area.

Major differences are seen in the size and condition of projectile points and the stone material types employed by the three groups of hunters, and in that one of the kills yielded evidence of ritual associated with the hunt.

CHAPTER 9

Cooper and Trends in Southern Plains Folsom Adaptations

The descriptive analysis of the three kill episodes has established the nature of the kills (arroyo traps), the sequence of activities associated with them, the size and composition of each bison herd, the season of their death, the technology employed to kill and butcher the animals, ritual practices associated with the kill, and the natural history of the bonebeds from the time of the kills to their excavation and analysis.

The significance of the Cooper site extends beyond a description of a series of Folsom-age bison kills in a single arroyo in northwestern Oklahoma. In the following sections current themes in Folsom archaeology are addressed from the perspective offered by the Cooper site materials: Folsom mobility as expressed through lithic assemblages; what bison remains can tell us; and shifts in butchering technology. Cooper also provides the opportunity to address issues pertaining to communal bison hunting. Finally, the ramifications of the painted skull as regards Folsom ritual are explored.

Folsom Mobility and Embeddedness of Lithic Technology

Recently, archaeologists have wrestled with reconstructing Folsom mobility and subsistence practices on the southern plains (Amick 1995, 1996; Bement 1995; Jodry 1987; Hofman 1991). Tool assemblages at kill and camp sites often include a variety of high quality lithic materials from sources separated by over 300 km. The various lithic materials manifest in any specific assemblage are interpreted as a direct indication of the past movements of the Folsom group. The area encompassed by the plotting of the various lithic sources equates to at least a partial mapping of the area traversed by a particular group

(Hofman 1991). In addition, the size of projectile points, the amount of reworking they exhibit, and the presence of nonfluted or pseudofluted points in the assemblage have been used to model a highly efficient and conservative lithic technology sustainable in a highly mobile system (Hofman 1991, 1992).

Likewise, analyses of bison kills and processing and Folsom camps have produced subsistence information consistent with the mobility reconstructions (Jodry 1987; Bamforth 1985; Boldurian et al. 1987; Kelly and Todd, 1988; Todd, Hofman, and Schultz 1990). Against the backdrop of lusher vegetation, higher carrying capacity for grazers, and low human population densities, Kelly and Todd (1988) have proposed a hunting and mobility model for early Paleoindian cultures. This model incorporates aspects of bison kill/processing strategies with mobility.

The model proposed by Kelly and Todd (1988:234–35) contains four basic parts:

> First, though continual range shift might have brought Paleoindians into new and different environments, it would not have required that new niches be occupied if Paleoindians were dependent primarily on terrestrial fauna.
>
> Second, Paleoindians should have made use of a landscape in a short-term and redundant fashion. . . . And since Paleoindians are postulated to have focused on faunal exploitation, the overall organization of resource extraction should have been constant from site to site.
>
> Third, Paleoindians needed a technology suited to a lifeway of high residential, logistical, and range mobility, yet which still fulfilled the needs of a hunting-oriented people. This means that Paleoindian technology had to be transportable and usable in "unknown" terrain yet hunting-specific.
>
> Lastly, . . . the role of Paleoindian kills in providing food products for long-term storage, and hence the expected pattern of animal-part utilization and processing, may have been markedly different from that of later hunter-gatherers. . . . A long-term repeated storage strategy would not be expected in the Paleoindian system.

Within this framework of mobility and subsistence, Kelly and Todd (1988:238) propose that Paleoindian groups, upon making a kill, would immediately begin to search for another herd. When a herd was located, the group would begin pursuit, taking with them any processed materials from the last kill. Pursuit took precedence over completion of the processing of bison remains for bulk storage.

Given the mobility aspects of this proposed model, what would the accompanying lithic technological system be like?

If, as Kelly and Todd suggest, finding bison for the next kill took precedence over complete processing of the last kill, then perhaps other factors such as lithic procurement would likewise take a back seat to the search for more bison. Such a situation is reminiscent of Binford's (1979) concept of embeddedness. According to Binford (1979:273), in such a system, the procurement of lithic material is conducted during the course of some other subsistence task (e.g., game searching) and tool production/maintenance is performed during other work schedules (e.g., processing of animals). One of the tasks repeatedly identified at Folsom processing sites is the retooling of weapons (Jodry and Stanford 1992), suggesting that point production and hafting occurred at the same time as bison processing. The recovery of redundant artifact classes at Folsom camps near kills indicates that the same tasks were performed at all camps (Kelly and Todd 1988). A similar situation is reported for the Hanson site, a camp site at a lithic source that may have been near a kill (Ingbar 1992). This is consistent with an embedded lithic procurement and production system.

That visits to a lithic quarry were embedded in the task of searching for bison is not a new idea about Folsom organization. However, when modeling the lithic technology and developing mobility systems based on lithics, the embeddedness of the lithic system is often lost. Reembedding lithic technology into the broader subsistence/mobility system may reduce problems encountered in applying lithic-based models to the archaeological record.

An Example

Recent characterizations of the Folsom mobility and subsistence systems include source mapping of the lithic types used in the manufacture of projectile points (Gramly 1980; Hofman 1991). The lithic materials represented by the projectile points are viewed as direct indicators of movement across the landscape between various lithic sources. In this scheme, the material comprising the highest percentage of the assemblage represents the last lithic source visited.

The composition of the assemblage is modified by the number of kills conducted since a quarry visit. Such kills result in the replacement and reworking of broken projectile points.

There are some underlying assumptions to these reconstructions. First, it is assumed that a visit to a quarry area leads to an immediate replacement of small, heavily reworked points (Hofman 1991:351) and to an increase in the use of a particular material—that of the quarry—in the projectile point assemblage. However, in a truly embedded system, the newly acquired stone would be employed only when tools broke or wore out. The newly acquired lithic material would be in the form of blanks, roughouts, and cores acquired from the source. If reconstructions of the mobility system are correct (Kelly and Todd 1988), the Folsom hunters would be in search of bison and would not disrupt this search for any length of time.

> Rather than putting up long-term stores after a kill, the most secure tactic would have been to begin an almost immediate search for further resources. . . . Survival security could be enhanced by moving the entire group to the new resource area, perhaps taking along only processed, easily transportable foods and abandoning foods and unused products from the previous kill. (Kelly and Todd 1988:238)

In this system, extensive refurbishing of the assemblage at a lithic source would occur only if a kill took place at or near the quarry. Perhaps the Hanson site is an example of this (Ingbar 1992). Such a kill would enable extended exploitation of a lithic source since the group would be processing the animals. Otherwise, only a quick stop at the quarry to obtain suitable materials (probably in the form of large bifaces) would be possible. These materials would be incorporated into the assemblage as the need arose. Knapping this material would occur as a general camp activity conducted while the group was searching for another bison herd or was processing the animals after a kill.

The lithic technology of Folsom groups has been characterized as a curative system (Bamforth 1986; Boldurian 1991; Brosowske 1996). A typical assemblage consists of highly curated lithic source material in the form of bifacial cores, large flakes that could be fashioned into a number of tools upon demand, formalized scraping tools, beaked tools, and projectile points. The projectile points often undergo numerous resharpening episodes. In addition to the curated assemblage, Folsom sites often yield numerous expediency tools made from flakes struck from the bifacial cores or from large flake blanks obtained at the quarry. These expediency tools usually consist of unifaces and unifaces with projections (often called gravers).

Modeling lithic acquisition and use during Folsom times will be differentially expressed in the curated assemblage and the expedient tool assemblage (Bamforth 1985). Because the archaeological record is predominantly composed of discarded items, the archaeologist is seeing the last decision regarding a curated item—that of discard. For a projectile point at a kill site, we assume (1) that the projectile is no longer considered usable and is discarded or (2) that the projectile was lost. Either way, the projectile point was part of a functioning curated system prior to its loss or discard at the kill site.

Utilized flake tools at the same kill site, however, are a component of the expediency tool assemblage and reflect the lithic material carried for the purpose of making such implements. Expediency tools are made from bulk material acquired at the quarry and reflect the last lithic source visited. Again, the decision to discard depends on the flake's usefulness in future retooling episodes. Many of the flakes recovered from kill sites are too small to have served as projectile point blanks, and thus were probably produced from a core specifically for the purpose of butchering the animals at the kill.

The Curated Assemblage

Since projectile points have been used to reconstruct Folsom mobility, a model is proposed based on the replacement of the curated projectile points in the site assemblage at kill/processing sites.

If a quarry visit is embedded in the act of searching for game, then it can be assumed that the hunters had already refurbished their weapons in anticipation of the hunt. In this instance the first infusion of a newly acquired lithic material into the curated assemblage might not occur until after the first kill following a quarry visit. At that time, broken or lost points would be replaced using material obtained from the lithic source. As a result, that particular knappable stone would see a percentage increase in the overall curated tool assemblage. Furthermore, that particular lithic material might not contribute significantly to the curated tool assemblage until several kill episodes had necessitated refurbishing the majority of the assemblage.

In this system, tools already hafted and determined usable would not be replaced simply because a new lithic source was available. The newly acquired lithic material would be employed when tools broke and needed replacement. Hence archaeologists might recover a single tool of a particular lithic source in an assemblage dominated by another source. In these instances, the usability of a point—not the material from which it is made—is the determining factor in whether the specimen is curated. Once a point is determined usable and time and materials have been invested in hafting it, it would require more than the timely availability of another lithic source for it to be summarily replaced.

The actual affect that an embedded lithic system would have on the curated point assemblage, then, is expressed as a direct relationship between the number of points of a particular lithic material and the number of retooling episodes since visiting that source. This relationship would change once another lithic source had been visited. At that stage, the first material would show a drop as it was being replaced by the new material type. As the group moves to yet a third source, the cycle begins again. Background noise includes possible infusion of groups from other areas of the plains in response to variations in bison movements.

Two generic lithic sources (Source A and Source B) can be used to illustrate this model (fig. 45). We enter the cycle immediately following a major kill and processing episode, as a result of which stores of large bifaces and flake blanks are nearly spent and a visit to a nearby lithic source (Source B) is warranted. At the last kill and processing stop, the group's hunting assemblage was retooled, so that it consists of many heavily reworked points. The stores on hand were adequate to retool enough spears for another kill episode if the opportunity presented itself. But, because the lithic stores were low, the search for bison was directed into the vicinity of the Source B lithic material. While in the process of looking for bison, the group stopped at the Source B quarry long enough to restock with large bifaces and flake blanks. Since the hunting weapons had already been retooled with the remainder of the Source A stores, there was no need to retool at the quarry.

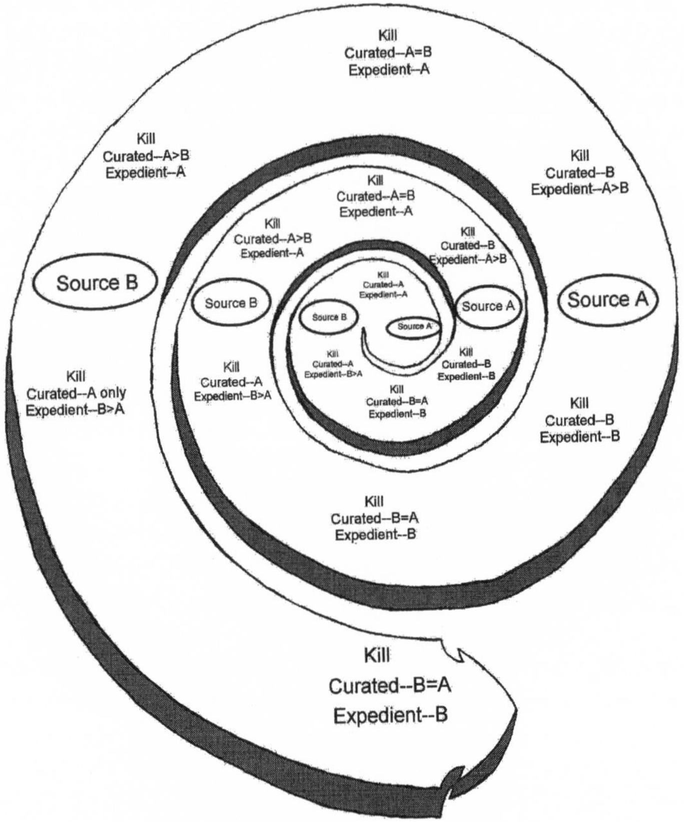

Figure 45. A model of lithic stone use, discard, and replenishment for curated and expedient technologies.

Following the quarry visit, the tool kit assemblage would consist of hafted projectile points made from Source A lithics and large bifaces and flake blanks made from the recently acquired Source B material. The first kill following the visit to Source B would leave at the kill site broken and lost projectile points made of Source A material. Flake knives and other expediency tools used in the initial butchering of the bison would be made of the recently acquired Source B material. Thus, any lost or broken butchering tools left at the kill site, along with any resharpening flakes, would be of Source B material. Retooling at the processing camp would include the manufacture of projectile points from the Source B lithic stores and use of expediency tools also made from Source B materials. Any points made from Source A material that were still hafted and deemed suitable for another kill would be maintained in the assemblage. Source B projectile points would be introduced into the assemblage only to replace points lost at the kill or broken beyond leaving resharpening as a viable option.

Upon departing this kill/processing camp, the group's lithic assemblage would consist of projectile points made of a mixture of Source A and Source B materials, and cores and flake blanks made of Source B cherts. As repeated kills are made, the projectile point assemblage witnesses a drop in overall percentage of Source A material as these points are replaced by Source B stores. The non–projectile point assemblage would continue to be dominated by Source B lithics.

This scenario could be changed if a kill had been made near the Source B quarry. Such a circumstance would allow the group to visit the quarry while processing of the animals continued. Because a kill had just occurred, any lost or broken points could be retooled using the newly acquired Source B material. And, as processing of these animals continued, large flake knives and other expediency tools made from the Source B materials could be employed. Upon leaving this site, the group's assemblage of projectile points would still be dominated by Source A cherts, since the Source B chert was used only to replace broken or lost components. The group, having replenished its stores (large bifaces and flake blanks) with Source B material, continues in search of bison for the next kill.

In this model, lithic material would be collected in the form of bifaces or flake blanks, and the projectile point assemblage would not see an immediate use of this material. However, at the first kill following a quarry visit, the new material would be used to replace broken or lost projectile points. Since kill sites usually contain far fewer projectile points than the total number of animals killed (Cooper Upper Kill 13 points/29 animals; Middle Kill 7 points/29 animals, Lower Kill 7 points/20 animals), it is assumed that the percentage of an assemblage lost during a kill is low. Hence, initial replacement of points with the new material would not constitute a major percentage increase of that lithic type after a single kill/retooling episode. However, the lithic type would see a steady increase in the assemblage after each kill, until at some stage, nearly all projectile points would be made from the type representing the last quarry visited.

The Noncurated or Expediency Assemblage

A different scenario is anticipated for the expediency tools in a given assemblage (fig. 45). The noncurated assemblage would almost immediately be dominated by the recently acquired lithic type—especially if, as Hofman (1991) predicts, raw material would be dwindling as a result of repeated retooling and processing activities after numerous kills. Hence, the amount of raw material retained by members of the group would dwindle. Thus, the quarry visit would target replenishing raw material in the form of bifaces (Boldurian 1990; Boldurian et al. 1987; Stanford and Broilo 1981) and flake blanks. The first kills following a quarry visit would already make use of the newly acquired materials to produce expediency tools since these tools are made at the kill. The noncurated tool assemblage would be dominated by recently acquired quarry lithic material while the curated assemblage would still be dominated by previously acquired lithic types.

The inverse relationship between curated and noncurated components of the assemblage would be visible only until the curated assemblage came to be dominated by the material obtained at the last quarry stop (i.e., after numerous retooling events). If enough retooling events took place, the entire assemblage would be dominated by the last source visited.

Archaeological Support of the Model

Although no direct link can be established between specific sites in the southern plains suggesting the round of a single group, if the model is applicable, then there should be redundancy in the archaeological record. Thus, the archaeological record should contain sites that can be plugged into the various positions. Turning to the archaeological record and the data provided by Hofman (1991), one trend that could support some aspects of this model is found in site assemblages containing Edwards and Alibates lithic materials. The Lipscomb bison kill site contains roughly 70% Edwards and 30% Alibates points (Hofman 1991:342). This kill occurred during the fall of the year. Moving farther to the east, the Cooper site, also a fall bison kill, has an assemblage from the Upper Kill containing 75% Alibates and 20% Edwards (5% is Niobrara jasper). This pattern appears to fit the model in that the percentage of Alibates projectile points increases as the distance from the Alibates quarry and the assumed number of retooling episodes also increase. Hence, as the pre-quarry Edwards chert assemblage undergoes attrition, it is replaced by Alibates material acquired at the quarry.

The noncurated assemblage at Lipscomb contains numerous pieces of Alibates, including several large flakes suitable for projectile point preforms (Hofman 1991; Hofman et al. 1991), even though the curated assemblage (projectile points) contains only 30% Alibates and is predominantly (70%) Edwards Plateau chert (Hofman 1991). Farther east, the noncurated assemblage in the Upper Kill at the Cooper site is entirely Alibates, whereas the curated component consists of 75% Alibates. Thus, the model presented for the noncurated and curated assemblages appears to reflect the archaeological samples from Lipscomb and the Upper Kill at Cooper. This model predicts that within several more retooling events after the Cooper kill, the curated and noncurated assemblage for this group will be nearly identical in composition, with a preponderance of both curated and noncurated tools made of Alibates Chert. Ability to determine the direction of seasonal movements will have an enormous affect on the closeness of fit of this model when applied to archaeological materials. On the southern plains, we do not have sufficient information at this time to evaluate the model. The Middle Kill and Lower Kill at Cooper have significantly different assemblages from that seen in the Upper Kill, indicating that they occurred at different stages in the stone-use cycle.

Effect of Embeddedness on the Reworked Assemblage

The presence of nonfluted or pseudofluted points and heavily reworked points in the Folsom curated assemblage provides another problem in modeling mobility patterns (Hofman 1991, 1992; Hofman et al. 1990). The manufacture and use of nonfluted points has been used to illustrate the conservative nature of Folsom lithic technology (Agogino 1969; Amick 1995; Judge 1973). The risk of projectile point breakage during manufacture is greatly increased by the fluting process (Hofman, Amick, and Rose 1990; Judge 1973; Kelly and Todd 1988). If lithic material is scarce, nonfluted points would appear to be an adaptive alternative to fluted points for bison hunting. Likewise, the rejuvenation or reworking of projectile points would conserve lithic raw material. Under this system, the number of nonfluted and heavily reworked fluted points should increase with distance from a source. But, as Hofman (1991, 1992) points out, it is the number of retooling events rather than the linear distance from a source that determines the amount of lithic material in the group. And indeed the archaeological record contains sites with high percentages of nonfluted, heavily reworked points near major lithic sources (Hofman 1991:345). The presence of nonfluted and heavily reworked fluted points at sites near lithic sources is not inconsistent with an embedded lithic technology. In an embedded system, usable points would not be replaced until they were broken, lost, or otherwise determined unusable, regardless of the proximity of a replacement source of material. The decision to discard a large number of nonfluted points most likely would be made at a kill that took place after a visit to a major quarry area. Thus, the assemblage at a kill just after a quarry visit would contain discarded nonfluted points and any broken or lost specimens. Fluted points made from the newly acquired lithic material would be incorporated into the assemblage during subsequent retooling events.

Again the Folsom points from the Upper Kill at the Cooper Site help illustrate the concept of embeddedness of Folsom lithic procurement systems. The recovery of small points illustrates that small Folsom points were not only perceived as still effective but in fact were effective: they came from among the skeletons of twenty-nine bison at the Cooper site.

The majority of points from the Upper Kill were made of Alibates. Following Hofman (1991:349), this would indicate that the Folsom group had most recently been at the Alibates quarry in the Texas Panhandle. Expedient large flake tools recovered from the kill are also made of Alibates, further strengthening the interpretation that these people had recently visited the Alibates source area. At least one of these flakes was of sufficient size to serve as a Folsom point blank. But, instead of replacing the several small, reworked Folsom points with new, larger points immediately following the quarry visit, this group employed the smaller points until they were no longer effective, or perhaps were lost in the kill. The use of large Alibates flakes for expedient tools in processing the animals at Cooper indicates that this Folsom group had the raw materials available to replace the small points still contained in the weapon assemblage prior to the Cooper kill. It is assumed that following the kill at Cooper, the lost or discarded small points were replaced by points made from Alibates procured at the quarry sometime earlier. Because the discarded assemblage at Cooper is dominated by Alibates, it is assumed that the overall assemblage was dominated by points made of this material. The number of kills prior to Cooper or when Alibates became the dominant lithic type is unknown. What is known, however, is that other lithic types, including Edwards Plateau chert and Niobrara were still in the curated tool assemblage even given the diminutive size of the points.

Discussion

This model, once again, is primarily concerned with the lithic assemblage and, in so doing, is removing lithics from an embedded position in the system. However, the principal theme espoused here remains consistent with the reembedding of the lithics back into the subsistence system. For example, if the Folsom group is primarily following or searching for bison, then their trek across the landscape could be quite erratic. Rather than a cyclical movement between two or three lithic source areas, the search path could place the group near the same lithic source time and time again. A group that consistently found itself near the Edwards Plateau source would have lithic assemblages dominated by that type regardless of the distance they eventually wandered from the source. This could explain the dominance of Edwards Plateau chert in the assemblages throughout West Texas. Only on occasion might the group travel into the area of Alibates in search of bison. On very rare occasions, this same group might continue northward into the vicinity of Niobrara material. The primary goal was to find bison; finding suitable lithic material was secondary.

Even though archaeologists emphasize the type of lithic material, the Paleoindians might have emphasized the tools. The deciding factor was not what type of stone the tool was made of but whether the implement was still perceived as capable of performing its task. This is not to say that Paleoindians did not have a preference for one lithic source over another. Instead, even given the availability of a suitable lithic source, individuals did not immediately replace every tool in their tool kit with the newly acquired material. Tools were replaced with specimens of the most recently acquired material when they were lost or broken. The decision was based on the assemblage, not the lithic type. The determining factor was the suitability of the assemblage to meet the perceived needs of the group. New lithic material was employed only when the assemblage was found lacking in some way.

Because of the difference in the uselife between expediency and curated tool forms, curated tools would reflect a greater number of lithic types in a system that routinely exploits different lithic source areas. On the other hand, expediency tools at a given site would be dominated by one lithic type, that of the last source visited.

If lithic procurement was embedded, then Folsom groups could move about the landscape following bison herds in any direction and not be concerned if they were near a lithic source until replenishment of the raw material dictated a quarry visit. Then, while in pursuit of bison, the group could stop by the nearest quarry. A highly mobile circuitous movement across the southern plains landscape would ensue. Only scarcity of bison (and perhaps extreme seasonal conditions) would force groups into other areas containing alternative lithic sources. Until seasonality studies are completed in more sites across the southern plains, the exact nature or direction of movements cannot be ascertained. The model of lithic procurement, use, and discard outlined here explains all patterns of stone uses seen on the southern plains except one: the lack of Alibates points and tools on sites near the Edwards Plateau. If Alibates were being picked up by the groups using Edwards Plateau chert, then Alibates tools and points should be transported back to the Edwards Plateau in use-assemblages. An alternative scenario is provided below. But first, the variation in other Folsom site attributes needs to be considered.

Variation in Folsom Sites

Folsom bison kill sites vary according to seasonality, number of animals killed, lithic raw materials, butchering techniques employed, physiographic/environmental setting, and landform use (table 40).

Table 40
Southern Plains Folsom Site Attributes

Map Ref.	Site Name	Type	MNI	Season	Edwards (%)	Alibates (%)	Other (%)	Butchery (heavy/light)
1	Cooper							
	Upper	kill	29	0.3*	75.0	20.0	5.0	light
	Middle	kill	29	0.3	100.0	0	0	light
	Lower	kill	20	0.3	57.1	42.9	0	light
2	Waugh	kill/camp	6	0.8–0.9	62.5	25.0	12.5	mixture
3	Lipscomb	kill	56	0.3–0.5	61.2	32.7	6.1	light
4	Folsom	kill	28	fall	20.0	18.8	61.2	unknown
5	Stewart's Cattle Guard	kill/camp	>8	fall	<0.1	0.8	99.1	heavy
6	Lindenmeier	camp/kill	13	unknown	0	0	100.0	heavy
7	Balckwater Draw	3 kills	2–5	unknown	61.5	6.6	31.9	heavy
8	Shifting Sands	camp		unknown	100.0	0	0	N/A
9	Bonfire Shelter	3+ kills	120	unknown	100.0	0	0	heavy
10	Lubbock Lake	kill/camp	3	spring	78.0	22.0	0	heavy
11	Lake Theo	kill/camp	12	0.4–0.5	64.0	8.0	28.0	unknown
12	Cedar Creek	unknown			76.1	13.4	4.5	
13	Bethel	unknown			68.0	16.0	16.0	

* 0.3 = three tenths of a year from calving season. Calving season is end of April through first part of May, so 0.3 (roughly four months) places season of death in August–September.

Sources: Waugh site: Hofman, Carter, and Hill 1992; Hill and Hofman 1997. Lipscomb site: Hofman 1991; Hofman et al. 1991; Todd, Hofman, and Schultz 1990. Folsom site: Hofman 1991. Stewart's Cattle Guard: Jodry 1987. Lindenmeier site: Wilmsen and Roberts 1978. Balckwater Draw: Boldurian 1981, 1991; Hester 1972. Shifting Sands: Hofman 1991; Hofman, Amick, and Rose 1990. Bonfire Shelter: Dibble and Lorrain 1968; Bement 1986. Lubbock Lake: Johnson 1987, 1997. Lake Theo: Harrison and Smith 1975. Cedar Creek and Bethel sites: Hofman 1987, 1991, N.D.

When sites are compared according to these variables, certain trends appear. The apparent link between large kills and a late summer–early fall seasonality is one pattern underscored by work at the Cooper site. A diametrically opposed pattern is seen in the association of small kills and winter–spring seasonality.

Spatial dichotomies exist in the use of toolstone sources. The kills on the Llano Estacado at Lubbock Lake and Blackwater Draw are dominated by Edwards Plateau chert almost to the exclusion of other stone types (table 40). Kills farther north and east such as at the Waugh site contain Edwards Plateau chert points but also have Alibates tools. Likewise, the larger kills have assemblages composed of Edwards Plateau and Alibates material.

Butchering tactics seem to vary according to regional setting, seasonality, and size of kill. The larger late summer–early fall kills are characterized by less disarticulation of the carcasses (Bement 1997) than are the smaller late winter–early spring kills, where extensive dismemberment is the rule (Johnson 1987).

What does this dichotomy of bison kill activity indicate about Folsom adaptation? Or, why are the larger kills spatially limited to the Oklahoma and Texas Panhandle area? The possibility that the larger kills are related to communal hunting at Folsom aggregation sites is discussed later. But this does not address the question of why the large kills are in the Cooper and Lipscomb areas. It is possible that the variation is tied to bison aggregation and movement cycles. Large kills of many species around the world correspond to cyclical aggregation and migration schedules of the prey species (Davis and Reeves 1990). Developing an understanding of the annual cycle of the prey species to interpret the actions of hunters better has been a dominant theme in plains archaeology (e.g., Frison 1970, 1987, 1991; Wheat 1972). And seasonal variation in bison herd composition, disposition, and movement is a common topic in discussions of bison kill sites (Bement and Buehler 1997; Chisholm et al. 1986; Davis and Wilson 1978; Dyck and Morlan 1995; Frison 1991; Speth 1983; Wheat 1972). In these studies, the emphasis shifts from social considerations to subsistence needs of the hunting groups. The two aspects, however, are probably intimately related.

To understand the annual cycle of past bison herds, analogs are sought in the modern herds. Relating modern herd dynamics to prehistoric behavior has problems often related to confinement and management practices affecting modern herds. But many of the actions of animals on large preserves provide models to be applied to prehistoric settings (Halloran 1961, 1968; McHugh 1958, 1972). Modern bison behavior is generally considered an appropriate analog for *Bison bison*. Hunters pursuing *B. antiquus* or *B. occidentalis* may have had to deal with behavioral characteristics somewhat different from those of the modern species. However, the redundant use of similar landscape features to kill modern and ancient bison species suggests that bison behavior related to handling has not changed significantly in the last 11,000 years. Bison kills of all ages can be found in arroyo traps, dune fields, at the base of cliffs, and possibly in constructed corrals. Other aspects of ancient bison annual movements, herd sizes, and behavior are less well extrapolated from an archaeological context.

Stable Isotope Analysis

Studies designed to compile data related to the movements of prehistoric *Bison bison*, let alone *B. antiquus*, have met with little success. One such study of *B. bison* utilizes stable carbon isotopes found in the bones to track bison movement from one grassland assemblage to another (Chisholm et al. 1986). Underlying this study is the metabolic relationship between the plant foods selected by bison and the carbon isotope ratio incorporated into the bone. The stable carbon isotopes contained in the bone collagen are directly relatable (linked) to the type of grasses consumed. If bison were to move between two habitats with different grass composition, then their bone isotope ratios would be at variance with the isotope composition of both grasslands. Of course, this assumes that the composition of the grassland is known, which is not always easy to accomplish when dealing with prehistoric areas where plant pollen, phytolith, or macrofossil remains are not preserved or where major shifts in plant communities are suspected. In areas where plant communities are stable and contain either an extensive mosaic of species or a single suite of species, the movement of bison from one area to another is not detectable in the bone isotopes.

The three kills at the Cooper site provide the opportunity to track changes in stable carbon and nitrogen isotopes in roughly contemporaneous herds. Unfortunately, no pollen and few phytoliths were preserved in the Cooper site deposits (G. Fredlund, personal communication, 1996). Thus, it is impossible to reconstruct the grassland composition near the site.

The presence of three closely timed kill deposits, however, provides a means to overcome this problem. Comparing the isotopes from individuals in one bonebed with those from the others should indicate if any of the herds are from distinctly different grassland areas. If samples from each of the three kills show no differences, then it can be assumed that the animals followed similar feeding and wandering cycles, which may or may not include migratory patterns. If differences are evident, this could support the possibility that the herds followed different patterns. Ultimately, differences could indicate the presence of resident and migratory herds.

Bone preservation is another concern in these studies. Bone that has undergone extensive chemical weathering contains diagenetically altered carbon isotopes. Such samples do not render acceptable results. Fortunately, relationships between carbon and nitrogen stable isotopes are known to indicate that diagenesis has occurred.

In the Cooper samples, the ratio of stable carbon isotopes between the collagen and apatite fractions of the bone is similar to that found in modern bone (H. W. Krueger, personal communication, 1996). A similar situation is seen in the ratio of carbon to nitrogen. Low preservation of carbon, however, suggests that some diagenetic alteration has occurred.

The stable isotopes, then, of six samples, two from each kill, are far from conclusive (table 41). A cross plot of the stable carbon isotope ratios from the collagen against the apatite shows two clusters (fig. 46). The first cluster, on the left side of the graph, contains two points. The second cluster contains four samples. Identified to bonebed and age of individual, the first cluster consists of a two-year-old from the Upper Kill and a two-year-old from the Lower Kill. The second cluster is composed of a five-year-old from the Upper Kill, two four-year-olds from the Middle Kill, and a four-year-old from the Lower Kill.

The reason for the separation of the two juveniles from the older individuals is not currently understood. A similar relationship between young and old is evident in a plot of *Bison bison* remains from the Texas Panhandle (Quigg 1992). The segregation based on age may be

Table 41
Stable Isotope Results

Lab Id	Kill	Age	$^{13}C_{apatite}$	$^{13}C_{collagen}$	$^{15}N_{gelatin}$
CCNR-83709	Upper	2.3	−2.9	−14.8	7.7
CCNR-82710	Upper	5.3	−2.0	−11.6	8.6
CCNR-82711	Middle	4.3	−1.2	−10.4	8.7
CCNR-82712	Middle	4.3	−1.7	−10.3	7.6
CCNR-82713	Lower	4.3	−1.4	−9.6	7.5
CCNR-82714	Lower	0.3	−2.8	−13.8	6.7

tied to fractionation of carbon from a diet of mother's milk. Further research is needed in this area.

A second pattern is the trend for the two Upper Kill samples to lie to the left of the other bone samples. The five-year-old from the Upper Kill is removed from the two Middle Kill samples by approximately the same distance as the Middle Kill samples are from the Lower Kill. The Lower Kill animal consumed a higher proportion of C4 grasses than did the two Middle Kill animals. The Upper Kill animal consumed even less C4 grasses than did the Middle Kill animals. Although not conclusive, this suggests that individuals from each of the three kill herds consumed grasses with different stable carbon ratios, which in turn suggests that each herd made use of different grassland areas or ranges. Additional samples are needed to confirm this trend.

Skeletal Growth as a Clue to Bison Herd Movement

Another study utilizes a ratio of the length of the femur to length of metatarsal by age to indicate growth differences related to forage quality rather than to genetics. This ratio was devised to explain differences in body size among ungulate herds of identical genetic composition inhabiting similar geographical regions (Klein 1964). In its application to deer populations on adjacent Alaskan islands where breeding populations intermingled, Klein found that genetic differences were insufficient to account for the observed somatic differences in the two island populations. His application of this ratio was altered to use hind foot length (hoof to proximal metatarsal) rather than just metatarsal length, to allow easier field measurements. However, the

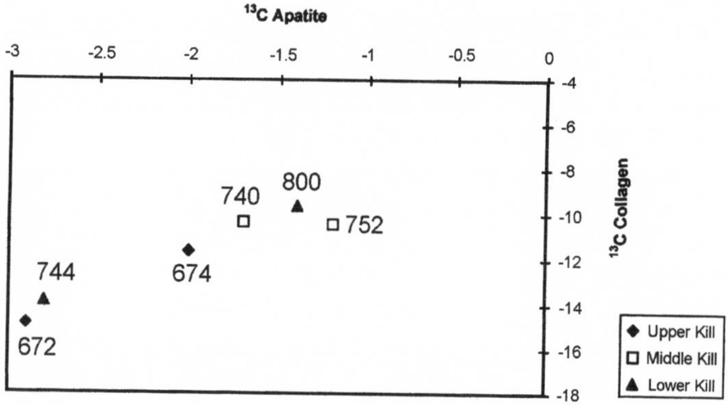

Lab #	BN	Kill	Age	^{13}C Apatite	^{13}C Collagen	^{15}N Collagen
CCNR-82709	672	Upper	2.3	-2.9	-14.8	7.7
CCNR-82710	674	Upper	5.3	-2	-11.6	8.6
CCNR-82711	752	Middle	4.3	-1.2	-10.4	8.7
CCNR-82712	740	Middle	4.3	-1.7	-10.3	7.6
CCNR-82713	800	Lower	4.3	-1.4	-9.6	7.5
CCNR-82714	744	Lower	2.3	-2.8	-13.8	6.7

Figure 46. A cross plot of stable carbon isotopes from apatite and collagen fractions removed from six Cooper samples suggests that there are differences between individuals from the respective kills.

femur: metatarsal ratio was the preferred ratio when available. The deer plot by sex showed better separation between males of the two herds than between the smaller females. However, the differences were also exhibited in the female groups (Klein 1964).

Applying this technique to bison populations is founded in studies such as Berger and Cunningham's (1994) analysis of the Badlands National Park bison in South Dakota. In this study, two bulls and three bison cows from a herd in Colorado were introduced to a herd in South Dakota in an attempt to provide greater genetic diversity in the breeding population. The Colorado animals were noticeably smaller and of different pelage characteristics than the individuals in the host herd, which was of Nebraska descent. Analysis of mtDNA revealed no genetic differences between the two bison populations, and the observed differences were attributed to habitat inequalities.

Initial plots of appendicular element lengths indicate the female animals from the Upper Kill are larger than females in either of the other two kill levels at Cooper (appendix). Radius lengths from female skeletons older than two years average 353.3 mm, 340.8 mm, and 338.0 mm for the Upper, Middle, and Lower kills, respectively. The Upper Kill radii are on average 15 mm longer than those from either of the other kills. Similar size differences are seen in the other long bones. The source of this variation is yet to be determined. Genetic analysis awaits funding. The possibility that environmental and not genetic factors were at work has been partially explored. The stable isotope analysis provides some indication that the herds killed at Cooper migrated from areas of the plains where grass composition was slightly different.

Applying the analytical technique of Klein (1964) to the bison remains from the Upper and Middle kills at Cooper provides interesting, and somewhat unexpected, results. The Lower kill was omitted from this analysis due to its small sample size. Plots of the ratio of femur length to metatarsal length against age yielded differing regression lines for the Upper and Middle kill animals (fig. 47). The regression line for the Middle Kill animals is considerably steeper than that for the Upper Kill population. This suggests that the Middle Kill population subsisted in a different nutritional niche than did the Upper Kill animals. The level of significance or robusticity of this analysis is difficult to evaluate until similar analyses are conducted on larger numbers of animals—preferably from living bison groups. These results are only presented to suggest that the animals from these herds were subjected to different nutritional and environmental conditions during growth.

The results of this analysis and the stable isotope analysis, combined with the near contemporaneity of the three herds, as indicated by trampled bone fracture morphology and geomorphological analysis (see chapters 5 and 7), leads to the conclusion that the Cooper herds came from different grazing pastures. Whether all herds were migratory or there is a combination of resident and migratory herds in the Cooper deposits cannot be ascertained at this time.

Folsom Hunting Adaptation

Communal Hunting

Bison hunting is an activity that can be accomplished by single hunters, small groups, or larger cooperative aggregates. For many time periods, there is a positive correlation between the number of animals killed and the number of hunters participating in the kill (Davis and Reeves 1990). Increases in time and energy required for preparation of a hunt are often met by increasing the number of participants. For example, the construction of a corral capable of containing and holding thirty bison requires the cooperative efforts of a large number of people. Additional coordination is necessary to accumulate the necessary number of animals and induce them to follow the constructed drive lanes into the corral, along a dead-end arroyo, or over a cliff. To meet the requirements of labor, historic Plains groups timed the large scale kills to enable aggregation of two or more bands of hunters. Timing the events made allowances for harvest schedules, bison aggregation cycles, and the seasonal needs of the groups (Driver 1990; Frison 1991, Frison and Stanford 1982; Frison and Todd 1987; Reher 1970; Reher and Frison 1980; Speth 1983; Todd 1987a, 1991). Planting, tending, and harvesting crops took precedence over bison hunting. Planning a large scale bison hunt during the time when bison herds were dispersed or absent from a region doomed the endeavor before it even began. Groups who relied on large amounts of stored foods for winter survival timed hunts with the onslaught of cold weather that would preserve the meat and took advantage of berry collection schedules so that pemmican could be made and stored for the winter. Any or all of these considerations affected the timing of large-scale bison hunts on the American plains. This is particularly noticeable on the northern plains, where the majority of hunts occurred during the fall and winter seasons (Todd 1987a; Frison 1991).

GENERAL CHARACTERISTICS OF COMMUNAL HUNTS. Are all large scale bison kills the result of communal hunts? This is a difficult question to answer. As we track hunting techniques back in time, it becomes even more difficult to address this question. Part of the problem rests in how we define communal hunting. Driver (1990:12) provides three traits of communal hunting:

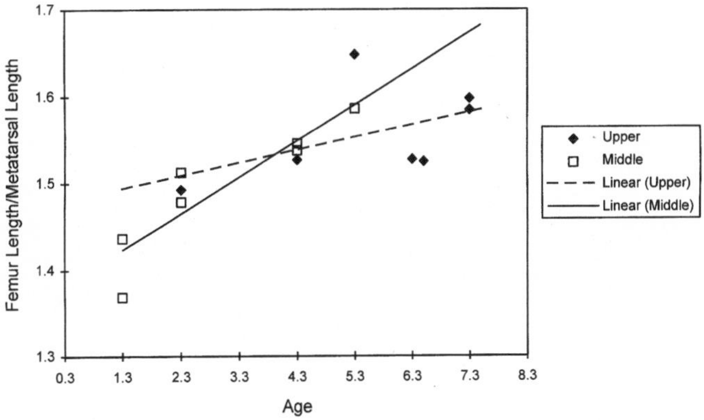

Bone #	Kill	Age	Side	Femur Length (mm)*	Metatarsal Length (mm)	Femur/Metatarsal Ratio
415	Upper	4.3	R	433	281	1.540925267
415	Upper	4.3	L	432	283	1.526501767
445	Upper	6.3	R	423	277	1.527075812
642	Upper	7.3	R	433	271	1.597785978
642	Upper	7.3	L	436	272	1.602941176
672	Upper	2.3	R	414	272	1.522058824
672	Upper	2.3	L	406	272	1.492647059
674	Upper	5.3	R	454	272	1.669117647
674	Upper	5.3	L	450	273	1.648351648
675	Upper	6.5	R	404	265	1.524528302
412	Upper	7.3	L	393	248	1.584677419
694	Middle	2.3	L	425	281	1.512455516
725	Middle	1.3	L	352	245	1.436734694
723	Middle	5.3	R	433	273	1.586080586
753	Middle	1.3	R	353	258	1.368217054
758	Middle	4.3	L	412	268	1.537313433
759	Middle	2.3	R	411	278	1.478417266
777	Middle	4.3	R	391	253	1.545454545
806	Middle	2.3	L	376	276	1.362318841

* femur length measured to head

Figure 47. The ratio of femur length (to head) divided by metatarsal length is plotted against age categories to illustrate possible differences in bison growth and nutrition between animals of the Upper and Middle kills.

(a) Participation by more than two hunters (usually many more than this).

(b) Active cooperation between hunters such that they work together, as opposed to passive cooperation in which hunters agree not to interfere with each other's activities.

(c) A system of hunting that requires all hunters to participate in a previously conceived plan.

This is a broad definition that could conceivably make the cooperative venture of killing a single bison a communal hunt. Missing from this definition is the social aspect imposed by assembling hunters who do not normally hunt together. Many historic communal hunts involved participants from different bands. Such aggregations allow ritual feasting and dancing, betrothals, trading, and the renewal of old acquaintances and obligations.

Communal Hunting at Cooper

Is there evidence that the kills at the Cooper site were communal? Following the three criteria of Driver (1990) it is easy to argue that each of the Cooper kills required (a) many more than two hunters, (b) working in cooperation, and (c) following a preconceived plan of action. Frison (1991) has demonstrated that an arroyo bison kill minimally requires one set of hunters to round up and drive the animals and another set to be in position to kill them. Evidence that the kills followed a set plan is rather obvious, considering the coordination that must have existed between drivers and killers. But was the arroyo in which the kills occurred the only one manned by hunters or were there hunters also positioned at the head of adjacent gullies? The most convincing evidence that this gully was the premeditated terminus of the drive is seen in the painted skull. If our reconstructed sequence leading to the painting of the skull and its subsequent trampling by animals of the Middle Kill is correct, then the ritual was performed in the predetermined locus of the kill. The possibility that hunters were positioned along adjacent gullies is not precluded by this situation, but that would entail additional people.

Communal kills, as defined by Driver (1990), could be performed by members of the same group. And, while this fits his criteria, many kills documented in the ethnographic and early historic sources coincide with the aggregation of more than one group or band (Verbicky-Todd 1984). In these instances, the large scale kill provided a means to feed a large number of people drawn together for social as well as economic reasons (Fawcett 1987). Such an intergroup or social aspect of "communal" kills adds another dimension not covered by Driver (1990). This fourth dimension is difficult to detect in the archaeological record and is assumed through analogy. One aspect of the social dimension is heightened ritual activity, often including feasting, dances, curing ceremonies, and ceremonies honoring the dead (Bement 1994b; Woodburn 1982). The painted skull at Cooper could fuel an argument of heightened ritual activity. But did similar rituals precede all hunts? If so, then this alone does not indicate heightened ritual activity.

Other lines of evidence for the amalgamation of more than one group might be drawn from the lithic raw material of recovered projectile points. Southern plains Folsom assemblages are usually dominated by implements made from Edwards Plateau chert from central Texas (Amick 1995, 1996; Hofman 1987, 1990, 1991). Points made from this material are often found over 400 km from the source (Hofman 1991:344). North of the central Texas area, additional lithic sources include Tecovas jasper and Alibates agatized dolomite. Tecovas Folsom points are seldom found, but Tecovas flake tools have been recovered in eastern New Mexico and the Texas Panhandle in areas near the source. Alibates is a more common component of some Folsom assemblages. It is used in the manufacture of projectile points and flake tools. Like Tecovas, the Alibates quarries are in the Texas Panhandle. Folsom assemblages in the Alibates area often include Edwards Plateau chert points and tools, yet sites nearer the Edwards Plateau do not include Alibates points or tools. In fact, only one Alibates Folsom point is known from a site near the Edwards Plateau (Tunnell 1977). North of the Alibates quarry area, the number of Alibates Folsom points increases; yet Edwards points are still common. The mechanism that allows the northern distribution of Edwards Plateau chert but inhibits the southern use of Alibates is not currently understood. Hofman (1991) proposes that Folsom groups leaving the Edwards Plateau area headed west and north in an annual round. As discussed previously, if the supply of Edwards Plateau chert were exhausted before the group returned to the Plateau, then alternative sources of stone, such as Alibates, would be sought. One problem of this model is the paucity of discarded Alibates points and tools in the plateau area. Were these materials jettisoned as the Edwards Plateau chert sources were approached?

An alternative explanation is that somewhere between the Edwards Plateau and the Alibates quarry was a boundary between two Folsom territories. Group composition and territorial boundaries were undoubtedly fluid and it is probable that territories overlapped. If this were the case, then it is possible that sites containing both Edwards and Alibates assemblages mark localities where members from both bands came together, perhaps for communal hunting. The distribution of sites containing both Edwards and Alibates assemblages suggests the location of this overlap or aggregation zone (fig. 48).

The social or fourth dimension of communal kills must incorporate a temporal factor, since the participating groups must have an agreed-upon time to meet. If bison hunting was a planned event at aggregations, then the scheduling of the aggregation should coincide with known bison movements or activities to ensure the presence of sufficient numbers of animals for successful hunts. The ability to determine the season of kill from bison dentition provides the means to determine the timing of aggregations.

Because of increased numbers of people to feed at aggregation sites, kills would probably contain larger numbers of animals than each group would normally procure on their own. Hence, the kills should contain large numbers of animals and should indicate a specific season of the year.

The distribution of Folsom bison kills of known seasonality indicates a cluster of large late summer–early fall kills in northwestern Oklahoma and adjacent portions of Texas (table 40). The lithic assemblages of these sites contain points and tools made from both Edwards and Alibates raw materials. The Middle Kill at Cooper is the only aberrant assemblage in this cluster, and this may be attributed to the small number of recovered points. If, for example, one of the Alibates points from the slump block actually belonged to the Middle Kill, this assemblage would also contain Alibates specimens. Sampling error related to the small size of the lithic sample may be affecting the results.

In addition to a temporal component, aggregation would rely upon selecting a meeting place that could be found by all groups concerned. Such a meeting place would allow access to sufficient amounts of food (i.e., bison), water, and wood. The meeting place may not have been a specific site but perhaps a broader area, such as a

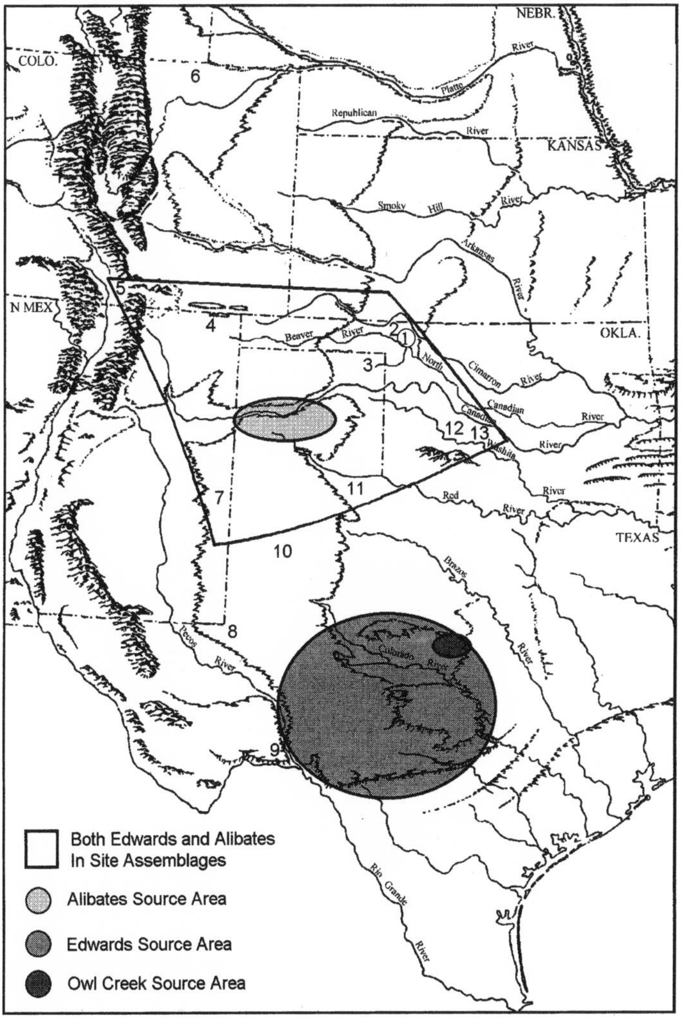

Figure 48. This map shows the zone in which Folsom sites contain both Edwards and Alibates raw materials in their assemblages. The numbers identify sites listed in table 40.

stretch of river. The groups would find each other by moving along a river course or divide. It follows that areas providing the requisite resources would be used repeatedly, although not necessarily for every aggregation or in successive years.

Recurrent use of an area, however, would allow repeated use of landforms where successful kills were made. The Cooper arroyo, with its three kill events, would be a predicted outcome of such a situation.

The Cooper kills indicate that the events occurred every three to five years. If aggregations were annual, then intervening years were spent at other locations or at least alternate arroyos were used. The Lipscomb site, 65 km from Cooper, could be a kill or kills (Schultz 1943; Todd, Hofman, and Schultz 1990) associated with another aggregation locus.

CLUES FROM BUTCHERING AND TRANSPORT DECISIONS. The effect of multigroup communal hunting on butchering and transport decisions is difficult to assess. Butchering patterns from small Folsom kills such as those seen at Lubbock Lake entail carcass dismemberment and meat stripping from the entire animal skeleton (Johnson 1987, 1997). The larger kills, including Cooper and Lipscomb, seem to rely upon a butchering process in which high quality meat packages were selected, resulting in little skeletal dismemberment. On the one hand, the switch from intense butchering to gourmet butchering—or from heavy butchering to light butchering (Reeves 1990)—could be the result of the number of animals at a kill. A Folsom group would require x amount of meat and bison products for subsistence. If the number of members in the group is held constant, and thus the meat/products requirement held constant, then the differences in butchering techniques could simply relate to the number of animals killed: the more animals killed, the less extensive the butchering necessary to fulfill the meat requirement (x) of the group. In this scenario, the amount of bison products obtained from heavy butchery of three animals would equate to the amount obtained from light butchering of a larger number of animals. The question is, how many gourmet-butchered animals equate to three extensively butchered animals? Are the kills at Cooper in excess of this number, to suggest killing by more than one Folsom group? The meat yield from a bison is roughly 45% of its body weight (Frison 1991; Halloran 1961, 1968;

Wheat 1972). Hence, roughly 50% of a bison carcass is usable foodstuff. If gourmet or light butchering removed half this amount from a carcass, it would take twice as many animals to meet the minimum requirement of bison products. The meat from six light-butchered animals would equal the meat from three extensively butchered.

The location of cut marks, spiral breaks, and other butchering damage on the bones from the three kills at Cooper may provide a means to quantify the amount of meat obtained from these kills. These marks have similar distributions in all three kills, clustering on the ribs and thoracic vertebrae, with possible marks also seen on the humerus, femur, and tibia. Marks are occasionally found on the radius/ulna, lumbar vertebrae, and pelvis (table 39). The single-carcass quantity of meat and fat associated with the bones displaying butchering marks (ribs, humerus, femur, tibia, and thoracic vertebrae) from each kill at Cooper, compared to that from a completely butchered carcass such as those found at Lubbock Lake, indicates that approximately 59.4%, 33.3%, and 64.6% of each carcass was potentially used in the Upper, Middle, and Lower kills, respectively, at Cooper (table 42). The breakdown of meat and fat from Emerson's (1993:142) food utility index model was used to figure the percentage of edible products from each skeletal element. Light butchering of twenty-nine animals from the Upper Kill, twenty-nine animals from the Middle Kill and twenty animals from the Lower Kill yielded at least 5.7, 3.2, and 4.3 times the amount of meat and fat obtained from extensive butchering of three animals, a kill the size of that at Lubbock Lake. Since the Cooper deposits are only a portion of the actual size of each kill, even greater yields are probable. Hence, even the selective butchering of animals at Cooper produces a surplus capable of feeding between 3.2 and 5.7 Folsom groups the size of the one at Lubbock Lake.

Although the switch in butchering technique from extensive to light may be related to the number of animals killed, the large kills at Cooper, and by extension at Lipscomb, could provide for the aggregate needs of at least three Lubbock Lake–size groups through gourmet butchering or six Lubbock Lake–size groups through extensive butchering. Although not conclusive, this discussion anticipates the presence of more than one group at the Cooper site on the basis of butchering technology.

Table 42

Cut Marks, Emerson's (1993) Food Utility Index, and Total Food Yield Comparison between Cooper and Lubbock Lake Butchering Techniques

Element	Utility Index	No. of Units	Total Carcass Utility	Percentage of Total Utility	Percentage of Bones with Cuts			
					Lubbock Lake*	Upper Kill	Middle Kill	Lower Kill
Skull	25.3	1	25.3	2.6				
Atlas	9.1	1	9.1	0.9				
Axis	9.1	1	9.1	0.9				
C. vertebrae	38.6	1	38.6	3.9				
T. vertebrae	47.4	1	47.4	4.8			4.8	4.8
L. vertebrae	45.1	1	45.1	4.6			4.6	
Sacrum-pelvis	34.7	1	34.7	3.5		3.5		
Caudal vertebrae	1.0	1	1.0	0.1				
Ribs	62.3	2	124.6	12.7		12.7	12.7	12.7
Sternum	32.4	1	32.4	3.3				
Scapula	27.5	2	55.0	5.6		5.6	5.6	5.6
Humerus	27.5	2	55.0	5.6		5.6	5.6	5.6
Radius-ulna	19.2	2	38.4	3.9				3.9
Carpals	10.7	2	21.4	2.2				
Metacarpal	6.5	2	13.0	1.3				
Anter. phalanges	4.0	2	8.0	0.8				
Femur	100.0	2	200.0	20.3		20.3		20.3
Tibia	57.7	2	115.4	11.7		11.7		11.7
Tarsals	30.0	2	60.0	6.1				
Metatarsal	16.1	2	32.2	3.3				
Post. phalanges	8.8	2	17.6	1.8				
Total	613		983.3	99.9	100.0	59.4	33.3	64.6
MNI			1		3	29	29	20
% used × MNI					3	17.2	9.6	12.9
Divided by Lubbock Lake MNI of 3						5.7	3.2	4.3

• Butchering at Lubbock Lake assumes that 100% of each of the three carcases was utilized. Hence the percentage of total utility provided for all elements applies to Lubbock Lake.

Shifts in butchering techniques could also relate to transport decisions. When the residential group established a camp adjacent to a kill—such as at Lubbock Lake and Waugh—transporting meat on bone was not a problem. A multigroup aggregation site established prior to a kill would require that meat/products be transported to the camp. A meat-stripping technique that leaves the bones at the kill would be an efficient technique in this situation. When used in conjunction with a gourmet technique, butchering time would be reduced to the extent that a processing camp would not be needed prior to transporting the meat masses to the aggregation site.

No evidence of a processing camp has been found in the vicinity of the Cooper kills. Of course, the extensive modification of the landscape by the Beaver River over the past 10,000 years may have removed any evidence. However, it should be noted that excavators recovered no debitage or tools suggestive of cooking or processing beyond the use and on-the-spot sharpening of flake butchering knives.

Gourmet butchering and lack of a nearby camp suggest that a habitation site was some distance from the kills. Locating such a site may be impossible. A large habitation site placed along the river for ease of access to water and timber would not have been preserved; flushing of floodplain deposits by the downcutting of the river valley would have destroyed any site in this setting.

In summary, the three kills at Cooper meet the criteria set forth by Driver (1990) for communal bison kills. However, if the criteria are extended to include the social aspect of aggregation of more than one group, then it must be demonstrated that the Cooper kills were the result of cooperation between hunters from two or more groups. Evidence for more than one group being present may be drawn from the presence of two spatially exclusive lithic types in the tool assemblages; from seasonal redundancy in the timing of the kills, utilization of a gourmet butchering technique, and repeated use of the same gully; and from the lack of a processing area adjacent to the kills, suggesting that the filleted meat masses were transported to a camp at some distance from the kills. The painted skull may manifest heightened ritual activity associated with aggregated groups. Without confirmation of the existence of a multigroup aggregation site in Folsom times (Hofman 1994), however, this must remain but one possible explanation of the available data.

Ritual and the Hunt

The 1994 excavation of the Cooper site uncovered a bison skull with a red zigzag design painted on its frontal (fig. 49). The archaeological context of the painted skull provides the opportunity to address questions involving hunting rituals and multiple use of specific locations for bison procurement. The age of the site raises for discussion the parallel use of hematite among North American Paleoindians and Old World Upper Paleolithic groups. The skull from Cooper is the oldest painted object in North America.

This unique opportunity to evaluate the role of usually intangible cultural or social aspects of Paleoindian life adds another dimension to the reconstruction of Folsom and other Paleoindian lifeways. Analysis of the painted skull hinges upon the contextual and technological aspects of painting a zigzag design on a Folsom-age bison skull and places this discovery within an anthropological context of ritual and the hunt.

Context and Technological Aspects

The painted bison skull was recovered from the lowest of the three bison bone deposits at the Cooper site. Trampling damage to the skull and adjacent bones and the fact that they were covered with articulated skeletons from the Middle Kill imply that the skull was painted just prior to the second use of the arroyo. As noted, this would have allowed nature time to clean and bleach the skull's surface. The alternative explanation would require that the skull be skinned, fleshed, cleaned, dried, and returned to its original position prior to painting during a ritual immediately following the first hunt. Since the skull with the zigzag line is from an animal from the first kill that was exposed at the time of the second kill, the former alternative is more likely.

Other bone from the lowest deposit was exposed at the time of the second kill, as is indicated by discovery of several long bones from the first hunt that have circular compression fractures such as those produced by trampling. The presence of trampled bones in the second bonebed indicates that bones were also exposed at the time of the third use of the arroyo. Since all the trampled bones in the second bonebed

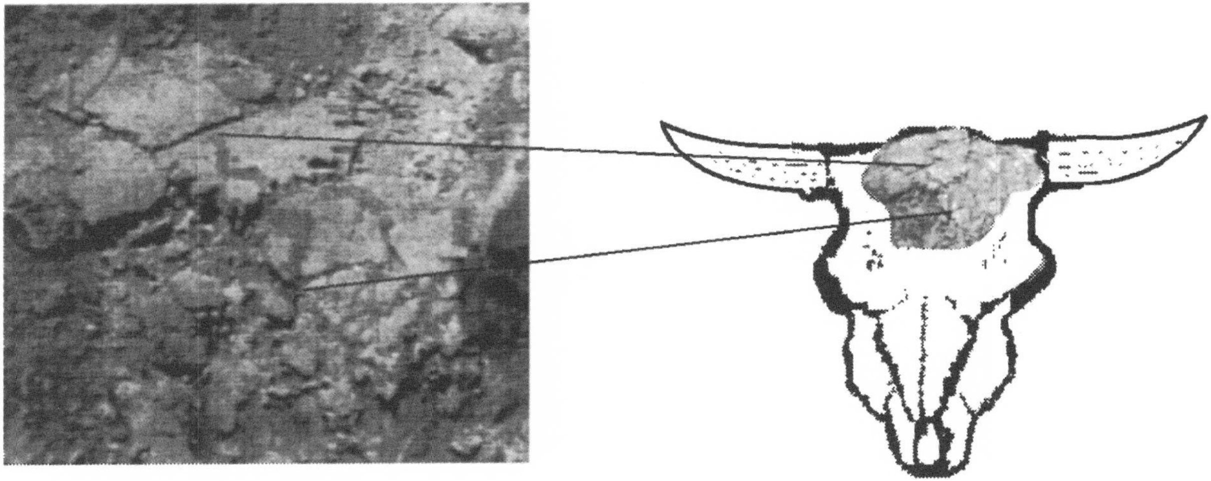

Figure 49. The power of the painted zigzag we came to call the lightning bolt is more readily appreciated on a reconstruction drawing of the Cooper bison skull.

are located along the edges and not in the center of the gully, where 30 cm of fill separates the second from the third kill, it is possible that a skull along the edge could have been exposed for use in a similar ritual prior to the third hunt.

Composition

To analyze the pigment on the skull, a pinhead-sized sample was collected from the skull and placed in a Gandolfi x-ray camera. The Gandolfi x-ray camera allows nondestructive analysis of single crystals under ten micrometers in diameter. This method rotates a single grain or crystal in the x-ray beam, thus exposing all available atomic planes to defracting positions. Requiring a sample barely visible to the naked eye, this technique is capable of identifying the mineral constituents of paint used by prehistoric artists (Russ, Hyman, and Rowe 1992). This technique was successfully employed in the elemental analysis of pictograph pigments in the Lower Pecos region of West Texas (Zolensky 1982:280).

The sediment surrounding the skull was analyzed to eliminate any possible soil contaminants. The defraction analysis of the pigment provides information on the constituents of the paint. This is the first step to the characterization of the hematite available to Folsom peoples occupying the southern plains. The high mobility purported for Folsom groups (Kelly and Todd 1988) suggests that hematite or ochre could be transported from distant sources. The possibility of tracing the origin of the pigment used on the Cooper skull is slender, given the widespread distribution of hematite and the general paucity of analyzed samples from known source areas. However, this analysis is a beginning in compilation of information regarding pigment composition from Folsom-age sites and provides a baseline for the study of additional pigment that may be found at Cooper, the nearby Waugh site (Hill and Hofman 1997), or any other southern plains Paleoindian sites.

RESULTS. Scanning electron microscopy (SEM) and micro-particle X-ray defraction (XRD) were utilized to characterize the pigment (Bement et al. 1997). SEM analysis was accomplished using a JEOL 35 SEM with EDS; the XRD analysis employed a Gandolfi camera. The sample was fastened to the end of a glass fiber and mounted in a rotation device that caused it to rotate simultaneously and at different angular velocities about two axes, yielding essentially a complete powder pattern from an unpowdered sample. A useful diffraction pattern was obtained after two days evacuating the camera to minimize air scattering of the X-rays.

The SEM analysis indicated that a scraping of the pigment included quartz, calcium (probably calcite), and a colloid-like silica mixture containing silica, aluminum, magnesium, potassium, and iron. In addition, a crystal of titanium oxide was present, along with trace amounts of phosphorus, probably from a bone chip.

XRD analysis revealed that the pigment was a mixture of iron oxides and hydroxides, including akaganeite (B–FeOOH), ferrihydrate (Fe_5O_7OH), lepidocrocite (y–FeOOH), maghemite (y-Fe_2O_3), and magnetite (Fe_3O_4), along with rutile (TiO_2), quartz (SiO_2), Manganoan calcite (Ca,$MnCO_3$), gypsum ($CaSO_4$), and orthoclase ($KAlSi_3O_8$). These mineral compounds are common in the Permian bedrock of this portion of the plains and a local source for the pigment is anticipated.

Paleoindian Use of Hematite

The Cooper site provides the opportunity to study the use of ochre in a context not previously documented for Paleoindians of North America. Ochre use has been identified in North American Paleoindian artifact caches, burials, and open camps but never before at a game-kill site (Roper 1987). Roper (1991) identified three contexts or situations in which ochre is found in Old World Upper Paleolithic and New World Paleoindian sites: burials, art and nonmortuary ritual contexts, and domestic contexts (Roper 1991:290). In the New World, the mortuary use of hematite has been demonstrated at the Anzick site (Lahren and Bonnichsen 1974) and the Gordon Creek burial site (Anderson 1966). At these sites, hematite covered the bones and associated tools. The bifaces and other tools contained in the Fenn cache in Wyoming, Simon cache in Idaho, and Richey-Roberts cache in Washington were rubbed or covered in ochre. In a domestic context, hematite or ochre has been found at Sheaman (Frison and Stanford 1982), Hanson (Frison and Bradley 1980), Lindenmeier (Wilmsen and Roberts 1978), Stewart's Cattle Guard (Jodry 1987), and Agate Basin (Frison and Stanford 1982). The domestic contexts include rubbed hematite nodules within the camp sites, hematite-stained grinding slabs, and hematite dust on the floors of suspected structures. A Paleoindian ochre procurement site has been found in Wyoming (Stafford 1990). The bison skull with the zigzag line from Cooper fits into the art and nonmortuary ritual category and is the first New World Paleoindian occurrence in this context.

In Europe, a mammoth skull decorated with geometric designs, including zigzags, was found at the Upper Paleolithic site of Mezhirich on the central Russian plain (Soffer 1985). Postcranial mammoth bones painted with geometric designs were also uncovered at Mezhirich and at Mezin. These Upper Paleolithic sites demonstrate the antiquity of the relationship between ritual and favored large game.

The Cooper skull was found in a kill site and in close proximity to the animal's skeleton, thus indicating that the skull had not been transported to or away from the site. The nonportable aspect aligns the Cooper skull with other kill-site phenomena, including the shaman pole found at Jones-Miller (Stanford 1984) and the possible shaman hut adjacent to the corral at the Archaic-age Ruby site (Frison 1991:208). The bone-filled pit at the Folsom-age Lake Theo site may be another example, although its context suggests a postkill ritual at the processing camp (Harrison and Killen 1978:20, 89). The implications of the nonportable nature of this example have yet to be fully considered or realized.

Contribution to Anthropology

The painted bison skull reemphasizes the role of culture in an act that is often seen only as subsistence. On the one hand, archaeologists view kill sites and the remains of animals at habitation sites as a means of quantifying a subsistence commodity—meat (Winterhalder and Smith 1981). Using equations that transform x number of animals into a quanity of kilocalories provides a means of predicting how long a group with a selected number of individuals can survive at a certain rate of consumption (Winterhalder and Smith 1981; Yesner 1981). On the other hand, archaeologists are constantly reminded that the ethnographic literature contains numerous examples of the social role of hunting and the rituals, taboos, and prestige that accompany this often more than subsistence activity (Fawcett 1987; Lowie 1963; McHugh 1972; Verbicky-Todd 1984).

In egalitarian societies, success or prowess at hunting is a means of achieving status (Binford 1971; Bloch and Parry 1982; Griffen 1969). Deer antlers and other proxy representations of game animals appear in mortuary contexts (Bement 1994b; Lukowski 1988). Pictographs and petroglyphs depicting hunting scenes have been found around the world (Davis and Reeves 1990; Keyhoe 1990; Kirkland and Newcomb 1967; Lewis-Williams 1980, 1981, 1982; Turpin 1992). Hematite is a common pigment source utilized in pictographs. It is also common in mortuary contexts, and, in some cultures, possesses power over other elements. Hunting magic or the ability to predict and influence in a positive way the outcome of a hunt is often found in the realm of a shaman (Turpin 1994). And it is in the context of the shaman or shamanic trance that the zigzag design on the Cooper bison skull finds its place among universal design elements often attributed to phosphenes and entoptic phenomena (Hedges 1982, 1994; Lewis-Williams and Dowson 1988; Oster 1970; Uher 1994). Phosphenes and entoptic phenomena refer to the bursts of light, seeing of stars, and such effects brought about by a blow to the head, by pressure on the eyes, or by certain hallucinogenic drugs. Zigzags and circles are common designs drawn by shamans following entoptic experiences often associated with rituals. But whether in the universality of the zigzag design, use of hematite, or association with a major subsistence act, the Cooper bison skull provides evidence of ritual in Folsom culture.

From this discussion, it can be seen that the study of the Cooper skull can contribute to research topics ranging from hunter-gatherer subsistence practices to social aspects of hunting, including hunting ritual. This example of ritual in Folsom culture serves to open the avenues of research to a time period in North America for which little is known of nonsubsistence activities. Parallels with the Upper Paleolithic use of hematite have been noted. The design element is commonly used and has been shown to be a universal component of imagery associated with shamanic trances. This Folsom example propels the context beyond a bison kill site into the sociocultural realm.

The painted skull is considered to have functioned as a good luck charm or talisman, drawing the bison herd into the desired arroyo and resulting in a successful kill—hence the subtitle "Where Lightning Bolts Drew Thundering Herds." Early historic bison hunters on the northern plains used similar objects. The majority of ethnographic accounts deal with bison herded into constructed corrals or pounds (short for impoundments) and the rituals associated with the building and operation of these structures (Verbicky-Todd 1984). Many of the rituals were invocations to the bison to draw them into the corral. Accompanying these rites, offerings were placed either at the entrance of the corral or at the base of a pole in the center of the pound. Sometimes items were suspended from the pole.

Cree and Assiniboine hunters placed tobacco, scarlet cloth, and bison skulls (often painted red), at the base of poles left in the center of the corral (Denig 1930; Verbicky-Todd 1984:44). These items were often destroyed by the trampling of bison hooves during a successful hunt. In such situations, the items become sacrificial offerings, used only once. Other objects including rocks or spirit rocks were used over and over again (Skinner 1914a, b).

The painted skull from the Cooper site serves as a reminder that past cultures were far from mundane. Acts that appear simply to involve the acquisition of food are interwoven with beliefs and emotions.

Importance of the Cooper Site

The Cooper site is a Folsom-age site containing three bison kill episodes. The existence at the site of three kill events is supported by geomorphology of the arroyo, sedimentation, stratigraphy, superimposition of weathered bone surfaces, morphology of trampled bone, variation in lithic assemblages, and variation in bison growth and size. The relationship between the intact primary deposits on the ancient gully floor and the secondary slump deposits on and within the Beaver River floodplain serves as a cautionary note to the integrity of other bone deposits.

Cooper is more than just another Folsom-age site. It serves as a catalyst in piecing together the variation observed in Folsom bison hunting and seasonal movement on the southern plains. With its three late summer–early fall kills, combined with those at Lipscomb and probably Lake Theo, Cooper establishes a link between seasonality and the activity of large scale bison hunting. The enigma of multiple, completely articulated skeletons discovered at the Lipscomb site is now grouped with the three kills at Cooper to define the modus operandi in butchering activity associated with large Folsom kills. With completion of the analysis of the Cooper bones, it is now known that meat was stripped from these carcasses without disarticulating the skeletons. The articulated skeletons no longer indicate waste from fortuitous overkill events. Indeed, articulated skeletons recovered at sites from any time period should be closely scrutinized for evidence of meat stripping. And it should be remembered that meat filleting does not necessarily leave marks on the bones, and it does not require specially crafted tools.

The identification of trampled bones in the Middle and Lower kills provides a means to help segregate the kill events at Cooper and to help identify multiple kills at other sites.

Presence of a black chert (Owl Creek chert) in the point and tool assemblages from the Lower and Middle kills ties these Folsom hunters with a source region in north-central Texas. Subsequent identification of a point made from this material from a surface find in central Oklahoma defines a territory or spatial tie that is different from that seen in other southern plains Folsom assemblages.

The consistent season of late summer–early fall for all three kills at Cooper and those at Lipscomb and possibly Lake Theo, as opposed to the inconsistent condition of the projectile point assemblages from these sites, indicates that Folsom lithic technology functioned independently from seasonal mobility patterns. Folsom hunters repeatedly made large late summer–early fall bison kills in the Texas Panhandle–western Oklahoma area regardless of the state of their lithic reserves. Relating the activity resulting in the patterns observed at this site to possible band aggregations remains conjectural but gives pause for reflection. Recovery of a painted skull is perhaps the most significant find, ushering the act of hunting into the realm of sociocultural belief systems. Cooper provides the reminder that Folsom hunting was more than simply a subsistence activity.

Appendix: Growth and Development of the *Bison antiquus* Skeleton: The Cooper Site, Northwest Oklahoma

The three kills at the Cooper site provide substantial data relating to herd demographics and growth patterns of *Bison antiquus*. In order to study growth and development, the age of each animal must be known. Age was determined by examining the eruption and wear patterns on the mandibular dentitions following the procedures of Reher (1974) and Todd (1987b).

Age Structure

The following descriptions present the dental age criteria derived from the mandibles for individuals from age group I (calf) through age group VIII (seven year old). None of the dentitions recovered from Cooper were from extremely old animals. The numbering of mandibular tooth wear facets follows the scheme defined by Frison (1982:243). Wear facet numbering increases in a posterior direction beginning with the labial anterior surface of the first cusp.

Group I (0.3 years old) n = 4

Group I includes four individuals with mandibular dentitions consisting of the dP2, dP3, dP4, and M1 (fig. 50a). All deciduous premolars are in wear with the exception of the endostylid and exostylid of the deciduous fourth premolar, which are 7.1–9.5 and 4.0–6.1 mm below occlusion, respectively. Eruption of the M1 varies from two-thirds to one-half the height of the dP4. No wear is present on any of the M1s.

Group II (1.3 years old) n = 7

In this group the dP2–4 are in full wear except the dP4 endostylid, which varies from just below wear to worn to an "o" shape (fig. 50b). The dP4 exostylid is in wear on all specimens. All facets of the M1 are in wear except the exostylid, which is between 7.2 and 9.0 mm below occlusion. Variation in the eruption of the M2 ranges from eruption of the first cusp with the second cusp at the level of the alveolus to both cusps erupted to half the height of the M1.

Group III (2.3 years old) n = 11

Group III dentitions have the dP2–4 in full wear (fig. 50c). DP3 is just barely hanging on by the roots. The roots of dP4 are beginning to show above the alveolus. The M1 is in full wear with the exostylid varying from no wear (3.1 mm below occlusion) to connected to the rest of the tooth by a loop of enamel. The M2 varies from full wear except exostylid (12.8–17.3 mm below occlusion) to wear on facets I–VI. The M2 exostylid is 20.0 mm below occlusion. The M3 is either just erupting or erupted to two-thirds the level of the M2 with the hypoconulid still below the alveolus.

Differential wear is seen between mandibles of the same individual. On one specimen, the right M2 cusps are in full wear and the exostylid is 8.6 mm below occlusion. In the left mandible wear is seen only on facets I–VI of the M2 and the exostylid is 12.8 mm below the occlusal surface.

Group IV (3.3 years old) n=10

The deciduous second and third premolars are replaced by permanent premolars in the Group IV dentition (fig. 50d). The P2 and P3 are erupted almost to the level of the other teeth, and P3 is just into wear. The dP4 is barely hanging on. Its roots are well above the alveolus and the P4 is visible. The cusps of the M1 are in full occlusion and wear on the exostylid forms an "o". The M2 is in full wear except the exostylid, which is between 7.3 and 14.0 mm below occlusion. The first and second cusps of the M3 are erupted and wear is found on

Figure 50. These mandibles are examples for each age group from group I (0.3 years old) to group VIII (7.3 years old). a = group I, b = group II, c = group III, d = group IV, e = group V, f = group VI, g = group VII, h = group VIII.

facets I and II or facets I through IV. The hypoconulid is at or above the level of the alveolus but not yet in wear.

Group V (4.3 years old) n = 7

All permanent dentition is erupted (fig. 50e). P4 is not yet in wear. All facets of M1 including the exostylid are in wear. All facets of M2 are in wear except the exostylid, which varies from 4.5 to 9.9 mm below occlusion. The M3 is fully erupted with the hypoconulid just below or beginning wear, but it is not attached to the rest of the tooth. The exostylid on the M3 ranges from 15.2 to 20.0 mm below the occlusal surface.

Group VI (5.3 years old) n = 2

All permanent teeth are erupted and in full wear (fig. 50f). The M2 exostylid is worn into an "o". The M3 hypoconulid is now attached to the rest of the tooth by enamel. The M3 exostylid remains 3.7–6.8 mm below occlusion.

Two additional age groups are tentatively identified in the Cooper material. Groups VII and VIII may contain individuals older than 6.3 or 7.3, but wear patterns on the mandibular dentition fall into two distinct groups.

Group VII (6.3 years old) n = 3

All teeth are in wear, including the M2 exostylid (fig. 50g). The only exception is the M3 exostylid, which varies from 2.1 mm below occlusion to just into wear forming an "o".

Group VIII (7.3 years old) n = 3

All teeth are in wear, including all exostylids and the M3 hypoconulid (fig. 50h). The base of the M1 enamel is showing above the alveolus. Only 13.2 mm of enamel height is left on the M1.

Comparison of these tooth eruption and wear patterns with those described for the Lipscomb and Scottsbluff bison (Todd, Hofman, and Schultz 1990) indicates that the Cooper animals died approximately

0.3 years after the calving peak. This provides a season of death for the Cooper animals at late summer or early fall.

Dentitions were recovered from fifty of the estimated seventy-eight animals contained in the three kills. Ages of the twenty-eight animals for which mandibles were not recovered could be determined by comparing the stage of epiphyseal fusion of their long bones with long-bone fusion in individuals aged by dentition. From the Cooper sample, Bement and Basmajian (1996) established a fusion chart that provides yearly age determinations from birth to five years old. All epiphyses of the appendicular skeleton are fused by the age of five (table 43).

The combination of dentition and epiphyseal fusion age determinations provided the basis for determining the age structure of the three herds killed at Cooper. The basic distribution of animals by age indicates that all three kill remnants were dominated by skeletally immature animals; that is, animals less than five years of age (fig. 51).

In addition to age, another component of bison herd demography is its sex distribution. Techniques to determine the sex of prehistoric bison rely on the fact that bison are and were sexually dimorphic. In this case, the males are larger than the females. Typically, the bones of mature animals are measured and sorted according to size. Elements commonly used in sexing are the metatarsals and metacarpals (Bedord 1974). A cross plot of the transverse width of the distal end against the product of the transverse width of the midshaft divided by the maximum length will produce two clusters if both sexes are present. The cluster of smaller measurements is interpreted to be female animals and the other cluster contains the males.

This technique does not produce reliable results for the Cooper samples because most of the animals are skeletally immature. However, sexual dimorphism means it should be possible to distinguish males from females by constructing growth curves from the long bones.

The Model of Growth and Sexual Dimorphism

In developing a growth trajectory for skeletal elements, the length of an element is plotted against its age. Skull measurements were plotted in this manner by Wilson (1974). This technique can be used for other

Table 43
Age of Complete Fusion for Select *Bison antiquus* Appendicular Elements

Element	Age
Proximal femur	5.3
Distal femur	5.3
Proximal tibia	5.3
Distal tibia	3.3
Calcaneus	5.3
Distal metapodial	3.3
Proximal 1st phalanx	2.3
Proximal 2nd phalanx	1.3
Proximal humerus	5.3
Distal humerus	1.3
Proximal ulna	5.3
Proximal radius	1.3
Distal radius	5.3

bones of the skeleton. For bones of the front and hind legs, maximum growth is seen at the time of epiphyseal fusion. Since bison are sexually dimorphic two growth trajectories are needed to plot the onset and continuation of dimorphic growth. Once epiphyseal fusion occurs, the bone length ceases to increase and remains constant for the life of the animal. Unlike body mass, which continues to increase throughout the animal's lifetime, bone length increases initially, then remains constant. Other skeletal attributes such as bone cortical thickness and articular surface width may continue to increase as a result of load stress from body weight.

Age assignments for the various positions along the growth curve are provided by plotting element length by age. In that the age of the animal is known (based on tooth eruption and wear or epiphyseal fusion patterns), the length of the element can be plotted for each age group (in this instance at yearly increments based on n + 0.3 years, since the youngest animal at Cooper was 0.3 years old). Such a cross plot for the radius defines two curves, one for males and one for females (fig. 52a). The steepest slope of the radius growth curves occurs between the ages of 0 and 1.3 years, and between 1.3 and 2.3 years. The curves nearly flatten between 2.3 and 3.3 years of age. By the time the Cooper animal is 3.3 years old, the radius is approaching maximum length even though the proximal epiphysis is not fused for another two years. Similar curves are defined for the tibia (fig. 52b).

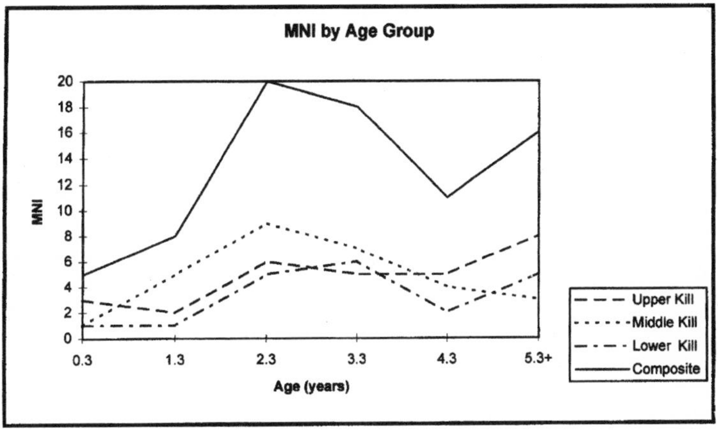

Figure 51. The distribution of Cooper animals by age and kill shows that all three kills are dominated by young animals.

This procedure can be completed for each of the elements of the appendicular skeleton. The curves for each element vary according to the length of time before epiphyseal fusion halts longitudinal growth. For example, the growth curve for the metacarpal levels out by the age of 2.3, and the slope of the curve is nearly equal between birth and 1.3 and 1.3 and 2.3 years of age. This curve does not exhibit the steep rise between birth and 1.3 that is seen in the curve for the radius or tibia.

From these plots, it is possible to identify male and female individuals. As is evident from the plots, females far outnumber males in all three kills. In each case, it is apparent that approximately 75% of the animals are females and no more than 25% are males.

The growth trajectory curves provide additional information about the Cooper herds. The Cooper plots contain no bulls over the age of five, yet the cows in each kill include animals in excess of seven years of age. This indicates that the herds killed by these Folsom hunters contained mature cows and immature animals of both sexes. Possible explanations for the absence of older bulls may be found in modern herd seasonal composition studies (McHugh 1958, 1972). Today, herds dominated by mature cows and immature animals of both sexes are found after completion of the rut, which occurs in mid-summer. The n + 0.3 age of the Cooper bison indicates that the kills

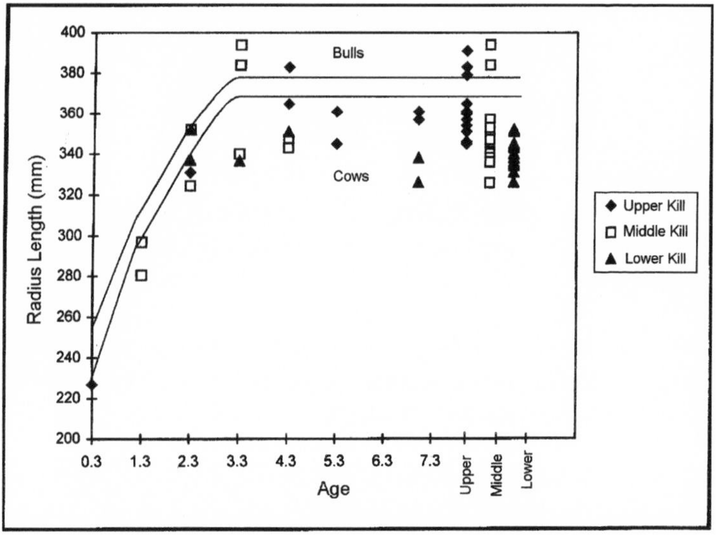

A

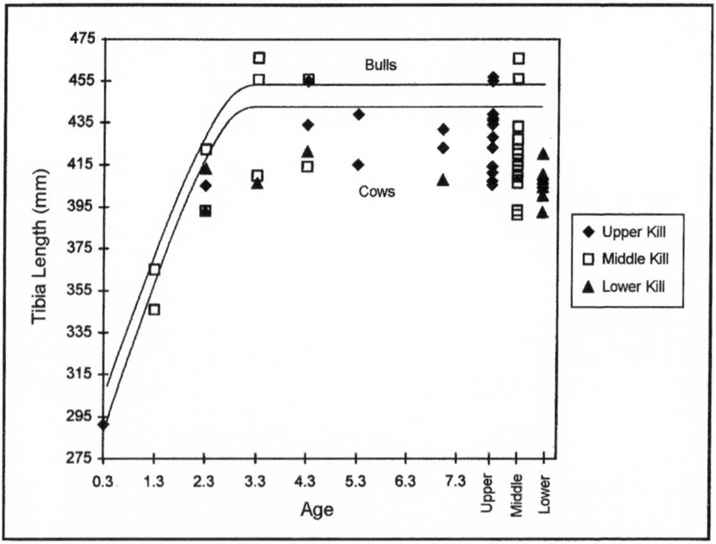

B

Figure 52. Plots of radius length by age (a) and tibia length by age (b) and possible growth curves describe growth in male and female *Bison antiquus*.

occurred during late summer or early fall, after the rut. Hence, the sex structure of the kills corroborates the seasonality indicated by the teeth.

Another pattern displayed in the plots of bone length by age involves the size differences between the females of each kill. In the plot of radius length, females greater than two years old from the Upper Kill are consistently larger than those from either the Middle or Lower kills. In fact, the smallest Upper Kill females are larger than the largest Lower Kill females. The range for Middle Kill female radii includes that of Lower Kill females but only overlaps with the lower half of the Upper Kill animals. It is possible that the range defined by the Lower Kill animals is skewed by small sample size. However, the range spread between the largest and smallest females in the Upper and Middle kill populations, respectively, is closely matched at 28 mm for the Middle Kill and 30 mm for the Upper Kill. The average female radius from the Upper Kill (mean length = 353.3 mm) is 12.5 mm longer than that from a Middle Kill (mean length = 340.8 mm) individual.

The analysis of *Bison antiquus* elements from articulated skeletons also provides a means to match elements from the same animal that were disarticulated through butchering or scavenger activity. Such refits are normally accomplished by sorting the elements according to age, sex, and side. In bone assemblages containing several individuals in each age category, these three variables may not be sufficient to rebuild skeletons. An additional variable to consider is the measurable size of the elements. If, for example, the length of a femur could be predicted based on the length of a metatarsal, this would supply another means of refitting elements. Todd (1987b, Todd and Frison 1992) demonstrated that this was possible when using the bones from mature animals. Cooper provides the opportunity to test the possibility that metrical refits are possible with immature animals as well.

To this end, scatter plots, regression, and correlation analyses were undertaken for select appendicular element measurements from the same individuals. As noted, the growth curves for the radius and tibia were nearly identical. The length of the tibia compared to the length of the radius from the same animal for a group of animals of all ages from 0.3 to over 7.3 years old produced a nearly 1:1 correlation. The Pearson's correlation coefficient between these two suites of measurements is 0.9938, indicating a strong correlation significant beyond .0001. The R^2 expressed by the regression line plot of these elements is 0.9876. This means that nearly 99% of the variability between these two elements is described by the regression line equation of $y_{tibia} = 1.1332 \times {}_{radius} + 22.373$. Stated another way, if the length of the radius is known and plugged into this equation, the length of the tibia can be predicted with a high level of accuracy. The same equation can be used to predict radius length if tibia length is known.

Scatter plots and regression analyses were conducted for the major limb elements. The resultant regression equations, correlation coefficients, R^2, and level of significance are provided in table 44. Surprisingly, the first plot between the radius and tibia produced the highest correlation coefficient and R^2. Other extremely high correlations were found between the femur and radius, tibia and femur, metacarpal and metatarsal, humerus and radius, and humerus and femur. The lowest coefficients were seen between the humerus and metatarsal and the humerus and metacarpal.

From these analyses, it is suggested that the lengths of bones of the appendicular skeleton from an individual of any age are highly correlated. And it follows that the length of one element can in most cases be predicted if the length of one of the other elements is known (Todd 1987b). Once the length is predicted using the equation with the highest correlation coefficient, that measurement can be compared with the measurements of elements to be refit. Elements with similar lengths to the value predicted would be possible fits.

The equations presented were developed from animals ranging in age from 0.3 to 7.3 years old. The high correlation coefficients suggest that these equations are applicable to animals of any age. Application of element length equations in a refit study has not been attempted. At Cooper, these equations will be used to try to refit bones from the slump block to skeletons along the edges of the primary deposits. Unfortunately, most of the bones contained in the slump are not complete and refits using bone length may not be possible.

Since many bones recovered from an archaeological site are broken, the total length of an element is often not available. However, if measurements of smaller segments of bones produced high correlation coefficients, then metrical refits would still be possible. To test

Table 44
Regression Equations for Appendicular Element Lengths

Equation	Pearson's	R^2	Sig. 2-tail
$y_{metacarpal} = 0.3112 \times_{radius} + 112.51$	0.8895	0.7913	.000
$y_{femur} = 1.2881 \times_{radius} - 24.811$	0.9784	0.9503	.000
$y_{tibia} = 1.1332 \times_{radius} + 22.373$	0.9938	0.9876	.000
$y_{metatarsal} = 0.3531 \times_{radius} + 147.15$	0.8325	0.6931	.000
$y_{humerus} = 1.0668 \times_{radius} + 36.192$	0.9209	0.8481	.000
$y_{femur} = 4.1988 \times_{metacarpal} - 505.34$	0.8889	0.7902	.000
$y_{tibia} = 2.7479 \times_{metacarpal} - 193.12$	0.8541	0.7294	.000
$y_{metatarsal} = 1.136 \times_{metacarpal} + 19.254$	0.9346	0.8736	.000
$y_{humerus} = 2.2124 \times_{metacarpal} - 155.35$	0.7340	0.5387	.004
$y_{tibia} = 0.8265 \times_{femur} + 67.443$	0.9770	0.9545	.000
$y_{metatarsal} = 0.2531 \times_{femur} + 163.65$	0.8151	0.6644	.000
$y_{humerus} = 0.884 \times_{femur} - 39.823$	0.9432	0.8897	.000
$y_{metatarsal} = 0.3411 \times_{tibia} + 129.27$	0.8496	0.7218	.000
$y_{humerus} = 1.0328 \times_{tibia} - 95.158$	0.9002	0.8104	.000
$y_{humerus} = 1.24 \times_{metatarsal} - 4.7111$	0.4701	0.2210	.123

Note: All femur and humerus lengths are measured to the head.

this possibility, the measurements of Upper Kill metatarsals were subjected to multiple regression analyses to see which measurements were highly correlated to length.

Growth of the Metapodials

Bison metapodials consist of a proximal articular surface that is fused with the diaphysis at birth. The distal epiphysis, however, does not fuse until an age of three (Bement and Basmajian 1996). The distal epiphyses of the Cooper animals are completely fused in the 3.3-year-old skeletons. With the fusion of the distal epiphysis, the maximum length of the metatarsal and metacarpal is reached. Beyond the age of three, the only growth seen in the metapodials is found in the width or girth measurements (transverse widths, anterior/posterior widths). The growth curve for the length of a metapodial increases sharply between birth and two years of age and then levels off by three years. After three years, there is no more increase in the curve. The growth curves for the transverse and a/p dimensions of the bone, however, continue to increase throughout the life of the animal. This growth pattern can be described in another way. A correlation matrix developed from the measurements of the metatarsal indicates that in individuals under three years of age, length is negatively correlated with transverse width and a/p width (table 45). In other words, growth in length outdistances growth in the other dimensions.

By three years of age, the inverse occurs. The transverse and a/p widths of the shaft and proximal and distal ends increase while the overall length of the element remains constant. From this, then, the length of the metatarsal cannot be predicted from width or girth measurements. Interestingly though, in animals over three years old, all transverse and a/p measurements with the exception of the midshaft a/p are highly correlated (R^2 values exceeding .92 in the metatarsals from the Upper Kill). This suggests that any width or girth measurements required for the type of analysis used in Bedord's sexing technique could be predicted even if that portion of the bone were damaged. The length of the metatarsal, however, cannot be predicted from other attributes of a broken metatarsal.

A similar study was conducted by Davis (1996) using the skeletal remains of domesticated sheep and the wild gazelle. In that study, Davis found that the highest correlation coefficients were found in measurements oriented along the same axis. In other words, high correlations were found between measurements of the length of elements. Likewise, measurements along the medial/lateral axis of different elements were highly correlated. Low correlations were obtained when measurements that crossed axes were compared. Hence, the length of a bone plotted against the transverse width of another element produced low correlation coefficients.

Regression analysis of the a/p and transverse width measurements for all the appendicular elements was not complete for the Cooper bison at the time of writing. An estimated 210 equations were being generated from measurements of the femur, tibia, metatarsal,

Table 45
Correlation Coefficient Matrix Derived from 32 Cooper Upper Kill Metatarsals

	Length	Proximal End Transverse	Proximal End A/P	Distal End Transverse	Distal End A/P	Midshaft Transverse
<3 year-olds						
Prox. trans.	0.677663					
Prox. A/P	0.445704	0.153709				
Dist. trans	0.476102	0.405639	0.855784			
Dist. A/P	0.469750	0.498765	0.137563	−0.11665		
Mid. trans	−0.30276	−0.46708	0.497345	0.642623	−0.60302	
Mid. A/P	−0.13445	−0.43390	0.280079	0.581587	−0.18334	0.616031
3+ year-olds						
Prox. trans.	0.080148					
Prox. A/P	0.196532	0.992129				
Dist. trans	−0.05749	0.984492	0.965427			
Dist. A/P	0.319819	0.969886	0.991515	0.923409		
Mid. trans	0.097231	0.993492	0.983113	0.964590	0.96580	
Mid. A/P	−0.21876	0.418371	0.347407	0.350963	0.329576	0.501854

humerus, radius, and metacarpal. Hopes are that once these are completed, equations useful in skeletal refit studies can be generated. The results of the appendicular length correlations suggest that this line of research will be fruitful and that similar analyses using *Bison bison* elements will be just as rewarding.

Glossary

Alibates agatized dolomite: High quality siliceous rock from the Texas Panhandle.

Apatite: The nonorganic component of bones.

Arroyo: Steep-sided, dry gully with little vegetation growing in the bottom.

Balk: Wall separating excavation units.

Bison antiquus: Ancient bison species with long straight horns, associated with Clovis and Folsom cultures.

Bison bison: Modern bison species.

Bison occidentalis: Ancient bison species intermediate between *B. antiquus* and *B. bison*.

Bull Probe: Hydraulic coring rig that pushes, rather than rotates, a hollow rod into the ground.

Clovis: Paleoindian culture that existed from 11,400 to 10,900 years ago.

Collagen: The organic component of bone.

Colluvium: Sediments that are transported by gravity and slopewash.

Datum: Fixed point on the ground used as a vertical and horizontal reference for an excavation grid.

Day Creek dolomite: Fine-grained chert found in northwestern Oklahoma and southwestern Kansas.

Diagenesis: Breakdown of the chemical components of bone, usually when it is buried for a long period of time.

Dip: When used in conjuction with "strike" to describe bones on the ground, refers to the downward slant of a bone along its longest axis.

Distal: Portion that is farthest from the body.

Edwards Plateau chert: High quality chert that occurs as nodules and plates in the limestone of central Texas.

Element: Bone in a skeleton; e.g., femur, humerus (fig. 53).

Entoptic: Pertaining to the interior of the eye.

Eolian: Windblown dirt, such as a sand dune.

Fossorial: Any of a number of animals that burrow or live in burrows.

Gleyed sediment: A gray zone that formed by microbial action on organic matter after the material was buried.

Hematite: Iron-rich sedimentary rock.

Hyoids: Group of nine bones that anchor the tongue in the mouth.

In situ: In place.

Knick point: Gully head cut. The actively eroding upslope end of the gully.

Malleolus: A small bone located in the hind leg between the metatarsal and tibia. It is the distal end of the fibula and is found in the tarsals.

Niobrara jasper (Also known as Smoky Hill jasper): High quality chert from northwestern Kansas and Nebraska.

Noviculo-cuboid: A small bone located in the hind leg between the metatarsal and tibia. It is the fused central and fourth tarsal bones.

Ochre: Iron-rich (iron oxide) substance prepared as paint.

Ogallala quartzite: Coarse-grained quartzites eroded from the Rocky Mountains and found in gravel deposits across the Great Plains.

Owl Creek black chert: Variety of Edwards Plateau chert that is black and has a restricted outcropping in the Fort Hood area.

Paleoindian: Any of a number of cultures found in North America that predate 8,000 years ago. Usually associated with the end of the Pleistocene.

Paleosol: An ancient ground surface with developed soil that is now buried.

Phosphenes: Bright flashes of light and images created by mechanical pressure on the retina.

Phytolith: Silica remains found in plants.

Pressure flaking: Method of shaping stone tools through application of force by pushing rather than by striking.

Proximal: Portion that is closer to the body.

Radiocarbon dating: Process of determining the age of an object based on the decay of carbon 14 isotope.

Riparian zone: Along a river.

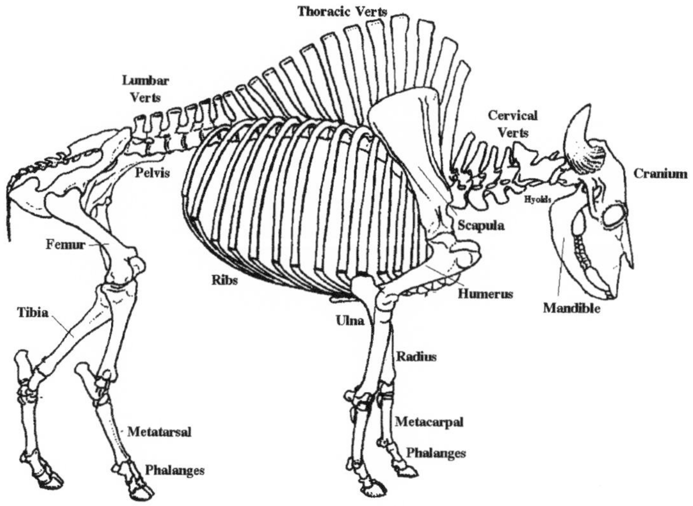

Figure 53. Bones of the bison skeleton.

Seasonality: Season of death, often determined by linking the age of an animal to the birthing or calving peak. For example, a bison calf determined to be 0.3 years old (4 months) would have been killed approximately 4 months after birth, which usually occurs in April. Thus death occured sometime in August, for a seasonality of late summer.

Slump: Dirt and debris that has fallen from the steep face of a bluff or stream bank.

Soft hammer percussion: A method of making stone tools that employs an antler or hardwood mallet to strike off flakes.

Spray foam insulation: Foam insulation packaged in an aerosol can; usually used to insulate around windows and other areas of the house.

Strike: When used in conjunction with "dip" to describe bones on the ground, refers to the compass direction of the bone's long axis. It is usually given in degrees off magnetic north.

Taphonomic agents: Any of a number of natural forces that can disarticulate, distribute, and destroy animal bone between the time of death and exhumation. Includes weather, roots, water action, and scavenging animals.

Tecovas jasper: Fine-grained chert from the Texas Panhandle.

Waugh site: Folsom-age bison kill and camp found in the Cimarron river drainage approximately 30 km north and west of the Cooper site.

Xeric: Dry, arid, usually used in describing environmental conditions.

Bibliography

Agenbroad, Larry D.

1978 *The Hudson-Meng Site: An Alberta Bison Kill in the Nebraska High Plains*. University Press of America, Washington, D.C.

Agogino, G. A.

1968 Archeological Excavations at Blackwater Draw Locality No. 1, New Mexico, 1963–64. *National Geographic Society Research Reports,* 1963 Projects, pp. 1–7.

1969 The Midland Complex: Is It Valid? *American Anthropologist* 71:1117–18.

Akoshima, Kaoru, and George C. Frison

1996 Lithic Microwear Studies of the Mill Iron Site Tools. In *The Mill Iron Site*, edited by George C. Frison, pp. 71–86. University of New Mexico Press, Albuquerque.

Amick, Daniel S.

1995 Patterns of Technological Variation among Folsom and Midland Projectile Points in the American Southwest. *Plains Anthropologist* 40(151):23–38.

1996 Regional Patterns of Folsom Mobility and Land Use in the American Southwest. *World Archaeology* 27(3):411–26.

Amick, D. S., J. L. Hofman, and R. O. Rose.

1989 The Shifting Sands Folsom-Midland Site in Texas. *Current Research in the Pleistocene* 6:1–3.

Anderson, D. C.

1966 The Gordon Creek Burial. *Southwestern Lore* 32:1–9.

Bamforth, D. B.

1985 The Technological Organization of Paleo-Indian Small-group Bison Hunting on the Llano Estacado. *Plains Anthropologist* 30:243–58.

1986 Technological Efficiency and Tool Curation. *American Antiquity* 51:38–50.

Banks, Larry D.

1984 Lithic Resources and Quarries. In *Prehistory of Oklahoma*, edited by Robert E. Bell, pp. 65–96. Academic Press, Orlando.

1990 *From Mountain Peaks to Alligator Stomachs: A Review of Lithic Sources in the Trans-Mississippi South, the Southern Plains, and Adjacent Southwest.* Memoir 4, Oklahoma Anthropological Society, Norman.

Bedord, Jean Newman

1974 Morphological Variation in Bison Metacarpals and Metatarsals. In *The Casper Site: A Hell Gap Bison Kill on the High Plains*, edited by George C. Frison, pp. 199–240. Academic Press, New York.

Behrensmeyer, A. K.

1978 Taphonomic and Ecologic Information from Bone Weathering. *Paleobiology* 4(2):150–62.

Behrensmeyer, A. K., K. D. Gordon, and G. T. Yanagi

1986 Trampling as a Cause of Bone Surface Damage and Pseudo-Cutmarks. *Nature* 319:768–71.

Bement, Leland C.

1985 Spray Foam: A New Bone Encasement Technique. *Journal of Field Archeology* 12(3):371–72.

1986 Excavation of the Late Pleistocene Deposits of Bonfire Shelter, Val Verde County, Texas. Texas Archeological Survey Archeology Series 1, University of Texas at Austin.

1994a The Cooper Site: A Stratified Paleoindian Bison Kill in Northwest Oklahoma. *Current Research in the Pleistocene* 11:7–9.

1994b *Hunter-Gatherer Mortuary Practices during the Central Texas Archaic.* University of Texas Press, Austin.

1995 The Retooling Index, Seasonality, and the Folsom-Age Cooper Bison Kill. *Current Research in the Pleistocene* 12:61–62.

1997 The Cooper Site: A Stratified Folsom Bison Kill in Oklahoma. In *Southern Plains Bison Procurement and Utilization from Paleo-indian to Historic*, edited by Leland C. Bement and Kent J. Buehler, pp. 85–100. Plains Anthropologist Memoir 29.

Bement, Leland C., and Susan Basmajian

1996 Epiphyseal Fusion in *Bison antiquus. Current Research in the Pleistocene* 13:95–97.

Bement, Leland C., and Kent J. Buehler

1994 Preliminary Results from the Certain Site: A Late Archaic Bison Kill in Western Oklahoma. *Plains Anthropologist* 39(148):173–83.

1997 (eds.) *Southern Plains Bison Procurement and Utilization from Paleoindian to Historic.* Plains Anthropologist Memoir 29.

Bement, Leland C., Marian Hyman, Michael Zolensky, and Brian J. Carter

1997 A Painted Skull from the Cooper Site: A Folsom Bison Kill in NW Oklahoma. *Current Research in the Pleistocene* 14:6–9.

Berger, Joel, and Carol Cunningham

1994 *Bison Mating and Conservation in Small Populations.* Columbia University Press, New York.

Binford, Lewis R.

1971 Mortuary Practices: Their Study and Their Potential. In *Approaches to the Social Dimensions of Mortuary Practices*, edited by James A. Brown. Memoir of the Society for American Archaeology 25:6–29.

1978 *Nunamuit Ethnoarchaeology.* Academic Press, New York.

1979 Organization and Formation Processes: Looking at Curated Technologies. *Journal of Anthropological Research* 35(3):255–73.

Binford, L. R., and J. B. Bertram

1977 Bone Frequencies and Attritional Processes. In *For Theory Building in Archaeology*, edited by L. R. Binford, pp. 77–153. Academic Press, New York.

Bloch, Maurice, and Jonathan Parry

1982 *Death and the Regeneration of Life.* Cambridge: Cambridge University Press.

Boldurian, Anthony T.

1981 An Analysis of a Paleoindian Lithic Assemblage from Blackwater Draw Locality No. 1 in Eastern New Mexico. Unpublished M.A. thesis, Department of Anthropology, Eastern New Mexico University, Portales.

1990 *Lithic Technology at the Mitchell Locality of Blackwater Draw: A Stratified Folsom Site in Eastern New Mexico.* Plains Anthropologist Memoir 24.

1991 Folsom Mobility and Organization of Lithic Technology: A View from Blackwater Draw, New Mexico. *Plains Anthropologist* 36:281–95.

Boldurian, Anthony T., George Agogino, Phillip H. Shelley, and Mark Slaughter

1987 Folsom Biface Manufacture, Retooling, and Site Function at the Mitchell Locality of Blackwater Draw. *Plains Anthropologist* 32(117):299–311.

Bonnichsen, Robson, and Marcella H. Sorg

1989 *Bone Modification*. Center for the study of the First Americans, Orono, Maine.

Bradley, Bruce A.

1993 Paleo-Indian Flaked Stone Technology in the North American High Plains. In *From Kostenki to Clovis: Upper Paleolithic-Paleo-Indian Adaptations*, edited by Olga Soffer and N. D. Praslov, pp. 251–62. Plenum Press, New York.

Brosowske, Scott D.

1996 Identifying Relative Levels of Mobility for Selected Southern Plains Hunter-Gatherers. Unpublished M.A. thesis, University of Oklahoma, Norman.

Brosowske, Scott D., and Leland C. Bement

1997 An Analysis of Resharpening Flakes from the Cooper Site. *Current Research in the Pleistocene* 14:99–101.

Buehler, Kent J.

1997 Where's the Cliff?: Late Archaic Bison Kills in the Southern Plains. In *Southern Plains Bison Procurement and Utilization from Paleoindian to Historic*, edited by Leland C. Bement and Kent J. Buehler, pp. 135–43, Plains Anthropologist Memoir 29.

Carter, Brian J., and Leland C. Bement

1995 Soil Investigations at the Cooper Site. *Current Research in the Pleistocene* 12:119–21.

Carter, B. J., P. A. Ward, III, and J. T. Shannon

1990 Soil and Geomorphic Evolution within the Rolling Red Plains Using Pleistocene Volcanic Ash Deposits. In "Soil and Landscape Evolution" issue, edited by P. L. K. Knuepfer and L. D. McFadden. *Geomorphology* 3:471–88.

Chisholm, Brian, Jonathan Driver, Sylvain Dube, and Henry P. Schwarcz

1986 Assessment of Prehistoric Bison Foraging and Movement Patterns via Stable-Carbon Isotopic Analysis. *Plains Anthropologist* 31:193–205

Cotter, J. L.

1937 The Occurrence of Flints and Extinct Animals in Pluvial Deposits Near Clovis, New Mexico, Part VI. Report on Excavations at the Gravel Pit, 1936. *Proceedings of the Philadelphia Academy of Natural Sciences* 89:2–16.

Curtis, Neville M., Jr., and William E. Ham

1979 Geomorphic Provinces of Oklahoma. In *Geology and Earth Resourcees of Oklahoma* by Kenneth S. Johnson, Carl C. Branson, Neville M. Curtis, Jr., William E. Ham, William E. Harrison, Melvin V. Marcher, and John F. Roberts. Educational Publication no. 1, Oklahoma Geologic Survey.

Davis, Simon J. M.

1996 Measurements of a Group of Adult Female Shetland Sheep Skeletons from a Single Flock: A Baseline for Zooarchaeologists. *Journal of Archaeological Science* 23(4):593–612.

Davis, Leslie B., and Brian O. K. Reeves (eds.)

1990 *Hunters of the Recent Past.* Unwin Hyman, London.

Davis, Leslie B., and Michael Wilson (eds.)

1978 *Bison Procurement and Utilization: A Symposium.* Plains Anthropologist Memoir 14.

Denig, Edwin Thompson

1930 *Indian Tribes of the Upper Missouri*, edited by J. N. B. Hewitt. Forty-sixth Annual Report of the Bureau of American Ethnology: 375–6256.

Dibble, David S., and Dessamae Lorrain

1968 Bonfire Shelter: A Stratified Bison Kill Site, Val Verde County, Texas. Miscellaneous Papers, no. 1, Texas Memorial Museum, Austin.

Dillehay, Tom D.

1989 *Monte Verde: A Late Pleistocene Settlement in Chile.* Vol. 1, *Paleoenvironment and Site Context.* Smithsonian Institution Press, Washington, D.C.

Dillehay, Tom D., and David J. Meltzer

1991 *The First Americans: Search and Research.* CRC Press, Boca Raton.

Driver, Jonathan C.

1990 Meat in Due Season: The Timing of Communal Hunts. In *Hunters of the Recent Past*, edited by Leslie B. Davis and Brian O. K. Reeves, pp. 11–33. Unwin Hyman, London.

Dyck, Ian, and Richard E. Morlan

1995 *The Sjovold Site: A River Crossing Campsite in the Northern Plains*. Mercury Series Paper 151, Archaeological Survey of Canada, Canadian Museum of Civilization, Hull, Quebec.

Emerson, Alice M.

1993 The Role of Body Part Utility in Small-Scale Hunting under Two Strategies of Carcass Recovery. In *From Bones to Behavior: Ethnoarchaeological and Experimental Contributions to the Interpretation of Faunal Remains*, edited by Jean Hudson, pp. 138–55. Occasional Paper no. 21, Center for Archaeological Investigations, Southern Illinois University at Carbondale.

Fawcett, William B.

1987 Communal Hunts, Human Aggregations, Social Variation, and Climatic Change: Bison Utilization by Prehistoric Inhabitants of the Great Plains, Ph.D. Dissertation, Department of Anthropology, University of Massachusetts, Amherst.

Ferring, R.

1989 The Aubrey Clovis Site: A Paleo-Indian Locality in the Upper Trinity River Basin, Texas. *Current Research in the Pleistocene* 6:9–11.

1990 The 1989 Investigations at the Aubrey Clovis Site, Texas. *Current Research in the Pleistocene* 7:10–12.

1994 The Role of Geoarchaeology in Paleoindian Research. In *Method and Theory for Investigating the Peopling of the Americas*, edited by R. Bonnichsen and D. B. Steele, pp. 57–72. Center for the Study of the First Americans, Oregon State University, Corvallis.

Figgins, J. D.

1927 The Antiquity of Man in America. *Natural History* 27(3): 229–39.

Fiorillo, Anthony R.

1989 An Experimental Study of Trampling: Implications for the Fossil Record. In *Bone Modification*, edited by Robson Bonnichsen and Marcella H. Sorg. pp. 61–72. Center for the Study of the First Americans, Orono, Maine.

Frederick, Charles D., and Chris Ringstaff

1994 Lithic Resources at Fort Hood: Further Investigations. In *Archeological Investigations on 571 Prehistoric Sites at Fort Hood, Bell and Coryell Counties, Texas*, by Mariah and Associates, pp. 125–411. Austin.

Frison, George C.

1970 *The Glenrock Buffalo Jump, 48CO304: Late Prehistoric Period Buffalo Procurement and Butchering.* Plains Anthropologist Memoir 7.

1974 (ed.) *The Casper Site: A Hell Gap Bison Kill on the High Plains.* Academic Press, New York.

1979 Observations on the Use of Stone Tools: Dulling of Working Edges of Some Chipped Stone Tools in Bison Butchering. In *Lithic Use-Wear Analysis*, edited by Brian Hayden, pp. 259–68. Academic Press, New York.

1982 Bison Dentition Studies. In *The Agate Basin Site: A Record of the Paleoindian Occupation of the Northwestern High Plains*, edited by G. C. Frison and D. J. Stanford, pp. 240–60. Academic Press, New York.

1987 Prehistoric, Plains-Mountain, Large-Mammal, Communal Hunting Strategies. In *The Evolution of Human Hunting*, edited by Matthew H. Nitecki and Doris M. Nitecki, pp. 177–211. Plenum, New York.

1991 *Prehistoric Hunters of the High Plains*, 2d ed. Academic Press, New York.

1996 (ed.) *The Mill Iron Site.* University of New Mexico Press, Albuquerque.

Frison, George C., and Bruce A. Bradley

1980 *Folsom Tools and Technology at the Hanson Site, Wyoming.* University of New Mexico Press, Albuquerque.

Frison, George C., and Dennis J. Stanford

1982 *The Agate Basin Site: A Record of the Paleoindian Occupation of the Northwestern High Plains.* Academic Press, New York.

Frison, George C., and Lawrence C. Todd (eds.)

1987 *The Horner Site: The Type Site of the Cody Complex.* Academic Press, Orlando.

Graham, R. W., and E. L. Lundelius, Jr.

1984 Coevolutionary Disequilibrium and Pleistocene Extinctions. In *Quaternary Extinctions: A Prehistoric Revolution*, edited by P. S. Martin and R. G. Klein, pp. 223–49. University of Arizona Press, Tucson.

Gramly, Richard M.

1980 Raw Material Source Areas and "Curated" Tool Assemblages. *American Antiquity* 45:823–33.

Griffen, W. B.

1969 *Culture Change and Shifting Populations in Central Northern Mexico.* Anthropological Papers 13. University of Arizona Press, Tucson.

Halloran, A. F.

1961 American Bison Weights and Measurements from the Wichita Mountains Wildlife Refuge. *Proceedings of the Oklahoma Academy of Science* 41:212–18.

1968 Bison (Bovidae) productivity on the Wichita Mountains Wildlife Refuge, Oklahoma. *Southwest Naturalist* 13:21–26.

Harrison, Billy R., and Kay L. Killen

1978 Lake Theo: A Stratified, Early Man Bison Butchering and Camp Site, Briscoe County, Texas. Special Archeological Report 1, Panhandle-Plains Historical Museum, Canyon, Texas.

Harrison, Billy R., and H. C. Smith

1975 Excavations at the Lake Theo Site, PPHM-A917, Briscoe County, Texas. *Panhandle-Plains Historical Review* 48:70–106.

Hayden, Brian

1979 *Lithic Use-Wear Analysis.* Academic Press, New York.

Haynes, C. Vance, Jr.

1993 Clovis-Folsom Geochronology and Climatic Change. In *From Kostenki to Clovis: Upper Paleolithic–Paleo-Indian Adaptations*, edited by O. Soffer and N. D. Praslov, pp. 219–36. Plenum Press, New York.

Haynes, C. Vance, Jr., Roelf P. Beukens, A. J. T. Jull, and Owen K. Davis

1992 New Radiocarbon Dates for Some Old Folsom Sites: Accelerator Technology. In *Ice Age Hunters of the Rockies*, edited by D. J. Stanford and J. S. Day, pp. 83–100. University Press of Colorado, Niwot.

Haynes, Gary

1980 Evidence of Carnivore Gnawing on Pleistocene and Recent Mammalian Bones. *Paleobiology* 6:341–51.

1982 Utilization and Skeletal Disturbances of North American Prey Carcasses. *Arctic* 35(2):266–81.

1983 A Guide for Differentiating Mammalian Carnivore Taxa Responsible for Gnaw Damage to Herbivore Limb Bones. *Paleobiology* 9:164–72.

Hedges, Ken

1982 Phospenes in the Context of Native American Rock Art. *American*

Indian Rock Art 7–8:1–10. American Rock Art Research Association, El Toro, California.

1994 Pipette Dreams and the Primordial Snake-Canoe: Analysis of a Hallucinatory Form Constant. In *Shamanism and Rock Art in North America*, edited by Solveig A. Turpin, pp 103–24. Special Publication 1, Rock Art Foundation, San Antonio, Texas.

Hester, James J.

1962 A Folsom Lithic Complex from the Elida Site, Roosevelt County, N.M. *El Palacio* 69(2):92–113.

1972 *Blackwater Locality No. 1: A Stratified Early Man Site in Eastern New Mexico*. Fort Burgwin Research Center Publication no. 8, Ranchos de Taos, New Mexico.

Hill, Andrew P.

1979a Butchery and Natural Disarticulation: An Investigatory Technique. *American Antiquity* 44(4):739–44.

1979b Disarticulation and Scattering of Mammal Skeletons. *Paleobiology* 5(3):261–74.

Hill, Andrew P., and Anna K. Behrensmeyer

1984 Disarticulation Patterns of Some Modern East African Mammals. *Paleobiology* 10(3):366–76.

1985 Natural Disarticulation and Bison Butchery. *American Antiquity* 50:141–45.

Hill, Matthew E., Jr., and Jack L. Hofman

1997 The Waugh Site: A Folsom-age Bison Bonebed in Northwestern Oklahoma. In *Southern Plains Bison Procurement and Utilization from Paleoindian to Historic*, edited by Leland C. Bement and Kent J. Buehler, pp. 63–83. Plains Anthropologist Memior 29.

Hofman, Jack L.

1987 The Occurrence of Folsom Points in Oklahoma. *Current Research in the Pleistocene* 4:57–59.

1990 Paleoindian Mobility and Utilization of Niobrara or Smoky Hill Jasper on the Southern Plains. *Kansas Anthropologist* 9(2).

1991 Folsom Land Use: Projectile Point Variability as a Key to Mobility. In *Raw Material Economies among Prehistoric Hunter-Gatherers*, edited by A. Montet-White and S. Holen. University of Kansas Publications in Anthropology 19, Lawrence.

1992 Recognition and Interpretation of Folsom Technological Variability on the Southern Plains. In *Ice-Age Hunters of the Rockies*,

edited by D. J. Stanford and J. S. Day. Denver Museum of Natural History.
1994 Paleoindian aggregations on the Great Plains. *Journal of Antrhopological Archaeology* 13(4):341–70.
N.D. Unbounded Hunters: Folsom Bison Hunting on the Southern Plains Circa 10,500: The Lithic Evidence. Paper presented at the international symposium "Bison Subsistence from Paleolithic to Paleoindian Times," Talouse, France, June 6–10, 1995. Paper in possession of author.

Hofman, J. L., D. S. Amick, and R. O. Rose
1990 Shifting Sands: A Folsom-Midland Assemblage from a Campsite in Western Texas. *Plains Anthropologist* 35:221–53.

Hofman, J. L., B. J. Carter, and M. Hill
1992 Folsom Occupation at the Waugh Site in Northwestern Oklahoma. *Current Research in the Pleistocene* 9:22–25.

Hofman, Jack L., Lawrence C. Todd, C. Bertrand Schultz, and William Hendy.
1991 The Lipscomb Bison Quarry: Continuing Investigation at a Folsom Site on the Southern Plains. *Bulletin of the Texas Archeological Society* 60:149–89.

Holliday, V. T.
1995 *Stratigraphy and Paleoenvironments of late Quaternary Valley Fills on the Southern High Plains.* Geological Society of America Memoir 186, Boulder.

Howard, E. B.
1935 Evidence of Early Man in North America. *Museum Journal* 24(2–3):61–175.

Hughes, David T.
1977 Analysis of Certain Prehistoric Bison Kills in the Texas Panhandle and Adjacent Areas. M.A. thesis, Department of Anthropology, University of Arkansas, Fayetteville.

Ingbar, Eric E.
1992 The Hanson Site and Folsom on the Northwestern Plains. In *Ice Age Hunters of the Rockies*, edited by D. J. Stanford and J. S. Day, pp. 169–92. University Press of Colorado, Niwot.

Jodry, Margaret Anne
1987 Stewart's Cattle Guard Site: A Folsom Site in Southern Colorado, A Report on the 1981 and 1983 Field Seasons. Unpublished M.A. thesis, Department of Anthropology, University of Texas, Austin.

Jodry, M. A., and D. J. Stanford

1992 Stewart's Cattle Guard Site: An Analysis of Bison Remains in a Folsom Kill-Butchery Campsite. In *Ice Age Hunters of the Rockies*, edited by D. J. Stanford and J. S. Day, pp. 101–68. University Press of Colorado, Niwot.

Johnson, Eileen

1987 (ed.) *Lubbock Lake: Late Quaternary Studies on the Southern High Plains*. Texas A&M University Press, College Station.

1997 Late Quaternary Bison Utilization at Lubbock Lake on the Southern High Plains. In *Southern Plains Bison Procurement and Utilization from Paleoindian to Historic*, edited by Leland C. Bement and Kent J. Buehler, pp. 45–61. Plains Anthropologist Memoir 29.

Judge, W. J.

1973 *Paleoindian Occupation of the Central Rio Grande Valley in New Mexico*. University of New Mexico Press, Albuquerque.

Keeley, Lawrence H.

1980 *Experimental Determination of Stone Tool Uses: A Microwear Analysis*. University of Chicago Press, Chicago.

Keeley, L. H., and M. H. Newcomer

1977 Microwear Analysis of Experimental Flint Tools: A Test Case. *Journal of Archaeological Science* 4:29-62.

Kehoe, Thomas F.

1990 Corralling: Evidence from Upper Paleolithic Cave Art. In *Hunters of the Recent Past*, edited by L. B. Davis and Brian O. K. Reeves, pp. 34–46. Unwin Hyman, London.

Kelly, Robert L., and Lawrence C. Todd

1988 Coming into the Country: Early Paleoindian Hunting and Mobility. *American Antiquity* 53(2):231–44.

Kirkland, Forest, and W. W. Newcomb, Jr.

1967 *The Rock Art of Texas Indians*. University of Texas Press, Austin.

Klein, D. R.

1964 Range-Related Differences in Growth of Deer Reflected in Skeletal Ratios. *Journal of Mammology* 45:226–35.

Kreutzer, L. A.

1992 Bison and Deer Bone Mineral Densities: Comparisons and Implications for the Interpretation of Archaeological Faunas. *Journal of Archaeological Science* 19:271–94.

1996 Taphonomy of the Mill Iron Site Bison Bonebed. In *The Mill Iron Site*, edited by George C. Frison, pp. 101–44. University of New Mexico Press, Albuquerque.

Lahren, L., and R. Bonnichsen

1974 Bone Foreshafts from a Clovis Burial in Southwestern Montana. *Science* 186:147–50.

Leonhardy, Frank C.

1966 Domebo: A Paleo-Indian Mammoth Kill in the Prairie-Plains. Contributions of the Museum of the Great Plains, no. 1, Great Plains Historical Association, Lawton, Oklahoma.

Lewis-Williams, J. David

1980 Ethnography and Iconography: Aspects of Southern San Thought and Art. *Man* 15:467–82.

1981 *Believing and Seeing: Symbolic Meaning in Southern San Rock Paintings*. Academic Press, London.

1982 The Economic and Social Contexts of Southern San Rock Art. *Current Anthropology* 23:429–49.

Lewis-Williams, J. David, and T. A. Dowson

1988 The Signs of All Times: Entoptic Phenomenon in Upper Paleolithic Art. *Current Anthropology* 29(2):201–17.

Lowie, Robert H.

1963 *Indians of the Plains*. Natural History Press, Garden City, New York.

Lukowski, Paul D.

1988 *Archaeological Investigations at 41BX1, Bexar County, Texas*. Archaeological Survey Report 135, Center for Archaeological Research, University of Texas at San Antonio.

Lundelius, E. L., Jr.

1989 The Implications of Disharmonious Assemblages for Pleistocene Extinctions. *Journal of Archaeological Science* 16:407–17.

Lyman, R. L.

1982 The Taphonomy of Vertebrate Archaeofaunas: Bone Density and Differential Survivorship of Fossil Classes. Ph.D. dissertation, University of Washington. Ann Arbor: University Microfilms.

1984 Bone Density and Differential Survivorship of Fossil Classes. *Journal of Anthropological Archaeology* 3(4):259–99.

McDonald, Jerry N.

1981 *North American Bison: Their Classification and Evolution*. University of California Press, Berkeley.

McHugh, T.

1958 Social Behavior of the American Buffalo (*Bison bison bison*). *Zoologica* 43(1):1–40.

1972 *The Time of the Buffalo*. Alfred A. Knopf, New York.

Meltzer, David J.

1993 *Search for the First Americans*. Smithsonian Books, Washington, D.C.

Morlan, Richard E.

1994 Bison Bone Fragmentation and Survivorship: A Comparative Method. *Journal of Archaeological Science* 21:797–807.

Myers, A. J.

1959 *Geology of Harper County, Oklahoma*. Oklahoma Geological Survey Bulletin 80.

1962 A Middle Pleistocene Stream Channel. *Oklahoma Geology Notes* 22:224–29.

Nance, E. C., J. D. Nichols, H. L. Kollmorgen, R. E. Daniel, H. L. Costilow, and K. T. Lofton

1960 *Soil Survey of Harper County, Oklahoma*. U.S. Department of Agriculture in cooperation with the Oklahoma Agricultural Experiment Station.

Nance, E. C., C. A. Steers, E. L. Cole, M. L. Miller, and C. F. Fanning

1963 *Soil Survey of Woodward County, Oklahoma*. U.S. Department of Agriculture in cooperation with the Oklahoma Agricultural Experiment Station.

Newcomer, M. H., and L. H. Keeley

1979 Testing a Method of Microwear Analysis with Experimental Flint Tools. In *Lithic Use-WearAnalysis*, edited by B. Hayden, pp. 195–205. Academic Press, New York.

Odell, George H.

1975 Micro-Wear in Perspective: A Sympathetic Response to Lawrence H. Keeley. *World Archaeology* :226–40.

1990 Brer Rabbit Seeks True Knowledge. In *Interpretive Possibilities of Microwear Studies*, edited by G. Graslund, H. Knutsson, K. Knutsson, and J. Taffinder, pp 125–34. Aun 14. Societas Archaeological Upsaliensis, Uppsala.

Odell, G. H., and F. Odell-Vereecken

1980 Verifying the Reliability of Lithic Use-Wear Assessments by "Blind Tests:" the Low-Power Approach. *Journal of Field Archaeology* 7:87–120.

Oster, Gerald

1970 Phosphenes. *Scientific American* 222(2):82–87.

Quigg, J. Michael

1992 Appendix I: Isotopic Data from Bison Remains. In *Historic and Prehistoric Data Recovery at Palo Duro Reservoir, Hansford County, Texas.* By J. M. Quigg, C. Lintz, F. M. Oglesby, A. C. Earls, C. D. Frederick, W. N. Trierweiler, D. Owsley, and K. W. Kibler, pp. I1–I13. Technical Report no. 485, Mariah Associates, Austin, Texas.

Reeves, Brian O. K.

1990 Communal bison hunters of the Northern Plains. In *Hunters of the Recent Past*, edited by Leslie B. Davis and Brian O. K. Reeves, pp. 168–94. Unwin Hyman, London.

Reher, Charles A.

1970 Population Dynamics of the Glenrock *Bison bison* Population. In *The Glenrock Buffalo Jump, 48CO304*, edited by George C. Frison, appendix II. Plains Anthropologist Memoir 7.

1974 Population Study of the Casper Site Bison. In *The Casper Site: A Hell Gap Bison Kill on the High Plains*, edited by G. C. Frison. New York: Academic Press.

Reher, Charles A., and George C. Frison

1980 *The Vore Site, 48CK302: A Stratified Buffalo Jump in the Wyoming Black Hills.* Plains Anthropologist Memoir 16.

Renaud, E. B.

1931 Prehistoric Flaked Points from Colorado and Neighboring Districts. *Proceedings of the Colorado Museum of Natural History* 10(2).

Root, Matthew J., and Alice M. Emerson

1994 Archaeology of the Bobtail Wolf Site (32DU955A): 1993–1994 Progress Report. Progress Report no. 26, Center for Northwest Anthropology, Department of Anthropology, Washington State University, Pullman.

Root, M. J., J. D. William, L. K. Shifrin, and E. Feiler

1995 Folsom Point and Biface Manufacture in the Knife River Flint Quarry Area. *Current Research in the Pleistocene* 12:65–68.

Roper, D. C.

1987 Plains Paleoindian Red Ochre Use and Its Possible Significance. *Current Research in the Pleistocene* 4:82–84.

1991 A Comparison of Contexts of Red Ochre Use in Paleoindian and Upper Paleolithic Sites. *North American Archaeologist* 12(4): 289–301.

Russ, J., M. Hyman, and M. W. Rowe

1992 Dating and Chemical Analysis of Pecos River Style Pictographs. *American Indian Rock Art* 18:35–42.

Schultz, C. Bertrand

1943 Some Artifact Sites of Early Man on the Great Plains and Adjacent Areas. *American Antiquity* 3:242–49.

Sellards, E. H.

1952 *Early Man in America.* Texas Memorial Museum and the University of Texas Press, Austin.

Sellards, E. H., G. L. Evans, and G. E. Meade

1947 Fossil Bison and Associated Artifacts from Plainview, Texas (with description of artifacts by Alex D. Krieger). *Bulletin of the Geological Society of America* 58 (10). Baltimore.

Skinner, Alanson

1914a Political Organization: Cults and Ceremonies of the Plains-Ojibwa. *Anthropological Papers of the American Museum of Natural History* 11(6):482–99.

1914b Political Organization: Cults and Ceremonies of the Plains-Cree. *Anthropological Papers of the American Museum of Natural History* 11(6):513–42.

Soffer, Olga

1985 *The Upper Paleolithic of the Central Russian Plain.* Academic Press, Orlando.

Speth, John D.

1983 *Bison Kills and Bone Counts: Decision Making by Ancient Hunters.* University of Chicago Press, Chicago.

Stafford, Michael D.

1990 The Powers II Site (48PL330): A Paleoindian Red Ochre Mine in Eastern Wyoming. Unpublished M.A. thesis, University of Wyoming, Laramie.

Stanford, Dennis J.

1978 The Jones-Miller Site: An Example of Hell Gap Bison Procurement Strategy. In Bison Procurement and Utilization: A Symposium, edited by L. B. Davis and M. Wilson, pp. 90–97. *Plains Anthropologist Memoir* 14.

1984 The Jones-Miller Site: A Study of Hell Gap Bison Procurement and Processing. *National Geographic Society Research Reports* 16: 615–35.

Stanford, Dennis, and Frank Broilo

1981 Frank's Folsom Campsite. *Artifact* 19(3–4):1–11. El Paso Archeological Society.

Stanford, Dennis J., C. Vance Haynes, Jr., Jeffrey J. Saunders, and George A. Agogino.

1986 Blackwater Draw Locality 1: History, Current Research and Interpretations. In *Guidebook to the Archeological Geology of Classic Paleoindian Sites on the Southern High Plains, Texas and New Mexico*, edited by V. T. Holliday, pp. 82–118. Geological Society of America, 1986 Annual Meeting, Department of Geography, Texas A&M University.

Todd, Lawrence C.

1987a Analysis of Kill-Butchery Sites and the Interpretation of Paleoindian Hunting. In *The Evolution of Human Hunting*, edited by M. Nitecki and D. Nitecki, pp. 225–66. Plenum Press, New York.

1987b Taphonomy of the Horner II Bone Bed. In *The Horner Site: The Type Site of the Cody Complex*, edited by George C. Frison and Lawrence C. Todd, pp. 107–98. Academic Press, Orlando.

1991 Seasonality Studies and Paleoindian Subsistence Strategies. In *Human Predators and Prey Mortality*, edited by M. C. Stiner, pp. 217–38. Westview Press, Boulder.

Todd, Lawrence C., and George C. Frison

1992 Reassembly of Bison Skeletons from the Horner Site: A Study in Anatomical Refitting. In *Piecing Together the Past: Applications of Refitting Studies in Archaeology*, edited by J. L. Hofman and J. M. Enloe. pp. 63–82. BAR International Series 578. Oxford.

Todd, Lawrence C., Jack L. Hofman, and C. Bertrand Schultz

1990 Seasonality of the Scottsbluff and Lipscomb Bonebeds: Implications for Modeling Paleoindian Subsistence. *American Antiquity* 55(4):813–27.

Tunnell, Curtis

1977 Fluted Projectile Point Production as Revealed by Lithic Specimens from the Adair-Steadman Site in Northwest Texas. In *Paleoindian Lifeways*, edited by E. Johnson, pp. 140–68. Museum Journal 17, Texas Tech University, Lubbock.

Turpin, Solveig A.

1992 Hunting Camps and Hunting Magic: Petroglyphs of the Eldorado Divide, West Texas. *North American Archaeologist* 13(4):295–316.

1994 *Shamanism and Rock Art in North America.* Special Publication 1, Rock Art Foundation, San Antonio, Texas.

Uher, Johanna

1994 Zigzag Rock Art: An Ethological Perspective. In *Contested Images: Diversity in Southern African Rock Art Research,* edited by Thomas A. Dowson and David Lewis-Williams, pp. 293–313. Witwatersrand University Press, Johannesburg, South Africa.

Vaughan, Patrick C.

1985 *Use-Wear Analysis of Flaked Stone Tools.* University of Arizona Press, Tucson.

Verbicky-Todd, Eleanor

1984 Communal Buffalo Hunting among the Plains Indians. Occasional Paper no. 24, *Archaeological Survey of Alberta.* Edmondton, Alberta.

Warnica, J. M.

1961 The Elida Site: Evidence of a Folsom Occupation in Roosevelt County, Eastern New Mexico. *Bulletin of the Texas Archaeological Society* 30:209–15.

Wheat, Joe Ben

1967 A Paleo-Indian Bison Kill. *Scientific American* 216:44–52.

1972 *The Olsen-Chubbuck Site: A Paleo-Indian Bison Kill.* Society for American Archaeology Memoir 26.

1978 Olsen-Chubbuck and Jurgens Sites: Four Aspects of Paleo-Indian Economy. In Bison Procurement and Utilization: A Symposium, edited by L. B. Davis and M. Wilson, pp. 84–89. *Plains Anthropologist Memoir* 14.

Wilmsen, Edwin N.

1968 Functional Analysis of Flaked Stone Artifacts. *American Antiquity* 33:156–61.

Wilmsen, Edwin N., and Frank H. H. Roberts, Jr.

1978 *Lindenmeier, 1934–1974: Concluding Report on Investigations.* Contributions to Anthropology 24, Smithsonian Institution, Washington, D.C.

Wilson, Michael

1974 The Casper Local Fauna and Its Fossil Bison. In *The Casper Site: A*

Hell Gap Bison Kill on the High Plains, edited by George C. Frison, pp. 125–72. Academic Press, New York.

Winterhalder, Bruce, and Eric Alden Smith (eds.)
1981 *Hunter-Gatherer Foraging Strategies: Ethnographic and Archeological Analyses*. University of Chicago Press, Chicago.

Woodburn, James
1982 Social Dimensions of Death in Four African Hunting and Gathering Societies. In *Death and the Regeneration of Life*, edited by M. Bloch and J. Parry, pp 187–211. Cambridge University Press, Cambridge.

Wormington, H. M.
1957 *Ancient Man in North America*. Denver Museum of Natural History, Denver.

Yesner, David R.
1981 Archeological Applications of Optimal Foraging Theory: Harvest Strategies of Aleut Hunter-Gatherers. In *Hunter-Gatherer Foraging Strategies: Ethnographic and Archeological Analyses*, edited by Bruce Winterhalder and Eric Alden Smith, pp. 148–70. University of Chicago Press, Chicago.

Zolensky, Michael
1982 Analysis of Pigments from Prehistoric Pictographs, Seminole Canyon State Historical Park. In *Seminole Canyon: The Art and the Archeology*, by Solveig A. Turpin, pp. 279–84. Texas Archeological Survey Research Report 83, University of Texas at Austin.

Index